THE VIKING AGE
IN DENMARK

The Viking Age in Denmark

The Formation of a State

KLAVS RANDSBORG

Duckworth

First published in 1980 by
Gerald Duckworth & Co. Ltd.
The Old Piano Factory
43 Gloucester Crescent, London NW1

ISBN 0 7156 1443 6 (cased)
ISBN 0 7156 1466 5 (paper)

*Photoset in Great Britain by
The Allen Lithographic Co. Ltd., Kirkcaldy
and printed by Butler & Tanner Ltd., Frome*

Contents

Preface

This book is the result of my interest in prehistoric and early historic societies and in social development in general; it is focused on the data of my home country, scanty though such data are. The general reader should know that much in the book is controversial. But I have devoted little time to polemics. I hope that the notes, lists and references will help the inquiring, and perhaps sceptical, student to gain a detailed understanding of specific problems. In general I have tried to maintain a continuous argument in the text.

I am grateful to my employer, the University of Copenhagen, for much support and indulgence, and to Washington University, St. Louis, Missouri, where a guest-professorate in 1975/76 gave me a chance to renew contacts and gain insights into the stimulating developments of American archaeology during the past decade. Short stays in England and continual friendly relations with English scholars have also been encouraging. In particular, I am obliged to Professor Colin Renfrew, the editor-in-chief of the series in which this book appears, for much sympathy. As always, the National Museum of Copenhagen and its personnel and a wide variety of Danish institutions have proved most helpful. Colleagues in the Netherlands and in Sweden too have all played a part. For information on unpublished data and for discussions I am indebted to Tove Hatting, M.A., of the Zoological Institute, University of Copenhagen, and to Bent Aaby, geologist of the Geological Survey of Denmark. Steen Hvass, M.A., Institute of Prehistoric Archaeology, University of Copenhagen, kindly permitted the reproduction of unpublished plans. Language corrections were efficiently carried out by Dr Richard Hodges, Department of Prehistory and Archaeology, University of Sheffield. Siri Louekari has assisted in the production of the original figures. The photographs are from the collection of the National Museum, Copenhagen. Finally, I am much obliged to Inger M. Bortolotti for assistance.

Copenhagen, August 1978   K.R.

*It is most certainly evident and thus free from doubt
that all things which are seen are temporal,
and the things which are not seen are eternal.*

(Anglo–Saxon Charter, 770 A.D.)

Chapter 1

THE VIKINGS AND THE STATE

A. The study of the Viking Age

There is an idea inherent in European civilisation that it is challenged by destructive forces, working from within and without. Tales of crises, and how they were overcome in the past, fortify the confidence we have in our own society and its continuance, albeit in the modified and changing forms which it has experienced through history.

The Viking raiders in western Europe a thousand years ago are no exception. Their eventual submission to what is seen as a part of the mainstream of cultural development – the Christian European state, which had developed on the foundations of the Roman Empire – remains a consoling fact. However, they also retained many aspects of earlier, more egalitarian societies. The Scandinavian states were small and their potential resources restricted. These limitatations resulted, despite eventual social development, in regional cultural differentiation.

A further part of the Viking story concerns their colonies in the north Atlantic. This enterprise satisfies the belief that the society was expanding naturally and, as with the raids in the west, was activated by a simple search for new gains. On the latter level, the Viking warrior is no more exciting and hardly more important to us than the American cowboy. Finally, another perspective has emerged – that of the Viking farmer and tradesman – due to our growing interest in culture and economy. Yet it tells us little in fact about the structure of Viking society, or about causes and consequences. It remains a partial picture unconcerned with inter-relationships.

The last decades of social thinking and research have led, above all, to an understanding of the systematic nature, often unconsciously determined, of human behaviour. Moreover, they have high-lighted the part played by adaptation in human society, with regard not only to tradition, but also to other social groups and to the natural environment. For instance, few scholars today would underestimate the decisive role played by population and economic factors in social institutions. This perspective has been reinforced by the use of quantitative methods, through which we have gained sophisticated insights into the dynamics of societies.

This, then, is our point of departure for the study of the Viking Age. The book is restricted to the investigation of one geographical area, within the Nordic tradition: wider Denmark, the Denmark of the Middle Ages (Fig. 1). The raids on the west, for example, can be seen in the light of Viking behaviour as a whole, and as part of the critical changes leading to and stemming from the foundation of a state in the area.

But the view that society is structured, a fundamental interest in production being basic to its survival, is not in itself sufficient for an understanding of Viking Age Denmark. We need to look both for a methodology and for a set of generalities about social behaviour which can be used as starting points for our investigation. One such is the concept of the state, and of other kinds of societies; further generalities deal with urbanism or with specific groups of societies.

B. The Vikings, a Danish perspective

The precise meaning of the word 'Viking' remains obscure. The word was used by the Scandinavians themselves, for instance, on one of the Danish tenth century runestones: a man is mentioned who died abroad in Sweden, accompanied by 'all the Vikings'.[1] A stone from about 1000 A.D. speaks of 'drengs' (literally 'boys') 'in Viking', i.e. on expedition.[2] Another contemporary monument ends by commemorating a man 'who died in the North in Viking.'[3] The western European texts of this period usually refer to the Scandinavians as 'Danes' or 'Normans'. The word 'Viking', therefore, may well be Nordic in origin, meaning a warrior on expedition or the expedition itself, though we should note that etymologically the word may indicate a socially deviating person.[4]

The term 'Viking Age' is normally applied to the period of Scandinavian history from about 800 to the mid-eleventh century, i.e. from the first raids on western Europe by Danes and Norwegians until the final collapse of Danish power in England. If we leave aside the political and military operations of the Norsemen outside Scandinavia and look specifically at the social history of Denmark, the period ought to comprise the eighth century, or at least part of it, while at the other end of the time scale the first half of the eleventh rather than the mid-eleventh century saw the end of the Viking era.

The state of Denmark, having attained its form and extension in about 1000, comprised the whole of present-day Denmark and southern Slesvig, the area from the Danish-German border down to the river Ejder (which was lost to Germany in 1864), as well as Skåne, Halland and Blekinge, the provinces lost to Sweden during the seventeenth century (Fig. 1). Environmentally, the central part of Denmark, including south-west Skåne, is composed of rich agricultural lands of much the same quality and appearance; more marginal soils are found to the west and to the north-east, in the forested parts bordering Sweden. In this book, then, we shall deal with the whole area from the eighth century until approximately the death of King Knud (Canute) in 1035.

The data we have at our disposal for this study are variable and, indeed, often rather incomplete. In most cases it has been necessary to investigate the minor details of the material because serviceable publications are few. For instance, the archaeological data are often dealt with in a stepmotherly way (by historians and archaeological synthesisers alike) except in works that present a specific monument or group of relics. Such publications, however, tend to lack a social perspective. As a result, anyone setting out to write a synthesis based on the considerable but varied information available, and with the economic and socio-political aspects as points of focus, is necessarily faced with a long and wearisome task.[5]

The written historical sources of the Viking Age proper concerning the Danish area are few, and they are not very illuminating about the structure of society. They do, however, supply crucial information of various kinds. Among other things, they point to the tenth century as decisive for the political development which led to the establishment of a hegemony (by the west Danish Jelling dynasty) over the whole of Denmark. They also inform us of the emergence of Christian institutions and the royal acceptance of this new ideology in the latter half of the tenth century.

The runestones are a surprisingly rich source for social reconstruction, particularly in regard to the temporal and geographical information they provide on dependants, lords and inheritance. Among other things, we gain insight into those new systems of quasi-vassalage which were to be significant in the foundation of the Danish state in about 1000. It is important to emphasise, however, that these 'feudal-like' aspects did not turn Viking society into a classic feudal state like, for example, contemporary France.[6] Instead, Denmark in about 1000 was socially similar to England before the Norman Conquest, with grants of land apparently being obtained in return for short-term, essentially military, obligations.

New climatic data combined with pollen analysis can now be used to reconstruct a landscape background to the subsistence economy and thus enable relative population estimates to be calculated. It is particularly important to note the new emphasis given by the Vikings to plant protein in the diet. The study of animal bones demonstrates some of the inter-relationships between the petty towns and the villages that supplied them. Until recently only a few remains of rural settlements from Viking Age Denmark were known. Now, many

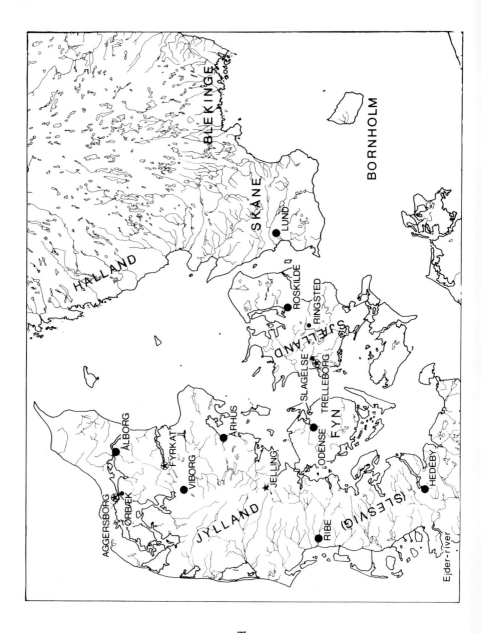

Figure 1 Danish provinces and
Viking Age localities

more have been examined, and these are dealt with here. These settlements have revealed, among other things, a completely new type of agricultural unit: the magnate farm, dating from the tenth century onwards.

Next follows a general, yet detailed, view of the data of the early towns; these data are essentially archaeological, and largely quite recent. The functional similarities and dissimilarities of these centres are outlined, while an attempt is made to bridge some of the gaps in the information. The well-known Trelleborg fortresses of the tenth century are then treated; the presentation has benefited from the recent exhaustive publication of one of the sites, Fyrkat in north-east Jylland[7] (Fig. 28 f. & Pl. I).

Concerning the graves, much older data are analysed, as well as the data from recent excavations. The classification of burials, for example, has enabled us to discover a number of personages who were in the service of the tenth century west Danish Jelling state or who at any rate belonged to its ruling echelons.

Finally, patterns of warfare and conquest within the social system, and some of the economic links with the outside world, are established by the help of the silver hoards – a major group of finds. The coins of these hoards disclose the fluctuations of trade, and here it has been necessary to extend the study as far as the Islamic world. Furthermore, through various developed techniques, the hoards are used to establish the varying amounts of silver surplus in the country. Thus it has been possible to link social development with relations of capital. The Viking raiders set out intentionally to acquire this wealth in western Europe at a time when trade diminished or when they were keeping up large and efficient military forces, as occurred in about 1000, and this accompanied the process of state formation. Thus warfare became an alternative economic strategy.

It has proved useful to divide up the book according to the categories of data. Such a 'Victorian' scheme may seem awkward when broader perspectives, as appears from the following section, are approached. However, the material is so complex and so difficult to present, partly because of its incompleteness, that it is the only feasible course.

If we turn to the background of the Viking Age, the late Iron Age in Denmark (from approximately 400 to 800 A.D.) presents some special problems.[8] As regards the second half of the period, the two hundred years preceding the Vikings show only few finds apart from some burials. Furthermore, there are very few settlement and fortification data and, in the late eighth century, only the earliest traces of townships (Hedeby and Ribe in south Jylland). This makes it extremely hard, if not impossible, to outline a firm social background to the Viking Age in Denmark. In Sweden and Norway the contemporary burial finds alone are much richer,[9] probably because of different social configurations. References to Danish circumstances in the

poems and myths about the pre-Viking Age – as, for example, in
Beowulf – can probably not be used for serious study of this society.
Apparently we are dealing here with a Germanic folk tradition
conditioned for local use. Moreover the texts are nearly all quite late in
the forms that have been handed down.[10]

If we go back to the early Danish Iron Age, from about 500 B.C. to
about 400 A.D., we are on firmer archaeological ground. The data
concerning settlements, graves, offerings, etc., are rich, but a
geographical and temporal overlap of the various types of material is
rarely observed. For instance, most of the wealthy graves are found on
rich agricultural soils, while owing to the circumstances of survival
settlements are almost only recorded from the sandy and marginal
soils to the west in Denmark. Many of the fields here were not tilled in
the period between the third and the present century. This factor,
among others, naturally complicates social reconstruction. However,
separate evidence from settlements and graves favours the idea that
these early Iron Age societies were more or less developed
'chiefdoms'. These societies experienced distinct differences in access
to wealth and subsistence goods, but without the signs of a true social
differentiation, at least when compared with tenth century society in
Denmark.

The links between the Viking Age and the early Middle Ages in
Denmark are also difficult to discern. From the written sources of the
early Middle Ages, however, some of which are now Danish in
origin, we possess a growing amount of information on political and
clerical history.[11] Furthermore, increased minting illuminates certain
aspects of economic history. Urban archaeology is progressing, but
the rural settlements of the early Middle Ages are almost completely
unknown; the Viking villages seem not to have continued into the
medieval period. Another classic archaeological source, the graves,
also tends to disappear from the picture, since from about 1000
cemeteries were established at the new parish churches, where the
ground is still in use today for burials and thus is extremely disturbed.
Furthermore, from the end of the tenth century Christian burial
customs prevent the deposition of grave goods. Pagan offerings,
needless to say, were long gone by the Middle Ages, though we
should note that wealth offerings actually declined drastically in the
middle of the late Iron Age (the sixth century A.D.). Only secular
hoards of valuables continue the Viking Age sequence.

The Denmark of the earliest Middle Ages was a more integrated
society than its northern neighbours, Sweden and Norway, and
throughout the Middle Ages Denmark was the leading Scandinavian
power. Vis-à-vis western Europe, the social and political extremes of
the Viking Age were ended by a combination of growing economic
and political strength of the west and various interior circumstances.
In Denmark the royal political apparatus was concerned with

governing the country at large and checking rival powers, such as the church. The developed town system was now directed primarily towards serving the local provinces, which in turn supplied provisions for the market. The country's exchange and trade were mainly with its Baltic partners and with Germany, the nearest west European area. In other words, Denmark found a balance between the limited size of its resources and its political aspirations. The country was now gradually becoming more like Christian western Europe, though we may note incidentally that in the eleventh and twelfth centuries it suffered, as England had done earlier, from 'barbarian' raids by Norwegians and Slavs, among others.

The ninth century Viking Age raids in the west would not have been possible in the twelfth century, for instance. Only the degree of integration of the country would have counteracted such radical movements. The different ruling groups in medieval society (king, church, aristocracy) were mutually dependent on each other but had different and opposing aspirations, each group trying to enlarge its control. King Knud's later campaigns in England, for example, would have been unthinkable in the twelfth century. The west would have been too strong, and the military and political power of the Danish king too weak, for such endeavours. In spite of the growing administration, relatively few resources were collected in the hands of the medieval sovereign; other magnates were the indispensable social basis for the royal power and, backed by holdings of land, were constantly challenging his position. Beneath these magnates the people would respond to excess burdens.

C. The state

The formation of the state, defined as a large, stable political unit with a high level of production, is crucial in the history of society.[12] Some states were truly 'primary'. They comprise the well-known ancient civilisations of both the Old and the New World, but most were and are 'secondary', developed in part through contact with an already established state. This is not to underestimate the decisive importance of the local society in the make-up of the secondary state – or of any state, for that matter. But within an economically related, and usually homogeneous, zone, the presence of a type of society with a high consumption of resources, like the state, inevitably involves neighbours in a process of trade, warfare, etc. A development is therefore initiated, transforming the local socio-economic structures, originally adapted to the local environment and tradition of society only.

This implies that the formation of secondary states may be more violent than primary developments. An obvious case is the European colonisation of non-state areas. The later history of states is dominated

by conflicts: by warfare with outsiders and by internal antagonisms
due to firmer control and to intervention in community affairs,
especially over different access to strategic resources, usually of
fundamental subsistence importance, and over wealth. In states
wealth and surpluses of production are of special importance because a
market economy usually exists.

The history of the study of the state can be traced back at least to the
Ancient Greek philosophers. Their focus was the power of the state
and how it should be exercised. During the Middle Ages and the
Enlightenment, philosophers discussed the role of God in worldly
power, though during the Enlightenment the state was often seen as a
social contract set up to protect society from evil, such as wars, or
encroachments on rights and property. The early Industrial Age
meant a growing concept of the state as an instrument of suppression;
this is clear in Marx, where any idea of the state as a social contract
gives way to the idea of governmental power serving the interest of
the propertied classes. Though Marx and many of his contemporaries
dealt with the evolution of state society basing their concept on early
historical and archaeological studies and, especially, ethnographic studies
of primitive societies, much of their research can no longer be upheld.
For example, the formation of primary states was completely
unknown to Marx, whose importance, along with that of other
scholars, lies in his early analyses of the function of the contemporary
state as an economic and social system. The tensions and antagonisms
of state society have frequently been emphasised, especially with
respect to its later development, but it should not be overlooked that
the structure of states, being stable societies, has survived internal and
external crises, even so-called revolutions, however important these
may have been in other respects.

In connection with the state the concept of the town, as a centre of
craft production, trade and markets, as well as governmental and
religious institutions, has been much discussed. The town, however,
though a characteristic of most states, is not synonymous with state
society. In Denmark, for instance, town-like structures precede the
true state, while many ethnologically-known states, for example,
have no towns, especially where trade is of little importance. Indeed, a
knowledge of social developments outside Europe has provided an
important perspective for our view of the Viking state, which would
otherwise be the feudal and quasi-feudal societies of western Europe,
which has conditioned so much previous thinking on the concept of
the state. The problem is that feudal western Europe (including England)
is a special variant of the state, resulting from the breakdown and
transformation of the Roman Empire. The Danish development differs
in building on a traditional background, while at the same time
Denmark is a secondary state formed with reference to the social
environment of western Europe. Furthermore, it should not be

overlooked that Denmark also has an eastern environment. The Slavonian and other areas were potentially important allies, and were trade-partners whose existence balanced the impact of the Frankish and German states. In short, it seems impossible to describe the secondary state development without taking into consideration both internal and external factors.

Traditional agrarian societies – in this context the societies that proved the basis of primary or secondary state formations – seem to have only a modest political body and a production directed basically at fulfilling the needs of local communities.[13] Nevertheless, exchange is an ancient institution in human history and may take place both between communities and within a smaller area where headmen or chiefs, whose position is inherited, regulate these processes as well as production as such. Moreover religion – the institutional explanation of the world and therefore a fundamental stimulus of production – is headed by leaders whose status is principally only insecure in times of factional clashes and warfare. Indeed there are strong links between warfare, raiding and trade among societies.

It is clear that a so-called chiefdom is a much larger society than a group of families inhabiting a relatively independent village or group of villages. The chief is in command of an apparatus of which the expansion of one or more sectors, like his revenue of trade or dictatorial rights in time of war, may transform society drastically – in spite of many checks on his power which he owes to the family character of a chiefdom. With respect to the formation of the primary states, a strong promotive factor of chiefly status and power may be the control of the agrarian resources in the confined, but potentially high, production environments of the 'core' areas, like Mesopotamia, the Valley of Mexico, etc. In these areas the instigation and maintenance of irrigation may be an important factor in the formation of a state. In other areas of the world competition for scarce resources during such circumstances as population pressure or inner antagonism may underlie the rise of a chief. This status of control may lead, under external impact, to the formation of a secondary state.

Since bureaucratic control is ultimately useless without physical power, and since power must be bolstered by economic institutions supplying payments and prerogatives, a discussion of the theory of the state may in the end lead to a discussion of economy and the control of the natural environment, the resources as well as the means of production. Indeed, as long as the followers of the chief, or king, are either just servants, living from his products, or themselves petty chiefs, backed by their own families and their claims and tenure of land, it is difficult to administer a large and highly productive society. A crucial point is reached when the followers receive their own economic base – for instance, as personal grants of land, as in early feudal western Europe. This was a process, however, which derived ultimately from the Roman Empire. Furthermore, natural resources, manpower and a powerful technology are needed to take the early state beyond the mere establishment of a tenuous, new controlling system. Even the western Roman Empire did not persist, not only because of the barbarian incursions, but also because of a technology too poorly developed to serve a society with growing problems of production, transportation, etc. And although Denmark did become a state in the Viking Age, the local resources never made it a powerful one. Indeed, its impact was stronger, as the early raids of the ninth century show, when it was still a loosely knit society, fragile on the level of integration, but stable on a local level owing to a self-sufficient economy.

These perspectives, however, serve only as a broad frame of explanatory theory for the history of the Danish Viking Age and as a point of departure for our research. In addition, a thorough knowledge of localised processes is needed to deal with the complex facets of social development. These processes are outlined in the following chapters.

Chapter 2

HISTORICAL SOURCES

A. Introduction

With the exception of the runestones, contemporary historical sources for Denmark in the Viking period are scarce and foreign. Documents are rare and most of our information comes from annals, chronicles and religious biographies, etc.; these vary in content and quality, and are often contradictory about the same event. Later writings are more copious, but like the Sagas and early Danish historiography they are even less reliable.[1] By comparison with the steadily growing archaeological data, the manuscripts, despite their extreme importance, can yield new information only through new interpretations of the few surviving texts.

For the present purpose it is first and foremost the sober Frankish Annals[2] and the biography of Archbishop Ansgar that provide an insight into the warfare and other events of the ninth century and the activities of the early Christian mission. For the further history of Christianity in Denmark and the political events of the tenth century a few German documents and chronicles (by Widukind and Thietmar) are useful. In addition we have a couple of important travel accounts (by Ottar and Wulfstan), and also King Alfred's geography from the turn of the ninth century. Of the later sources Adam of Bremen's History of the Archbishops of Hamburg-Bremen, written in about 1070, is so thorough that it will always hold a central place. English texts play a relatively small part except for the late conquest period, when England shared rulers with Denmark and Danish institutions can be illustrated by comparison with the rich English sources.[3]

An extensive historical literature has been composed on these scarce communications, and it need hardly be mentioned that both the use of the texts themselves and the later interpretations of them cause problems. We must not only employ methods of historical source criticism, but also remain open to information that may seem less momentous or even less reliable in the present state of knowledge. The use we can make of the texts is dependent also on the whole body of theory about the past in which we can apply the general historical data.

Here we shall concentrate on the contemporary sources of the Viking Age, investigating principally the character and development of the social and political institutions. In the texts these occur in connection with warfare and diplomacy and various events relating to the Christian mission and the ports of trade. This is the only type of information that contemporary western European societies were interested in, and that they therefore recorded, for the north. It is striking how long such views of history have served both rulers and scholars in western societies. In general little has been written about subsistence, though rural property was almost the only major source of wealth. (Here we depend on archaeology.) Political government and ideological guidance, which characterise all state societies, were enforced by the military apparatus and the bureaucracy; government also controlled external affairs and the regulation of trade and monitored the religious institutions. Agriculture and the unequal access to wealth were things taken for granted and legally circumscribed by the state; they are a characteristic found in all societies with class distinctions. At the end of the Viking Age, Denmark was just such a society; but it remains to be questioned whether it was so at the time of the first intensive contacts with western Europe.

B. Major historical events

In about 800 the Danes appear as a military power on the Continent and the first Danish raids at sea were launched on the west.[4] In connection with the Carolingian expansion into the Saxon lands across the river Elbe, the north was brought into direct contact with the Franks, and a Danish king, Godfred, is mentioned (in 808) as an enemy attacking the Slavonian Abodrites (a tribe living mainly to the east of present-day Lübeck). The Abodrites were allied with the Franks during the reign of Charlemagne. Godfred already received duties from the emporium of Reric (Alt-Lübeck?), but raided the lands of the Abodrites, replaced their rulers and collected taxes. Reric was destroyed during this raid and its merchants carried to the port of Hedeby, at which point Godfred was intent on securing the Danish border. From here, stretching across the foot of Jylland, he made his army build a wall (Danevirke) 'from the waters of the Baltic to the Western ocean', as the Frankish Annals explain (*see* Translations).

Godfred was murdered (by one of his followers) in 810, but the fighting continued in the following years, and in 815 a Frankish army even entered Jylland for a few weeks in an attempt to overthrow the sons of King Godfred, who were fighting a King Harald of another royal lineage. Harald aspired to royal power supported by the Franks, who later (in 826) gave him a fief as a base in north-west Germany after his baptism. The same year Ansgar undertook his first Danish mission, though with no immediate result.[5] Before his death in 865, however, churches were built at Hedeby and Ribe ports in south Jylland, and at Birka in Sweden (*see* Translations). Of the Danish churches we know that permission was granted by two kings (a father and son) both of the name Horik, who supplied the plots for the buildings. The elder Horik, a son of Godfred, was also said to possess absolute mastery in Denmark; in 854, however, he fell to warring pretenders. In 857, during the reign of Horik II, a pretender named Rurik (a relative of Harald), so the text tells us, received the part of the Danish kingdom that lies 'between the sea and the Ejder'.[6] The Ejder is the Danish/Saxon border-river, but the exact geographical position of the area in question is impossible to ascertain, though it may, for example, have been a western (Frisian) part of south Slesvig. More important is the fact that we may have the first Danish example of something that resembles the continental fief. Furthermore, the province of Rurik controls the western access to Hedeby (cf. Fig. 1), and it is probably no accident that practically the last ninth century source we have for conditions in Denmark deals with border and trade negotiations between Ludwig the German in 873 and the Danish kings.[7]

The Danish raids on the west escalated in the last two thirds of the ninth century, with fighting in Frisia, Saxony, Francia and England. Several 'kings' are mentioned as leaders of the Vikings, and some of them have the same names as kings in Denmark, though further identification cannot be satisfactorily made. Some of the armies settled abroad permanently, especially in England, where Danish kingdoms were established in the eastern half of the country, in the Danelaw ('Danelagen'), in the last third of the century. To what extent bonds with the homeland were maintained is disputed, as is the magnitude of the settlement. At the beginning of the tenth century, Danelagen fell to the English, but in the same decades Danes received Normandy as a fief from the Frankish king.[8]

For more than fifty years around 900 there is no contemporary historical information about Denmark at all. But in 934 the continental (now German) attacks on south Jylland were renewed,[9] and in the same period the mission intensified its impact on the north with the nomination in 948, by the German king, and later emperor, Otto I, of the bishops for the towns of Hedeby, Ribe and Århus, all of which are situated in Jylland. (In 988, at the latest, a bishop is also nominated for Odense on Fyn.)[10] To what extent these early nominations are real – whether the bishops actually reached their seats – is unclear, since the Danish king did not adopt Christianity until about 960.[11] A letter of immunity (exemption from taxes) to the bishops from the emperor in 965 (renewed in 988) follows a standard formula for Germany and probably does not apply to Danish circumstances. According to this letter, the emperor is collecting taxes in Denmark, keeping officials there, and exercising judicial authority, which is not in accordance with the rest of our information of the period.[12] Consequently the mention of slaves, copyholders, etc., cannot be taken to describe Danish economic conditions of the tenth century.

A few names of kings are known from the period. The Danish king at the time of the raids in 934 was Knuba, who may have been of Swedish descent (though his queen was Danish). He is said to have been baptised after his defeat.[13] Other kings were Gorm and his son Harald, who are referred to on the runestones of Jelling in Jylland (Pl. XIII) – the same Harald who accepted Christianity in about 960 and who declared that he, for himself, won the whole of Denmark and Norway (cf. Fig. 3).[14] This Harald, however, was attacked in 974 by Otto II, who took the Danevirke wall and erected a fortress at the border, which fell to the Danes in 983.[15] Harald died in 987 at the latest and was followed by his son Sven, who from 994 onwards participated in the renewed attacks on England. In 1013 Sven was nominated king of England but died soon after and was succeeded by Knud the Great (Pl. XVI). Knud lived until 1035, ruling Denmark, England and Norway like his father.[16] In their relations with the ecclesiastical institutions it is significant that they personally nominated bishops, sent from England, first to Skåne (Sven) and later to (Knud) Sjælland, and also to Fyn.[17] With Knud's son Hardeknud, who died in 1042, the period of the North Sea empire definitely ends, but by this time Denmark, in its medieval extent, has become a unified state with a homogeneous population possessing firmly established Christian institutions and a military and bureaucratic apparatus to sustain the political establishment.

Furthermore, we have entered the eleventh century, for which the archaeological data once again are poor.

C. Political units

The extent and character of the political units in the Danish Viking Age are difficult to grasp from the written historical sources, but a few details seem clear.

The power of King Godfred, in 800, was based on the rallying of military forces, and as far as we know, it had two purposes. The first was to gain wealth from taxation and plundering in neighbouring areas. The second was to secure the income from trade by protecting Danish ports, and at the same time to prevent foreign powers from crossing the borders. If the rigidly straight Kovirke wall, immediately to the south of Hedeby (Pl. VIII & Fig. 21), is Godfred's contribution to the Danevirke system (which we have little reason to doubt), it tells us about the discipline and organisation of the army. A royal official was put to watch the wall, as the sources also disclose.[18]

The two King Horiks at least had an official in Hedeby, called in the German texts 'comes', count, to regulate social order and collect taxes.[19] Moreover, at Hedeby, royal power, probably initiated by Godfred, is seen in the establishment of the central settlement with its fixed plan containing larger and smaller streets (Chapter 5 D and Figs. 22-3). To protect Jylland against Charlemagne, Godfred could have chosen to fortify the older and more irregular main wall to the north of Hedeby. Instead, the incorporation of Hedeby leaves no doubt of its growing importance. It was not a market settlement on the border to the Saxons and the Slavs, but a port controlled and regulated by a Danish king.

To what extent Godfred's behaviour is normal for the age, and to what extent it is a result of the Frankish military pressures and other contacts with the west, remain in doubt. Border walls were certainly erected much earlier (cf. Chapter 5 E), and the same goes for raids into foreign parts.[20] The settlements of Hedeby and Ribe were already established in the eighth century (Chapter 5 D); yet the growth of Hedeby at the time of King Godfred must be the result of more trade and manufacturing, which in turn would yield larger revenues to the potentate; and the military rallying needed to oppose Charlemagne's land army, which had just subdued Saxony and constituted a threat far beyond any other to Denmark, must have had political and economic consequences too. For instance, the military occupation may have increased, and it is a question whether the connected expenses were met by the income from tax and toll as well as from raids. If not, the insecurity and wars of the ninth century may ultimately have forced the kings to grant land to their followers in return for military service, or as in the Rurik case (857) perhaps to solve other problems. Such a development would be a clear step away from the society of ranked families in the various parts of the country which we believe to have existed in Denmark before the changes of the Viking Age. Other economic changes would come from the creation of a market for foodstuffs among the urban populations, and perhaps even the armies, and yet other changes from the creation of craft production and exchange, particularly in luxuries, in the towns. Previously these activities must have taken place at the political centres and at periodic markets.

These perspectives raise the question of the size of the political units in Denmark in the Viking period, where the high level of warfare may easily have led either to fragmentation or to integration. Godfred's successful struggle with the Franks would be a factor favouring co-operation, and at a peace meeting (at the Ejder river) in 811, the year after the murder of Godfred, a gathering of twelve high-ranking Danes and the same number of Frankish counts met to conclude peace.[21] Among the Danes were three persons of the name Osfrid; these are further characterised respectively by their nickname, father's name and province. The third Osfrid was from Skåne, which must mean that Danes to the west and at the border, as well as to the east, were involved in the fighting. Whether Skåne was an integrated part of Godfred's kingdom, however, is not certain. The geographical characterisation, as compared with the family ones, would favour the view that Skåne was outside the realm.

The Frankish army, entering Slesvig in 815, marched on for a week to the coast, across from which lay the sons of Godfred with their forces on an island three miles (4.5 kms) away. This island was probably Fyn, which might have been the centre of Godfred's kingdom. This perhaps is confirmed in the Frankish Annals for 819, which document King Harald's return to power in Denmark. Instead of crossing the border at Hedeby, or sailing to south Jylland, Harald travelled through the land of the Abodrites (east of later Lübeck), whence he sailed to his homeland. For the year 821 it is added that Harald was accepted as co-regent by the sons of Godfred. Furthermore, we know that Godfred and his sons made raids in the Baltic, as far as the Oslo-fjord area to the north of Kattegat, in about 813, while a Danish raid on Frisia to the west in 810 was apparently led by some other chieftain. Finally, it may be mentioned that the only ninth century runestone erected for a woman, assuredly of high rank, was set up on Fyn by a man with the royal name of Godfred.[22]

Of King Horik II, the grandson of Godfred, it is said that both Hedeby and Ribe were within his kingdom (about the mid-ninth century), but his realm may well have been much larger.[23] In 813 Vestfold (west of later Oslo) is described as being at the farthest north-western border of the realm of Godfred's sons.[24]

In the countryside we must rely on the runestones to tell us about the social structure. Here we find titles like 'gode' and 'thul' (cf. Chapter 3). A gode is a pagan priest and a thul probably the same, although the word means 'speaker', possibly implying a secular connotation. That the gode also had secular duties is disclosed by the Glavendrup stone on Fyn, where the deceased is both a gode and a thegn, a royal vassal (Pl. X).[25] The Glavendrup monument is erected by the wife, Ragnhild, who came from Sjælland and was married there too, either before or after her marriage on Fyn.[26] This reveals the close-knit connections between the magnate families from various provinces. Earlier, another gode from Fyn, Roulv, occurs on four different runestones scattered over the island;[27] this gives some impression of the size of the geographical space that these officials and other personages commanded. In the next chapter we shall discuss the early runestones at length.

Shortly before 900 a Norwegian (Ottar) sailed from north Norway to sell his products, mainly furs, at Hedeby, 'a Danish port lying on the border between various peoples'.[28] Leaving south Norway, he kept 'Denmark' on the port side (i.e. the province of Halland) and, thereafter, on the starboard side, Jylland and Slesvig, and many islands, and on the port side 'the island' belonging to Denmark. This shows that Halland to the east was also part of the Danish nation.

Another traveller, Wulfstan, left Hedeby about the same time, going eastwards.[29] He mentions the 'lands' of Langeland, Lolland, Falster (all islands) and Skåne as belonging to Denmark. 'Bornholm came thereafter; it had its own king,' Wulfstan then mentions the province of Blekinge, part of medieval Denmark, and a number of other 'lands' as belonging to the 'Swedes' (but not to 'Sweden'). This account indicates existing minor kingdoms in the Danish area, but Wulfstan may have considered Bornholm neither Danish nor Swedish, which, according to the text, is possible.

The two travel books appear in King Alfred's English version of Orosius' *History of the World*, a work of late Antiquity. Among Alfred's contributions to the book is a geography of Europe which says that Denmark is divided into the areas of the 'Northdanes' and 'Southdanes'. The Northdanes lived on the continent and on the islands, meaning Skåne, Sjælland, etc., and the Southdanes to the west on the North Sea, in Jylland, etc.[30] This interesting division probably corresponds to the oldest known dialect border through the Store Bælt,[31] and it is also known from a tenth century runestone on the island of Lolland (to the east) which speaks of Special Swedes, Swedes living outside their homelands, and also Southdanes.[32] That only the eastern part of the country is called 'Denmark' in Ottar's account is perhaps due to the circumstances of his description.

Later historical sources talk about Swedish kings holding land in Denmark in about 900,[33] a claim that cannot be completely discarded since a couple of runestones at Hedeby mention the same persons as the texts, of which one seems to be the king, Knuba, whom the Germans were fighting in the attack on the Danes in 934.[34] This perhaps is confirmed by the runestone from Lolland mentioned previously.

A foreign population group would have had to integrate into the local milieu, even if the foreigners were rulers. In the present case all we know is that Knuba was married to a Dane, a daughter of an Odinkar, a name known to have been used by lineages with royal connections. The possibility occurs that in the incident of the Swedish 'kings' we may have a parallel to the grant of land to Rurik in south Jylland. Another parallel may be seen in the Danish kingdoms and fiefs of foreign lands in other areas of western Europe. At all events, it is impossible to conceive of rulers not belonging to the local society if they did not possess estates of their own with which to maintain themselves. This again would continue the break-up of traditional tenure of land and perhaps even turn it into a kind of commodity which, if not sold, could be granted in return for services such as

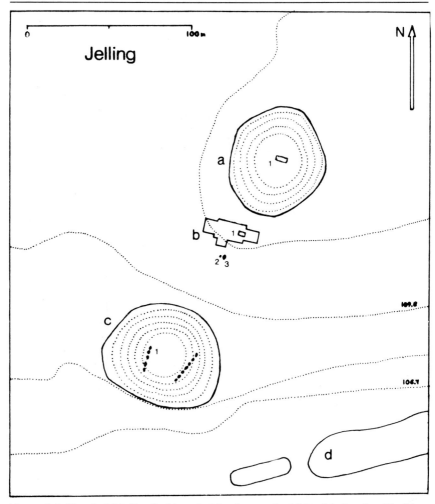

Figure 2 Jelling (mid-Jylland). (a) = the Northmound with burial chamber (1); (b) =
the medieval stone church with Viking Age burial chamber (1) beneath (the stave
churches are not shown), (b 2) = King Gorm's stone (*DR* 41), (b 3) = King
Harald's stone (*DR* 42), (cf. Fig. 3); (c) = the Southmound, covering remnants of a
stone-setting, probably a ship-setting (1); (d) is ponds

guarding the border. In the Knuba case the chronology of Danish kings
may suggest that King Gorm, the father of Harald, was ruling at Jelling
in the 930s and was the overlord of the Hedeby magnate, whose son
was also a 'king' according to the runestones set by his Danish mother.

King Gorm, his wife Thyra and their son Harald are tied to the
locality of Jelling by the two well-known runestones standing next to
the Romanesque parish church between two giant mounds (Pl. XII-
XIII and Fig. 2).[35] The Northmound holds a wooden chambered tomb
divided into two parts with remnants of very fine tenth century

Figure 3 A. King Harald's stone (*DR* 42)

equipment for a man and a woman. This grave has been opened and carefully closed again with additional boards. Below the present church are the remnants of three wooden churches, the earliest and largest of which is contemporary with another chamber tomb holding the secondary burial of two bodies, apparently a male and a female, each of very high rank, to judge from their exquisite garments and jewellery. Under the Southmound are two rows of boulders in a narrow angle; in between the mounds were big stones, probably all belonging to a ship-setting in connection with the Northmound, or rather with the ancient Bronze Age barrow inside the mound. It is into this barrow that the chamber tomb has been dug.

The oldest runestone is of the usual size. It was erected by King Gorm over Thyra, his wife, 'the adornment of Denmark'. The second stone, the largest runestone in Denmark, reads: 'King Harald bade be made these kumls (this monument) after (in memory of) Gorm his father and after Thyra his mother, that Harald who won for himself Denmark all, and Norway, and made the Danes Christian' (Fig. 3).

It is reasonable to conceive that King Gorm 'bade be made' his stone

Figure 3 B. King Harald's stone

in connection with the burial chamber in the Bronze Age barrow of the Northmound and with the pagan stone-setting. The Northmound itself must have been finished by Harald, since Gorm, most probably, was buried here too. At a later date the mound was opened to transfer the bodies to the chamber, which was built on the site of the already planned first wooden church. This may also be the date at which the large runestone was erected, which now stands at the entrance to the church, as well as the Southmound. Another possibility is that only the first part of the inscription was made at the same time as the Northmound, the mound being the 'kumls' (monument) of Harald for his parents. (If the Northmound alone cannot be termed kumls (plural), the southern mound may be of the same date or the stone itself conceived as a part of the monument. Anyway, to judge by the age of the mosses on the stones of the ship–setting, the Southmound is some twenty or thirty years later.) The second part of the text, concerning Norway and Christianity, would then have been written at the time of the transfer of the bodies, the building of the first church and, perhaps, the partial 'destruction' of the pagan ship-setting by the

Figure 3 C. King Harald's stone

Southmound. This is not completely impossible, to judge from the inscription and its relation to the pictures of the stone.

King Harald must have died no later than 987. According to later tradition he reigned for fifty years,[36] which is consistent with the fact that only he, according to Adam of Bremen, is mentioned during the period of Adeldag's archbishopric at Bremen (936-988), while Gorm is mentioned under his predecessor Unni (915-936). Harald's conversion and baptism seem to have taken place in about 960 – of his own free will, since no German pressure is recorded at that time. Nor is the missionary Poppo said to have had any connection with Germany.[37] (According to the legend, Poppo carried red-hot iron before Harald to prove the power of Christ.) Before 960 Harald must have been hailed as a distant lord of at least a part of Norway and won, for himself, all of Denmark. The remark about Norway may throw some light on the claim of 'Denmark all'. (We take Denmark, as indicated above, to comprise roughly the area of medieval Denmark.) Control of Norway cannot have been of the same kind as control of Denmark, nor of the same kind as contol of mid-Jylland. The words 'for himself' are also interesting, since they may indicate the final disappearance of other heirs to the throne. Harald is carrying the same name as the expelled Harald of the early ninth century and may have been of the same royal lineage, but we have no actual evidence of continuity between the two centuries.

Harald's conversion to Christianity at first sight seems strange. We have indications of a royal Odin-cult in pre-Christian Denmark, and religious and secular powers were traditionally integrated.[38] In a Christian system priests and bishops of an international church assume parts of the royal power. Furthermore, the pagan Nordic ideology accords far better with local circumstances than the transcendence of Christianity. Harald, however, by favouring his southern social environment, would be less easily overrun by the German emperor Otto I, who sought European supremacy from a firm base of power. We may conceive of Harald imitating Otto's idea of the king's considerable influence on religious affairs and on the Christian officials. In the short run this may have been against the plans of Germany, but in the long run western Europe would benefit from having northern opponents whose societies were of the same developed, and vulnerable, kind and not, like the Germanic tribes of the Roman period, for instance, a constant threat to their centres of power. In fact there is no sign that Harald had to submit to the Germans, who throughout the period mention the Danes as being outside the German realm and as a constant menace. Like Otto, Harald sought to secure his borders and realm by fortifications and fortresses and, as we shall see later, military settlements. Yet it was apparently internal opposition that finally overthrew the old King Harald, and several sources mention his son Sven as participating in the rebellion.[39]

By the reign of Sven at the latest the major parts of medieval Denmark must have been fully integrated. In the historical sources this may appear from the marriages of King Harald (whose mother was Danish) and his son Sven. Both of them married women from outside Denmark – Sven a daughter of the Polish king, and Harald a daughter of a prince of the Slavonian Abodrites – and both marriages, political in nature, are notably with royal houses opposing the Germans.[40] Fighting in Scandinavia had now reached the level of nations, and indeed without a united Denmark it would have been possible neither for King Sven nor for his son Knud to maintain power on both sides of the North Sea.

As in the ninth century, the runestones are virtually our only source for the political and social structure of the country (Chapter 3). On the tenth century stones we have quite a number of titles which seem to refer to the royal power, to the hird (the housecarls), to the vassals and to various other institutions; but the pagan are gone.

The immediate retinue of the kings (and queens) and other magnates are the housecarls. Additional high-ranking servants comprise managers of land ('landhyrde'), agents ('bryde'), skilled craftsmen ('smed') and ships' captains ('skippers'). More numerous are thegns (thane, in English), vassals, and drengs (literally 'young men'), minor vassals. The titles 'landmand', 'bomand' (residing man, perhaps petty landman), and 'bonde' (farmer) seem to be those of a vassal, probably with different duties from those of the thegns and drengs, of which the drengs at least disclose connections with the army. Drengs are also captains of warships ('styresmænd', steersmen) and follow the king and other magnates in combat. Finally, a high-ranking man, perhaps a royal adviser, is known.[41] Bishops, earls, counts of towns, commandants of forts do not occur; and we conclude that the late stones refer first of all to a system of royal vassalage, comparable with the contemporary, but much more extended, English system. The numerous tenth century stones are simple texts of succession, and most probably of inheritance too. They lack the pagan expressions of the earliest stones, but they preserve much of the traditional ethos at a period when Denmark was becoming a west European society.

Chapter 3

RUNESTONES AND PEOPLE IN A CHANGING SOCIETY

A. Introduction

The written historical sources for Denmark in this period are almost all foreign, and we consistently lack a local perspective. The only texts from the country itself are the brief inscriptions on the runestones, which in addition have some of the same qualities as the archaeological material. The stones are spread throughout the area and we can give the inscriptions a geographical dimension. Furthermore most of the texts refer to succession to titles and rights over land, enabling us to view the politics and social structure of the rural economy.[1]

Runic letters were in use in Denmark at least six hundred years before the beginning of the Viking Age, but the runestones themselves cannot be earlier than 700–800 since they are written in the so-called younger 'futhark' (alphabet) appearing on artefacts of the eighth century onwards. This alphabet is simpler to write than the earlier one and seems to have developed in daily life, or in the trading and administrative sectors. At the end of the tenth century dots were added to some of the letters to facilitate reading; this may mean that communication by then was becoming more complex. It is striking how the development of the runes corresponds to the social growth of the country. That runestones were introduced late into Denmark, apart from the marginal eastern province of Blekinge, is strange, since the custom in Norway and Sweden is much earlier.[2] This suggests that we are not dealing with a simple process of diffusion. Their occurrence appears to be connected with the emergence of new social categories, or new social conditions, where the monuments should sustain the position of the successor of the deceased. It is not certain that any of the Viking Age stones were raised over a living person, and in most cases it was a member of the closest family who had it raised, usually a male following another male.

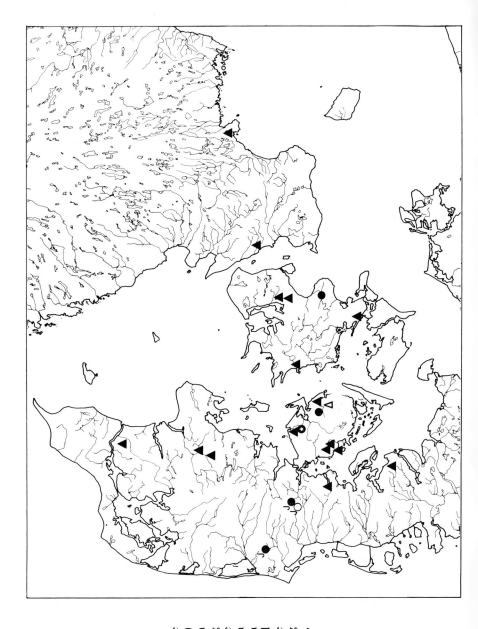

Figure 4 Distribution of the early runestones (triangles) and the transition stones (in Jylland of the Læborg group, on the islands of the Glavendrup group). Open signature: stone raised over a woman. Star: stone raised over a thegn. J = a stone referring to the Jelling dynasty. (Appendices I, II, III & V.)

B. *Chronology and content*

A chronological classification of the runestones can be made based on a number of traits. The philologist picks up the type of language, while the runologist is more interested in the alphabet and in the appearance of the inscription, including ornamentation; both study the content of the text. The absolute chronology is established by comparison with texts on artefacts and, within more narrow time scales, by the so-called historical runestones, referring to known personalities and events.

The earliest group of stones comprises here the 'Helnæs-Gørlev' and most of the 'Pre-Jelling' stones of the standard classification of 1942 (Appendix I and Fig. 4).[3] The monuments are undecorated, while they still show some archaic runes, and the texts are in general short, written in Old Danish, but with a few so-called Primeval Nordic elements from an earlier period without national characteristics in the written language. The content is a name with various additions, not infrequently magical, but usually of a close family relation, often to the erector of the monument. The stones mostly come from Fyn and neighbouring areas in the middle of Denmark.

Three late stones of the early group, two of which are connected with ship-settings, have more copious inscriptions (Appendix II).[4] Glavendrup (Pl. X) in north Fyn mentions the god Thor, whose 'hammer' became the symbol of the tenth century pagan reaction against Christianity. This stone is erected over an honourable thegn (vassal) and heathen priest (gode) by his wife and sons, the heirs to his position and property. 'Sote' wrote the runes 'for his Lord'. The text ends with a curse threatening anyone who destroys the stone or moves it away.

Contemporary with the Glavendrup stone, or perhaps a little later, is a group of monuments from mid-Jylland (of which one, Læborg, has a Thorshammer ornament), mentioning a Thyra, without doubt the wife of King Gorm (Appendix II).[5] Gorm's own stone for the queen belongs to the so-called Jelling group, which includes no old runes and is written in Old Danish without earlier elements (Appendix IV, Fig. 5).[6] In the same group are King Harald's stone for his parents, Gorm and Thyra, from about 960, and the monuments connected with King Knuba fighting the Germans in 934.[7] The early stones are not definitely connected with historically known persons, but they seem to lie in the ninth century or even the eighth century. The so-called 'After Jelling' stones, on the other hand, are historically connected with King Sven, the son of Harald, and are dated to about 1000, though some may have been erected even later at the time of Sven's son, King Knud (Appendix VI; cf. also III, and Fig. 6).[8]

The 'After Jelling' group of runestones is defined by the occurrence of he late runes with dots, among other details, but both this type and the Jelling type are characterised by inscriptions of the firm formula

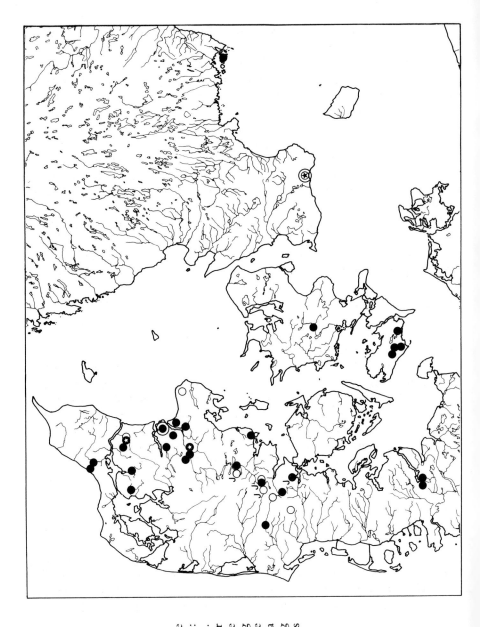

Figure 5 Runestones of the Jelling type. Open signature: stone raised over a woman. White star: stone raised over a thegn. Black star: stone raised over a dreng. Ring around the signature: stone raised over a fælle. J = a stone referring to the Jelling dynasty proper. (Appendices III, IV & V.)

'NN made this monument (or the like) for NNN, his . . . (family or other relation) . . . (possibly further characterising, etc.)' and the lapse of magical elements. A few stones refer to Thor or are found with pagan ship-settings, for instance Gorm's Jelling stone.[9] Other monuments, especially of the 'After Jelling' group have Christian elements. Other traits are the often quite rich ornamentation (cf. King Harald's Jelling stone) and a freer arrangement of the text ribbons on some of the 'After Jelling' monuments, in waves, along the margins of the stone, compared with the standard arrangement of the words in parallel rows.

The late inscriptions clearly take the form of statements of succession and refer sometimes directly to ownership of land, which of course is the basic source of wealth in the Viking period.[10] Typically, the erector of the stone is mentioned first, while titles are usually used only when reference is to the deceased. Indeed titles gradually become more common, most of them apparently of various types of vassals to the king and other magnates. Consequently, in the 'After Jelling' period non-family relations become more common.

The geographical spread of the Jelling runestones is as follows: two come from Hedeby, and a few more from the island of Lolland, while the majority are from mid-Jylland, to the north of the Kongeå river, and north-eastern Jylland (Fig. 5). The 'After Jelling' stones are concentrated in north-eastern Jylland, with a small group around the city of Århus and a larger one to the west and north of the later town of Randers; in addition, a significant cluster has been found at the Skåne city of Lund, and a similar one is known in south Skåne. A couple of monuments are from Hedeby. Only a few Jelling and 'After Jelling' group stones are found in other areas of Denmark (Fig. 6).

On the island of Bornholm the many runestones differ from the others, both in time and style. They belong runographically and in terms of language to a period around 1050 and even later, and are paralleled by most of the Swedish stones whose appearance they copy.[11] In terms of their content, these stones continue the trends of the 'After Jelling' type with the same kind of inscription; many, however, are Christian, while a number of titles occur, though none mention non-family relations.

C. The socio-political sphere

The first problem in dealing with the runestones and socio-geographical questions is the representative quality of the data. In general this is a critical archaeological question, but here we may feel sure that the spreads in time and space correlate with the original ones, since runestones cannot have been moved far from their Viking Age sites; in addition, they are hard to destroy completely. Indeed the very

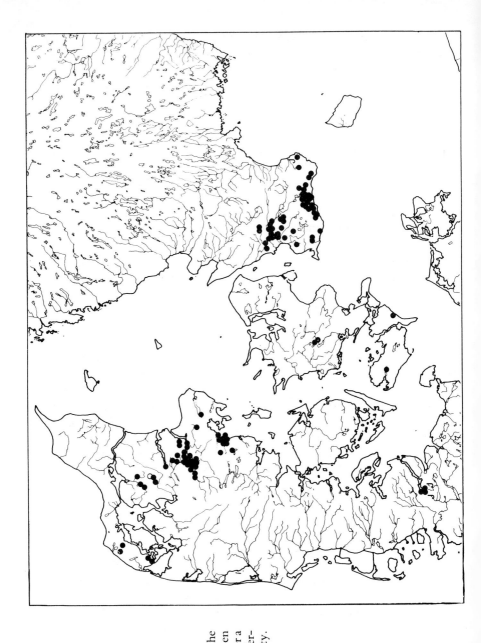

Figure 6 Runestones of the 'After Jelling' type. Open signature: stone raised over a woman. J = a stone referring to the Jelling dynasty. (Appendices III, V & VI.)

different distributions in Denmark of the chronological groups are the strongest point in favour of the sample being identical with the original scatter.

The early stones, of Helnæs-Gørlev type, etc., show a striking concentration in the Danish population medians, perhaps with a bias towards the south-west (Fig. 4). The distribution is rather coastal, except for mid-Jylland, and corresponds to the areas of good soil (and much forest). We have already mentioned the fact that all memorial stones bolster the position of the bereaved; this is clearly so on the stones which include the member of the family who had the stone erected and who is taking over the inheritance, be it a position or a land-holding, or very likely both. At the same time the appearance of the memorial stone bearing an inscription of about 700 or 800 must signify a larger society, though the use of runes carries a magic element in itself. We have very few clues about who the deceased were, except that they were males of the higher social echelons, like the 'gode' and the 'thul' who held important religious, and, apparently, also secular, positions. So far the development might have taken place entirely within the traditional society, and it is significant that the mentioned titles appear with names of peoples and localities. The Glavendrup thegn, however, cannot be understood within this framework alone.[12] Thegn is an Anglo-Saxon title for a royal vassal, who, in exchange for certain, basically military, duties is granted land which is inheritable.[13] What speaks in favour of a similar position open to the Danish thegn is not only the contemporary contact with England and comparable political and military conditions, but also the notion that Alle, the 'gode' at Glavendrup, was the thegn of the lith, the troop of warriors. But otherwise it is not until the Jelling group proper that we find firm support for an idea of royal vassalage, or royal dependence of a quasi-feudal kind.

On the other hand we cannot exclude the possibility that even the ninth-century stones were erected for people whose rights of land differed from the traditional ones. First, the employment of the runestone custom may show this in itself, and secondly the distribution-pattern could indicate the emergence of centralised power. The stones are usually placed close to the modern high roads that join on Fyn, which we have mentioned above as a possible centre of Denmark during King Godfred's reign. This spread cannot possibly be considered random.

Kings have a constant need for military power and protection, and in times of intense unrest these kings' warrior retinues may have grown considerably. Furthermore, the need for local support and control will have had to be augmented; this problem was perhaps solved by grants of free land to ex-housecarls and other servants (as the word thegn, 'servant', seems to have meant originally). The coastal distribution may find its explanation here, and we cannot help but be

reminded of the Danish 'herreds' division, the germ of which goes
back to some time in the Viking period. The 'herreds' seem originally
to have been military districts, each probably with a stipulated
obligation to man one or more warships.[14] Already King Godfred was
in command of a fleet, as is reported by the Frankish Annals; in 804 he
arrived at Hedeby with his fleet and all the cavalry of his kingdom to
meet Charlemagne. In 815 a Danish fleet of '200' (20?) ships, under the
command of the sons of Godfred, prevented a Frankish army from
landing on Fyn. Unfortunately nothing is said about how these navies
were rallied, but we believe that considerable Danish forces were
pledged to unite under such circumstances, a fact reflected perhaps in
the presence of Osfrid of Skåne at the summit meeting on the Ejder in
811. Finally, the forested areas of central Denmark could yield new
estates for royal followers without coming too much in conflict with
the local rights to land.

Whether we see the early runestones as reflecting a development
within the traditional society, or as a new institution, the distribution
needs to be explained. It is in this central area – and not, for instance,
on the border with Saxony, or in the area of the early ports, Hedeby
and Ribe – that the need is evidently felt to reinforce support of certain
personages and their positions – indeed perhaps even the first kings of
a paramount rule.

Denmark in the Viking Age is a well confined and relatively
homogeneous environmental entity. On most sides it is surrounded
by the sea, but in the south-west a narrow land corridor led to Saxony,
and in the north-east the fertile soils of the southern and western parts
of Halland, Skåne, and perhaps Blekinge, gave way to the thinly
populated and heavily forested soils of the Danish/Swedish borderlands. Within this zone competition, possible conflicts and any
imbalance in the societies would be felt most in the population
medians, merging on Fyn, since here, in the middle of such an area, the
number of potential opponents would have been largest. On the other
hand, co-operation and unification of societies at this point could
diminish conflicts more than in any other area.

The possible reasons for such disturbances are manifold. Some
disturbances would be slow, like the population growth, others faster,
like the Frankish pressures in about 800, or the result of an influx of
wealth from increasing trade. Perhaps we should favour a two-step
development, where population growth and competition for resources and wealth and trade revenues led to a political centralisation
in central Denmark. A factor like Charlemagne's engulfing of the
Saxons and assault on borderlands would then leave even the strongest
political body with military problems and imperatives, including
grants of land to maintain the allegiance of close followers.

We have pursued quite stubbornly the idea that the persons
mentioned on the early runestones were connected with royal power.

The primary reason for this assertion lies in the complementary distribution of the subsequent Jelling-type stones, where we are relatively well-informed about kings and their dependants. In addition, the transition-stones of the Glavendrup and Læborg groups are found in the zone stretching from north Fyn to southern mid-Jylland which constitutes the main border between the early stones and the Jelling type (Figs 4-5). Apparently we are dealing with the diffusion of one and the same general phenomenon, the runestones marking its introduction and then disappearing. The reason for the disappearance may lie in the fact that of course we are dealing not only with succession to social positions but with a new kind of rights to land. The moment these rights of tenure are established, however, they follow the regular channels of family inheritance. This is not to say that the political milieu was the same in both the ninth and the tenth centuries. Indeed, as we may observe from the style of the inscriptions, the ideological milieu was certainly not the same. And socially, it is apparent that the successor who benefits from the inheritance and position is indicated more regularly on the later monuments.

We return to the model of internal competition. In the initial period possible conflicts were based on central Denmark, which was the first area to become integrated. In the tenth century the spread of Jelling-type runestones to more marginal areas, and the existence of the Jelling political centre itself in southern mid-Jylland, speaks of the incorporation of these perimeter areas (Fig. 5). We infer that the development in the Fyn zone put pressure on the marginal areas. (This was at the time of major Danish attacks on western Europe.) The periphery might have countered through a traditional system of alliances, but in such cases geography favours the heart of an area, and the outcome was employment in still larger portions of the perimeter, of the advancing system of royal vassalage and new holds on land. (A parallel case is Charlemagne's engulfing of the Saxons.) At the end of the Viking period, not only was Denmark a linguistic and cultural entity, and a system of political alliances, but it was united under one rule and, as we shall see from the following chapters, it also had an economic system that differed greatly from the days of Godfred. The movement of the centre of political gravity to the west was probably the result of the growth of the early towns, which were exclusively western, and a rural economy directed, among other things, at supplying the towns. It can also be taken to represent a reaction against the Fyn-zone personalities of the Godfred line and an assumption of power by new dynasties, such as the petty Swedish dynasty in Hedeby and the Jelling kings further north. During the reign of King Sven of the Jelling line, the 'After Jelling' stones are found both to the west and to the east in Denmark, and we consider the process of integration to have been largely completed, except, perhaps, for Bornholm and Blekinge. The kings may have been fighting each other, but the antagonisms all served to develop a new social system, eventually with towns, and ultimately to create a true hegemony.

The Jelling-type stones, as we have noted, are clear witnesses of family heirship. The inheritor was now as important as the deceased, and we get the impression that the ruling families were detached from the rest of the population. Moreover, we no longer hear of names of localities or peoples in connection with titles. One major group of stones is from the southern mid-Jylland around Jelling. Compared with the early monuments, situated near the coast, these are raised inland, and half of them are attached directly to the dynasty family (Figs 4–5). In the outer scatter of stones – comprising, as viewed from Jelling, north Jylland, Sjælland-Lolland as well as south Slesvig – we have no monuments for the Jelling dynasty itself; only a Lolland text speaks of Southdanes (Jyder/Jutlanders). Furthermore, these latter stones are basically coastal, which is why we see a difference between the homeland and base of the ruling family and the estates of the dependants which, as in the ninth century, often lie at the sea.

At least six of the stones in the central part of Jylland are raised for women, but only two in the peripheral areas, while the ratio of deceased men is about six from the central to twenty-two from the outside scatter (cf. Appendix V). That only a few, very high-ranking women seem to have had property of their own underlines the social importance of southern mid-Jylland. At the same time we can understand how the Jelling kings and followers, and perhaps the Swedish kings too, at Hedeby, bolstered their power by marrying the daughters of the local magnates.

Outside the central cluster and its royal personages we have the majority of dependants, who were given land mainly on the coast. In the periphery there also lay the fortresses and other defences of the mid-tenth-century Jelling rulers: Aggersborg on the Limfjord, Fyrkat at present-day Hobro in north-eastern Jylland, Trelleborg on the west coast of Sjælland and some of the Danevirke walls at Hedeby (cf. Fig. 1).

In terms of occupational and rank titles, apart from 'king', we have from the centre only one example, a 'bryde' (agent of an estate), who must have been of high rank, perhaps a royal bryde, since he mentions his own title, like kings, and raises a monument for his wife.[15] From the periphery comes one 'landmand', a royal vassal,[16] two thegns (not counting Glavendrup),[17] one 'dreng' (young man, a minor vassal)[18] and two 'skippers' (ships' captains).[19] The titles all belong to the deceased, except for one of the skippers. Also from the periphery come two non-family, or 'fælle' (cf. fellow), relations, one of them with the dreng.[20] The word 'fælle' comprises 'fæ', property; it appears in connection with one of the thegns too, who bequeathed his land to his foster son.[21]

The 'After Jelling' stones from about 1000 A.D. are rich in titles, and most discussions of their meaning – for instance those concerned with thegns and of drengs – have their starting point here.[22] In the following we shall pay considerable attention to the geography of the stones. It must be emphasised that much of our conception of the stones as monuments of succession to titles, position and land, and of the idea of the relations between the kings and the magnates and dependants of the stones, stems from the observations we shall now deal with.

We take as a point of departure the Skåne material, since this, of the two main clusters of runestones, is from an area that is almost devoid of earlier stones (Figs 7–8). In north-eastern Jylland, which will be discussed below, we have a strong continuation from the Jelling period. Two Jelling – and one 'After Jelling' – type monuments from here even seem to have been written by the same master of runes.[23] On the other hand, there is evidence that the Jylland and Skåne stones are probably contemporary. For instance, two monuments, one erected in Jylland and one in Skåne, stand to four brothers who have the same father.[24] Other observations, however, suggest that some of the Skåne stones are later than the Jylland ones. For one thing, King Sven appears on two Jylland stones and his son Knud apparently, on a single stone from Skåne.[25] More important, the new way of arranging the text, on ribbons following the margin of the stone, is four times as common in Skåne as the traditional parallel ribbons, while in Jylland the old style is found on slightly more than half the stones. Furthermore, the Skåne examples of the parallel-line text come from the western cluster around the city of Lund, whereas it seems to be practically unknown in the south Skåne cluster.[26]

Looking at the relations between the dead person and his heir on the Skåne stones, it is surprising that the small cluster along the fertile southern coast divides in two parts or sub-clusters (Fig. 7 B and 8 C). To the west we have ten (perhaps eleven) dead brothers, another male relative, who is mentioned neither as a father, nor as a son, two 'fæller' (fellows) as well as a single husband at the northern edge of the group. To the east we have four dead fathers (there is also someone who is said to have a son, 'the dreng of Knud') and two husbands. The distribution is strange, considering that we are dealing with a settlement of well-established landowners. A possible solution is that the men to the west in this southern cluster may in fact have been married and may even have had sons, but their holdings were not passed on to the family at large, only to their brothers. And even the brother may not, of course, always have been a full brother: on at least one Skåne stone the word 'brother' stands for foster-brother.[28] It is conceivable that the men of the western sub-cluster did not own their land without restrictions, but paid a kind of rent, or rather service, probably to the king. It may have been a duty only a man of younger age could succeed to, and in case of death the brother, or another closely related person of equal standing, would be picked to take over the holding or 'fæ', perhaps as the 'fælle' of the deceased. Otherwise it is unlikely that

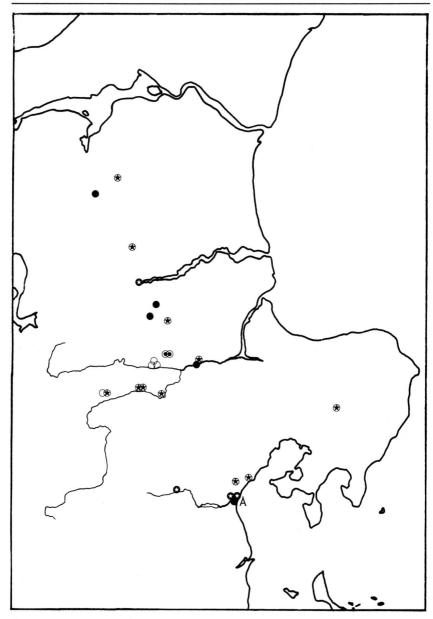

Figure 7 A. 'After Jelling' stones in north Jylland. Black dots: stone raised over a
father or a husband (small dot, with ring). Black star: stone raised over a brother,
etc. Ring: stone raised over a son, etc. White star: stone raised over a fælle. Å= the
city of Århus

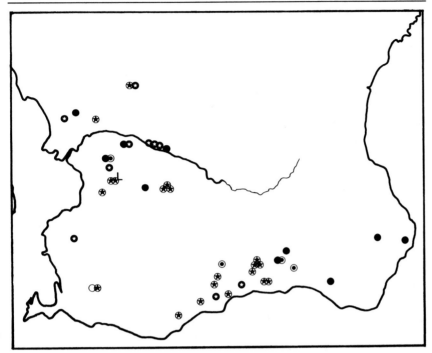

Figure 7 B. 'After Jelling' stones in Skåne. Signatures as in Fig. 7 A. L = the city of Lund

a regional pattern would emerge, covering a period of some twenty-five or fifty years, and made up entirely of men whose fathers, mothers and wives were all gone at the time of death and whose sons were not old enough to take over their position. A suggestion is that the persons represented in this sub-cluster were connected, for a couple of generations, with the active manning of the longships of Kings Sven and Knud in the Baltic district. Furthermore, roads were maintained; someone, for instance, is cited as responsible for building a bridge.[29] In return a grant of land was given, which must have comprised at least as much as a village, or the equivalent, as we learn from one of the stones where the brother 'had' this.[30] Another brother was a ship's captain, and one of the fæller 'did not flee at Uppsala (in Sweden), but fought as long as he had weapons'.[31] Three, perhaps four, brothers and the male relative referred to were drengs, in this connection possibly captains of warships ('styresmænd', steersmen), like the fælle and dreng Erik who fell during King Sven's siege of Hedeby.[32]

In about 1025, after the conquest of England, the obligations may have discontinued and the holdings have fallen to the family at large, as in the case of the eastern persons of the south Skåne cluster. In the eastern sub-cluster, apart from the father of a dreng mentioned above, we have three thegns, a bomand (residing man, perhaps a petty

Figure 8 A. 'After Jelling' stones in north Jylland. Black dot (big) : stone raised over a
thegn. Small dot (with ring): stone raised over a dreng. Star: stone raised over a
person who 'died'. Å = the city of Århus

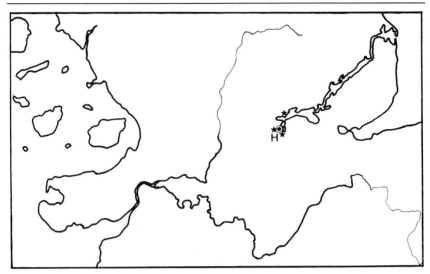

Figure 8 B. 'After Jelling' stones in southernmost Jylland. Signatures as in Fig. 8 A.
   H = the city of Hedeby

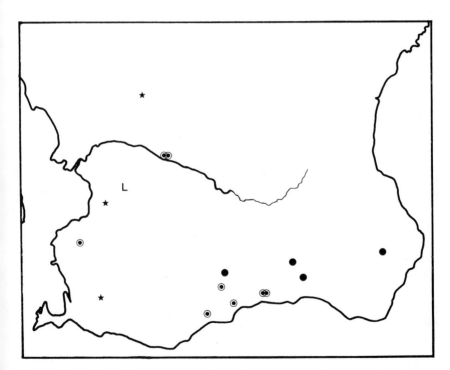

Figure 8 C. 'After Jelling' stones in Skåne. Signatures as in Fig. 8 A. L = the city
   of Lund

'landmand', a vassal-title, or a royal bailiff) 'the most generous with food', and a bonde ('farmer', or rather magnate), whose monument contains a curse against anyone destroying it.[33] In addition we have the thegn from the northern edge of the west sub-cluster, the 'first of thegns'.[34] Other surnames, indicating high rank, go with the bonde, 'the sharp' and one of the three thegns, 'the far-seeing'.[35] God is asked to help the soul of two men: 'they are lying (i.e. are buried) in London'.[36]

To the east in the south Skåne cluster we have in sum a group of high-ranking persons whose position and property is inherited through the normal family channels and who apparently own their land without restrictions. Only the bomand, if he is in fact a bailiff, speaks of direct obligations.

Like the drengs, the thegns and the bonde have the apposition 'very good'; one thegn, however, is 'first'. The bomand is 'best', perhaps an alliteration on *b*omand (the following line of the text is '*m*ad' (food) *m*ildest). Furthermore, the landmand we meet below is 'good'.[37] The positions of direct subordinates like managers of land (landhyrde), agents (bryde), craftsmen (smed), ships' captains (skippers) (of lords) and housecarls (literally 'home-taken') are, on the other hand, never 'good'. It is clear that the 'good' apposition, and related ones, only refer to masters, to the king's 'good men', his dependants or more probably his vassals. 'Good' denotes a close but rather equal relationship, as when it occurs in connection with relatives. The 'good' thegns, drengs, etc., are of high rank, but so are many other persons without the 'good' apposition, and its absence does not, in itself, denote a lower standing. The 'fæller', for example, are never 'good'.

The other cluster in Skåne, perhaps the oldest, is around the city of Lund, King Knud's Scandinavian capital, and is founded in the same decades shortly before 1000 (Figs 7 B and 8 C). In the city itself we have only two stones: one is raised over two brothers and 'good' landmen, while the other mentions the building of a church.[38] The cluster has an even spread of dead brothers (eight in all), a single male relative who is neither a father nor a brother and fathers (four), and also a single husband; due south a single son occurs. An interesting group of brothers comes from the Hällestad stones.[39] The first monument was set up by Eskil for Toke, the son of Gorm, his gracious lord who did not flee at Uppsala; drengs raised the stone for their brother – 'they went the closest to Gorm's Toke'. In this case we meet a lord whose father carried a royal name (perhaps as a grandson of King Gorm, and a brother or cousin of King Sven, the son of Harald). The lord is also a 'brother' of the drengs, but obviously not a kin brother. The second stone of the group is for a brother who was Toke's housecarl, and the third raised by a housecarl of Toke for Toke, his brother. In these cases, particularly the last, 'brother' may mean brother-in-arms. In the first case Toke may be the leader of a unit in the fleet and the drengs his captains; in the second we may see a brotherhood of housecarls and their lord, probably the same Toke. But there is no indication that housecarls and drengs are synonymous.

Another interesting aspect of the western brothers (around Lund) is their connection with the expression 'he died' followed by a geographical specification, indicating a death far away from home like the Toke of the Hällestad stones and a couple of possible cases from southern Skåne.[40] In addition we have seven dead 'fæller' in the Lund cluster, three of whom are also drengs, and a person who 'had ship' together with the erector of the monument, whose brother, incidentally, 'died farther north in viking'.[41] 'In viking', i.e. on an armed expedition, were also a couple of the drengs-fæller.[42] An interesting stone is set up by a son for his father along with the fælle of the father.[43] With the results of the western part of the southern cluster in mind, we may view this stone as a verification of the idea that the persons of the set brother-dreng-fælle (the drengs connecting the other two terms) might in fact have been married, though the family at large did not inherit the property. It may also demonstrate a change towards the usual family inheritance occurring concurrently with a lapse of the warrior-duties. The other father-stones in the cluster may be seen in the same light (or as normal vassals with family-inheritance). It is perhaps significant too that the west cluster in Skåne has more fæller and more deaths abroad than the apparently later southern stones, where brothers dominate. Apart from the two landmen in Lund, the only title and position held by seniors is a solitary bonde from Dalby (a bishop-seat some time during the eleventh century);[44] no thegns are known from the cluster around the city of Lund.

To summarise some of the typical combinations of titles and family terms, we should note that the thegns, fathers and husbands are concentrated to the east in the southern Skåne cluster. To the west in the southern cluster we have drengs who are brothers, while the drengs in the Lund cluster occur as 'fæller' only. Furthermore, the brothers at Lund often died abroad. The number of observations is small, but interestingly enough the same sets of expressions appear on the 'After Jelling' stones in Jylland.

From Hedeby we have at first a stone raised by one of King Sven's housecarls for his fælle Erik, who died 'when drengs sat round Hedeby' (were laying siege to the city); moreover Erik is noted as having been a steersman (captain of a warship) and a 'very good' dreng (Fig. 8 B).[45] Another monument was set up by King Sven for one of his housecarls, who had been to the west but had died at Hedeby.[46] The last text is for someone who died abroad and was buried in England.[47] As in the Lund cluster, so in this urban context, we have the title dreng connected with fælle and notions of deaths abroad, or far from home. Taken as a whole the solitary Hedeby texts strongly resemble the information on the Hällestad monuments, King Sven being in the same position as Toke, Gorm's son. Only, it is perhaps less clear whether the dead persons were settled at Hedeby. At this time runestones are completely absent from the Jelling area, succession being no longer a problem here. To the north in Jylland a cluster occurs at the city of Århus, on the east coast (Figs 7 A and 8 A). Southern connections are given by a stone with the word 'Hedeby' on it – perhaps another fallen warrior from the siege?[48] A second stone is for a fælle and 'very good' dreng, who died of '*men most non-knave*' (but no geographical locality is given), and who 'had ship' together with a named person, possibly the successor to the ownership.[49] A third monument from the city of Århus is also set up for a fælle, who died . . . 'when kings fought'.[50] To the west of the city is a text apparently containing a geographical locality and raised for a high-ranking follower, perhaps like a fælle in terms of inheritance. A brother who died in the east is commemorated by a 'smed' (craftsman) of a lord;[51] and a manager of an estate ('landhyrde') belonging to a person with the surname 'Norwegian', also in the Århus cluster, is commemorated by his kinsmen.[52] Other family-stones are few: one was raised for a father and one for a male relative, not mentioned as father or as son. Finally, an interesting monument is set up by a craftsman (smed) for the person who liberated him from slavery 'and gave him gold' (or perhaps 'lineage') (cf. Chapter 6 E). The same 'smed' erected a monument to a brother of the landmen from the city of Lund, but this stone stands in the north-eastern Jylland cluster, to which we shall return.[53]

In spite of the variations, the Århus group is parallel to the Lund cluster (and to the Hedeby stones) in terms of the dreng-fælle, and brother and 'died' combinations. We also lack the dreng-family type and the thegns, etc.

To the north of the Gudenå river as far as the Limfjord there exists a belt of stones similar, not surprisingly, in some ways to the southern Skåne cluster. It includes one dreng, who is a brother, and two who are sons, and we lack the expression from the urban clusters 'he died' and a geographical locality. Of a deceased fælle there is only one example, and in this case it is combined with dreng. There are a number of thegns and other lords, including a high-ranking 'man of tidings' (royal advisor?), two ships' captains and a manager of land (literally 'land-herds-man'), who, like the smed (craftsman) above, is raising the stone though.[54]

In the previous Jelling period the stones of this area contained a landmand, two thegns, a single fælle and in addition a son who 'died' in Øresund.[55] This resembles the scatter we have just described, and with a possible time-overlap in mind it is safe to say that we cannot depict any temporal difference. We lack clear indications of a settlement of active younger warriors like, for example, the southern Skåne west sub-cluster, possibly because of the status of north-eastern Jylland as an 'old' province in the Jelling state. Looking at the family terms of both the Jelling and the 'After Jelling' type we also have a quite even scatter of fathers, brothers, sons, etc., throughout the area. This does not imply that north Jylland and south Skåne were differently organised, only that family inheritance played a stronger role in Jylland. Two of the four drengs are sons, and one of these is remembered by the mother, who could not take over warrior duties.[56] Moreover the thegns and drengs seem to be scattered quite evenly throughout the cluster; at any rate we cannot discern any significant differences for this group alone. On the other hand, there is a general tendency for the drengs to be closer to towns than the thegns; the latter are missing from the clusters around Lund, Hedeby and Århus, while in north-eastern Jylland and southern Skåne they are concentrated in the farthest, and most inland, area to the north and east, where drengs are noticeably lacking. In addition, the thegns are also farther from each other, as if they had larger estates than the drengs. The dreng-lands were close to the coasts and cities. The obligations of a dreng – and of other similar persons of his social status – were characterised by mobility, chiefly comprising manning and supplying the fleet; this brought the dreng companionship with other people besides his own family; it also, of course, took him abroad, where he might die, and yet gave him, like the thegn, a substantial grant of land which eventually fell fully to his family.

In addition to the clusters, only a few solitary stones occur. Of the more interesting are two from Thy in the north-westernmost part of Jylland, mentioning housecarls.[57] The same woman raised a stone over her husband who was the housecarl of Finulv, and yet another over a husband, or father, who was also someone's housecarl and had been killed. In these examples we seem to meet the settled, and probably 'retired', housecarls, their earlier occupation being deemed a designation of honour, although it may also have carried a grant of land. Finulv is comparable to King Sven and the Toke, Gorm's son, of the Hällestad stones in Skåne.[58] He is perhaps identical with the father of a woman who in north-eastern Jylland set up a monument (with a curse against any possible destroyer of the stone) for an Odinkar, the honourable and lord-faithful,[59] also a name from the royal lineages.

From the island of Lolland comes a father, 'the Jutlander', and thegn, a usual combination in the far countryside.[60] More surprisingly, perhaps, is a brother, who 'died' (on Gotland?), a combination we otherwise have only from urban clusters, on a stone from the island of Falster.[61] The text, however, shows a connection in its dialect with the Skåne stones, and the dead brother may have belonged to the settlement there as well.

On the many, and late, Bornholm runestones, set out in a contemporary 'Swedish' style, we meet drengs and a thegn, and even a bonde.[62] The 'good' bonde is a father; of the 'good' thegn we note only that he is remembered by another male person, but the dead 'good' drengs clearly rest in a family context: a son was killed off the coast of Blekinge and a brother killed 'outrageously'. The third dreng, a son, apparently also 'died'; the stone is raised for a brother of the dreng too, but, interestingly enough, the latter does not carry the dreng title. This shows clearly that 'dreng' connotes an occupational position.

On Bornholm, dreng obligations may as usual have been required at a relatively young age, warfare and expeditions being all part of the life of drengs. Only one other Bornholm stone is raised for a 'dead' person, a father who drowned, with 'all the ships' captains'.[63] But whatever the duties, property was inherited by the family at large. The Bornholm stones are probably connected with the Christianisation of the island and its incorporation under the administration in Denmark after the middle of the eleventh century.[64] One of the latest stones mentions an archbishop and should be twelfth-century in date.[65] The thegns and the drengs, as well as the 'dead' expressions, cluster on the south-western quarter of the island of Bornholm, and royal vassals may have been restricted to this area. The remainder of the monuments on the island are normal family-stones, although a surprisingly large proportion have been raised for women. The possibility occurs, as in southern mid-Jylland in the Jelling phase, that newcomers bolstered their position and received land by marrying daughters of Bornholm magnates.

The other historical sources basically describe the actual political behaviour of the societies whose underlying variables we try to reveal. And although political information, in a broad sense of the word, is of paramount importance, the runestones are the first data to give us a pattern of development of social offices in a geographical space. In this way we have been able to make statements about the course of conflicts and formation, by the kings, of a system of dependants, whose position was bolstered by grants of land to which succession was marked by these stones. In other words, we can now approach the questions of production and distribution to study the underlying factors and constraints, from the climate and soil, on the pattern of settlement, as well as the organisation of towns, all of which conditioned the economy.

Chapter 4

SUBSISTENCE AND RURAL
SETTLEMENT

A. Climate and settlement

Over the past two thousand years Denmark has witnessed a number of minor and major climatic fluctuations, among them the well-known cold period subsequent to the Middle Ages, 'the little Ice Age'. The medieval period itself (1000-1500) was warmer, especially in the beginning, and so was the preceding Viking Age, while the centuries around 500 were cold. We are dealing with changes of the order of only one degree centigrade, or rather less, on a yearly basis; but they were of great consequence.

The climatic fluctuations have, logically, a bearing on the plant cover, on the quality of the harvest and on the nutrition of animals and human beings; but it is difficult to discern the relationships for past periods, although we are dealing with almost the same variables as today. One reason is incomplete climatic and botanical-zoological knowledge, another the problem of isolating human impact from natural factors when reading the record.

Recent studies of raised bogs in Denmark have shown that the degree of humification, which is dependent on the humidity of the bog, and in turn entirely related to the climate, apparently changes at approximately 260-year intervals, as measured in a negative direction (Fig. 10).[1] Visually, these changes are accompanied by transitions from layers of dark peat with a high degree of humification to layers of light peat with a low degree of humification, deposited under colder and/or more humid periods. (In each case it is uncertain whether a lower temperature or a higher precipitation is the prime factor responsible.) The 260-year regularity is independent of the magnitude of the individual changes that make up the long-range climatic trends, but it serves a practical purpose as a comparison with other climatic series.

Some of the most rewarding climatic research is carried out on

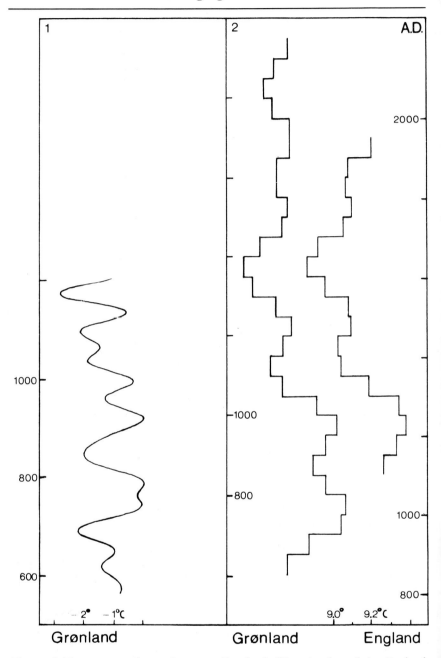

Figure 9 Temperature-fluctuations on Grønland (Greenland) and in England. Greenland temperatures: Godthåb. (Based on Dansgaard et al.)

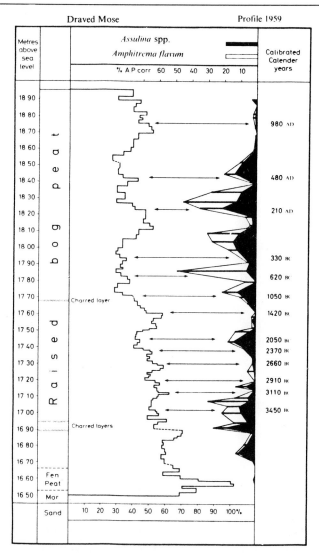

Figure 10 Fluctuations in the degree of humification (to the left) in Draved bog, south Jylland, and the frequency of two species of water-loving plants (to the right). (After Aaby)

Greenland, where the ice-cap contains an extremely long record (Fig. 9).[2] So-called oxygene-isotope studies of temperature fluctuations have demonstrated a clear congruence – on the level of medium-sized frequencies – between the variations in temperature on Greenland and those of post-medieval north-west Europe. The movements on the low-frequency level – periods of more than 200 years – are also parallel to each other; but here there is a time lag of about 250 years between Greenland and, for instance, England (after 1100), which has the best

European meteorological data for earlier periods. For instance, the medieval warm climate ends in Greenland in the beginning of the eleventh century, but in England it ends in about 1300 according to the historical record. Furthermore, the Greenland curve shows the same trend towards poorer conditions of weather, at intervals of about 250 years, as the Danish bogs.

We shall not investigate the reasons, but only note that there seems to be a correlation between climatic periods and transgressions of the sea.[3] According to the Greenland medium-frequency curve, the temperatures seem to be high in the eighth century, before the onset of the Viking Age, low in the ninth and in general warm again in the tenth, with a cooling in the eleventh (Fig. 9). By comparison these changes should also hold true for north-west Europe. On the long-term level in Greenland, eliminating the 250-year time lag, we also have a cold ninth century, the period of the Danish raids on west Europe, a warmer trend throughout the tenth century and a drop towards a lower yearly average in about 1100.

Returning to the humification of the Danish bogs, there is support here from comparisons of temperature between Greenland and north-west Europe for prehistoric periods. To a high degree the changes towards a colder and/or more humid climate in the bog-series turn out to be parallel to the cold recessions of the Greenland temperature curve.[4] This reveals temperature as the main factor behind the fluctuations in humification, and we tend to read the humification curve of Denmark, especially in outline, as a scale of temperature differences.

In Draved bog, for instance, in south-western Jylland, we have a drop in humification in the later part of the Bronze Age (Periods IV-V, about 1100 to 700 B.C.) (Fig. 10). At exactly this time the distribution of burials shows that marginal lands in western Jylland have been given up.[5] The next drastic recession takes place around 200 A.D., at a time when a large number of early Iron Age settlements, especially on the poor lands to the west, were abandoned, and the field system was changed.[6] The centuries at the turn of the first millennium B.C. on the other hand, were warm and probably dry, and rich in settlements on the same soils. Apparently the problems of a colder climate in south Scandinavia were greater than the benefits that sandy soils would gain from possible increase in precipitation. The climatic and environmental data show that a poorer harvest, the leaching out of the soil for nutrients and mulldrift have caused the settlement system in the west to break down. In south Jylland, Olmer's dyke, protecting the rich eastern areas from the west, was set up in the third century A.D.[7] The same date applies to an underwater blockade from the Haderslev inlet, fifty kilometres to the north-east of Olmer's dyke.[8] Moreover we know of a number of sometimes very large offerings of weapons and other equipment for war parties in the bogs of the western border of the rich clay area in central and western Denmark.[9] All this points to an increase in hostilities, probably centring on the west.

We do not believe that these changes altered the general character of the societies, which was much the same during both the Bronze Age and the early Iron Age (as compared with the period of the Viking Age state). For instance, valuable objects were being disposed of in large quantities in graves and sacred places, like the bogs, never to be regained. It is striking how both these practices disappear around 400–600, at the onset of the late Iron Age and the development of more stable societies which eventually lacked these glaring, but redundant, ways of underlining personal status, either at individual burials or in public rituals like the bog-offerings.

Nor should the differences between the burial and the common public ritual be overlooked. Rich burials tend to be concentrated in the early Bronze Age warm period and to disappear during the late Bronze Age climatic recession, only to return before the turn of the millennium at the optimum of the early Iron Age.[10] They vanish again after about 300 A.D., where offerings, often of weapons, are common. Furthermore, the late Bronze Age and the beginning of the early Iron Age have many offerings of valuable objects. In short, there seems to be a correlation between periods of expansion of the settlement, stable subsistence production and conspicuous individual graves. The periods of recession stress public rituals and communion, and may in some ways have a firmer social system; but squandering of wealth in individual graves was suppressed, probably as a result of more concrete systems of inheritance.

These considerations cannot be directly applied to the end of pre-history. The Viking Age does have a number of wealthy graves and lacks bog-offerings; but the graves are all from the tenth century and refer to new statuses within the west Danish Jelling state. Between about 600 and 900 rich graves (as well as bog finds) are practically unknown, although the settlement was markedly expanding during the Viking Age climatic optimum and even during the preceding one or two centuries; this is apparent, in particular, from the many new place-names. The ninth century, however, may have been a period of some hardship, to judge from the Greenland evidence. The decades after the death of King Godfred in 810, with internal struggles for power, accompanied by the raids on western Europe and some settling abroad, would then fall within a shorter period of recession. The political expansion of the tenth-century Jelling dynasty, on the other hand, was bolstered by fine climatic conditions for subsistence production. To conclude this sector, we should point out that King Olaf 'Hunger' of Denmark late in the eleventh century reigned during years of severe crop failure, which fits into another recession in the Greenland series of temperature. Such detailed evidence has not been produced from the study of bogs; yet these yield the prime data for the

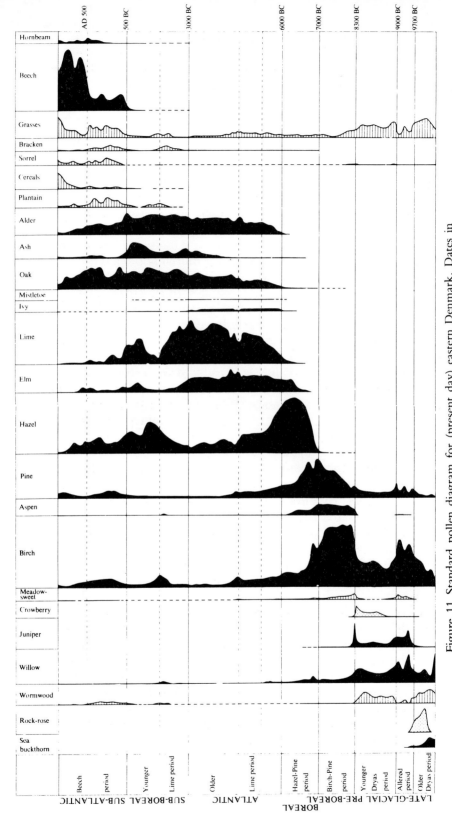

Figure 11 Standard pollen diagram for (present day) eastern Denmark. Dates in uncalibrated C^{14}-years. (After Iversen)

important reconstructions of the Danish landscape. In particular, the pollen of plants has proved a critical source for these studies.

B. Landscape and cultivation

In the Iron and Viking Ages the presence of man in the pollen picture of nature is clearer than in the previous periods.[11] The colder and more humid climate of the Iron Age, helped by forest clearance and animal grazing, led slowly to poorer soil. On the more acid and humid ground, beech was doing better than oak and other types of trees, which were dominant during the Neolithic and the Bronze Age. The open land became commoner, for instance, on the poor soils of west Jylland and east Skåne, and heather spread, especially on sandy soils. Bogs also became more frequent. In short, man accelerated the interglacial climatic-botanical cycle through his clearings and farming, but the development was not without fluctuations, including crises for both nature and human culture.

In the pollen diagrams of south Scandinavia the expansion during the warmer centuries at about the turn of the first millennium B.C. is clearly marked by the promotion of grasses and other plants which do not tolerate shade (Fig. 11). In the second quarter of the first millennium A.D. this phase discontinues and is followed by a forest regeneration during the cold, and possibly also humid, third quarter of the millennium which precedes the warmer Viking Age. Parallel to these trends, the pollen curve for the cereals – especially barley and wheat – first shows an increase (compared with the Bronze Age) followed by a recession, in the forest regeneration phase, and is terminated by a sharp increase in the last quarter of the first millennium. This, however, is partly due to the more common use of rye, very rich in pollen, from the Viking Age onwards. Oats, like rye is a more appropriate cereal for cold periods and poorer soils, and yet it is less common; it had an important bearing on the feeding of the many Viking horses.

Apart from the pastures, the animals may have been fed from leaves and from hay. Alder, for instance, growing on moist soils, shows a decline, in spite of the rather damp weather conditions in the Iron Age, which probably means that alder swamps were being converted into hay meadows. The first broad scythes are accordingly dated to the second half of the first millennium B.C.; the leafknife dates to more or less the same time.[12] In the coldest phases of the Iron Age it was especially important to gather winter fodder for the stalled animals. The longer scythe, however, seems to occur later – in the first half of the first millennium A.D.[13] If this scythe (along with the short scythe) is used for harvesting grain, instead of the older sickle, a reason may be the use of straw for feeding animals.

We have already mentioned the expansion of grasses, and it is not surprising to find ribworth plantain indicating cattle grazing as a feature accompanying the development of the early Iron Age (500 B.C. to 400 A.D.). In the Viking Age species of grass were again expanding, along with cereals, after the forest regeneration phase; now, however, the ribworth plantain was markedly decreasing. This shows that Viking Age farming put much less emphasis on animal protein than earlier periods. The intensive growing of plant protein led to a higher nutritional output. It is hard to conceive of this as anything but a response to population growth. Furthermore, forest grazing may have become more important, but if so it suggests the stress placed on cereal production. Finally, the size of the animals, except for horses, was decreasing in the Viking Age, probably as a result of poorer nutrition.[14] This development was not isolated, for to the south of Denmark the growing of cereals expanded during the last quarter of the first millennium A.D.[15]

From the Viking Age we have several examples of the use of a heavier plough – the mouldboard wheeled plough – which turned the ground when working, and in the Middle Ages became at least a partial substitute for the older 'ard'-types, which only made furrows in the ground.[16] One example of its use from Sjælland stems perhaps from as early as the seventh or eighth century A.D.,[17] but south of Denmark we have even earlier indications of the mouldboard plough.[18]

The human influence factor in the pollen diagrams of southern and central Scandinavia has been tentatively described by an interpretation of the pollen curves of trees and of light-demanding plants (Fig. 12).[19] Four early stages of growing human impact are developed, lying parallel to each other in the different areas with little, or no, time lag in between. That some temporal distinctions do exist is probably due to the population growth, conditioning the impact. The first stage is the

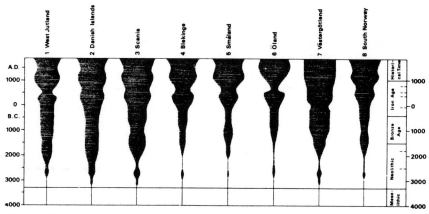

Figure 12 Diagrams of the human influence on the vegetation (shaded). Dates in uncalibrated C[14]-years. (After Berglund)

Neolithic landnam, which, for example, is earlier on the Danish islands than in, say, southern Norway. The second stage is the great influence from the beginning of the so-called Middle Neolithic period (3000 B.C.) onwards. The third corresponds to our expansion during the milder climatic conditions around the turn of the first millennium B.C., and the fourth to the latest Iron and Viking Age growth, continuing to the early Middle Ages, and also very visible in the diagrams for areas south of Denmark. An additional, final stage corresponds to the modern, post-medieval expansion.

The correlation between the major climatic optima and the periods of expansion of the open land for fields and pastures suggests that better harvests, in the first place, created a population growth which later caused inroads to be made into the forested area. The reverse must have happened at the onset of poorer climatic conditions. However, the depression around 500 A.D. may have been felt so strongly in the densely settled and centrally organised country that it was decisive in enabling a larger part of the population to survive. This was perhaps achieved by the change in the subsistence strategy leading to the expansion of cornfields at the expense of pastures.

The third stage, or early Iron Age, seems to have culminated earlier on the sandy and more rapidly leached west Jylland soils than in those areas further to the east and north in Scandinavia. This is in accordance with the settlement data. Moreover the expansion after the depression around 500 A.D. is slightly earlier in west Jylland than in the eastern parts of Denmark. We have already outlined the possible pressures on the east in the early Iron Age due to these circumstances. For the latter half of the first millennium A.D. the west may have served as an area of colonisation, partly through a renewed period of slash-and-burn agriculture. Forest regeneration is certainly very pronounced. Southernmost Jylland, for instance, is strongly resettled,[20] and in 700, or shortly after, the first Danevirke walls were constructed at the border with the Saxons (Chapter 5 E).

It is clear that the entire Viking Age experienced a growth in population, but it is equally clear that this development started much earlier than the political evolution leading to the formation of the state of Denmark at the close of the tenth century. In the centuries at the turn of the first millennium B.C. the size of the open land was almost as large as at the beginning of the Viking Age, but owing to the wide-scale concentration on cattle-rearing the population was probably somewhat smaller. The early Iron Age did not see any social formation which we would term a state with the Viking Age in mind. In this perspective the population density and pressure on the resources must have played a role in the creation of the high degree of political control of the Viking period, though we are not able to connect the onset of population growth with a particular social development. Just as supercooled water may freeze at an accidental touch, so the political development we have described in previous chapters could come true only when certain conditions of population and production were fulfilled. If we look to the south of Denmark, the Carolingian expansion also took place during a population growth. A large, dense population may cause problems of production, but it is none the less a prerequisite for the military and economic power of a stable state.

C. Domesticated animals and distribution of food

The data for the study of Iron and Viking Age animals come mostly from refuse of food in the settlement deposits and are made up of smaller and larger fragments of bone. Furthermore, some animals come from burials, especially dogs and horses, and to a lesser degree sheep, but they have no interest in a production and consumption context.

The biggest problem, when studying the fragments, is how to relate to the original numbers of cattle, pigs, sheep and horses.[21] Dogs are rare, like wild mammals, and the ratios of the fragile bones of birds and fish too uncertain to build on, as their retrieval has varied a great deal. In general only fragment numbers are published, but in modern investigations other types of analysis are used. The animals in question have practically the same number of bones; but the size of the single bone varies, and large animals may produce many more fragments than small ones. On the other hand, the fragile bones of smaller animals may break more easily. To avoid these uncertainties some students have used the weight of the bones as a critical factor for interpretation. This measurement probably has some bearing on the amount of meat from an animal, but it is difficult to use for archaeological sites because of the variable weight loss for different species and under different preservation conditions.

A still more developed and time-consuming methodology calculates the minimum number of individuals, a technique independent of the degree of fragmentation. This is probably the most satisfactory treatment, but it has been carried out only on a few samples.

In addition to the study of animal ratios it is important to look into variables such as the age of slaughter, especially with respect to sex, the presence or absence of various parts of the animal (for instance, the fleshy parts) and even diseases. (Such studies are only rarely made.) Some anatomical features, however, stand out clearly. The cattle, pigs, sheep/goats and horses were much smaller than today.[22] Racial differences may account for some of the variation, but mostly it is due to poorer nutrition of the Viking Age animals. In the Middle Ages cattle, pigs and sheep were even smaller, but the horses were a little larger. Compared with the early Iron Age, Viking Age horses are larger and have longer legs – they probably represent a different race –

while the cattle are poorer than the relatively stout animals from the centuries around the turn of the first millennium B.C., a period of climatic optimum with an extensive use of pastures.

As indicated, if we want to analyse the Viking Age subsistence animals with respect to type of settlement, etc., and, at the same time, have data of some dimension and quality, we are left with bone fragments. The number of reliable sites and samples are about twenty in all, including a few which date a little beyond the strict Viking Age in Denmark and adjacent areas; basically they comprise rural settlements, towns and fortresses.

Often fish bones and bones of wild birds are neglected, and only a few sites display more than one per cent of wild animals. In general, the towns and fortresses seem to have a slightly higher proportion of wild mammals than the villages. Hunting may perhaps have been the prerogative of the higher social echelons, but the towns and fortresses may also have been so dependent on outside supplies of meat that they utilised any possibility of self-sufficiency. It is notable, for example, that the Slavonian town fortresses of east Holstein, close to Denmark, have a high percentage of wild mammals.

Dogs also are few; if cattle and minor domestic animals are considered, they amount only rarely to more than one or one-and-a-half per cent of the bone fragments. Incidentally, the dogs vary in size and breed, though small specimens are most common. Cats are known, but they also are rare. Domesticated birds – fowls, geese and possibly ducks – are also relatively rare, but their presence or absence in the material, like fish and wild birds, is dependent to a large extent on the conditions of preservation. As to size, the hens too are smaller than today's specimens.

Horses also are rare, though only in towns, where they obviously have not been eaten. In the rural settlements fragments of horse bones amount to about ten to fifteen per cent of the mammals (not including dogs). In the following discussion the 'towns' comprise the settlements of Hedeby, Ribe and Århus in Jylland and Lund in Skåne. The Viking Age deposits below the medieval town of Viborg in north Jylland seem to stem from a rural settlement. The different frequency of horse remnants gives rise to a further study of the percentages of cattle, pigs, sheep/goats and horses. It transpires that there is a strong negative correlation between the percentages of cattle and pig bone fragments for the rural settlements, which means that a high cattle index is followed by a low pig index and vice versa (Fig. 13 and Appendix VII). Between sheep/goat and horses a similar link is apparent, but it is less strong. Other possible combinations are less, or not at all, significant, and we may reduce the data to two factors, cattle-pigs and sheep/goats-horses. A possible explanation of the combinations is that the first group relates primarily to 'food' while the second has more to do with 'utility' (wool and transportation).

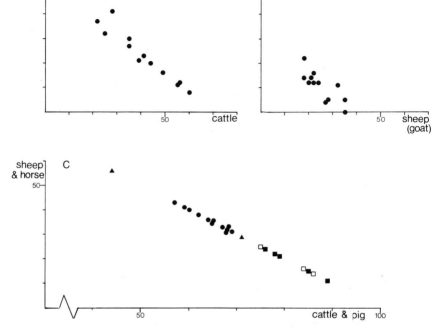

Figure 13 A. Percentages of bone fragments of, respectively, cattle and pig from rural settlements (Appendix VII). (Sample: cattle, pig, sheep, goat and horse)

Figure 13 B. Percentages of bone fragments of, respectively, sheep (and goat) and horse from rural settlements (Appendix VII). (Sample as in Fig. 13 A.)

Figure 13 C. Percentages of bone fragments of, respectively, the cattle-pig and the sheep (and goat)-horse group from rural settlements (dots), towns (black squares), east Holstein Slavonian fortress-towns (open squares) and fortresses (triangles). (Appendix VII.) (Sample as in Fig. 13 A.)

Both groups supply meat, milk, hides and draught power, though to quite varying degrees. From distribution maps of the ratio cow/pig, it is seen that pigs are dominant in the central Danish provinces, the most forested region, while cows are frequent in the open lands of west Jylland and east Skåne. Apparently the environment determines what meat animal is kept most often, and though cows may graze in woods these are the natural pig area. No clear picture emerges from the sheep/horse ratio, while the distinction between sheep and pig provinces, the sheep being dominant in west Jylland, for instance, is the most obvious of all.

Going back to the sites, it is seen that the towns have more than 75 per cent cattle and pig bones (and less than 25 per cent sheep, etc.), while the rural settlements have less than 70 per cent cattle/pigs fragments (Fig. 13 and Appendix VII). Among the rural settlements

are the Viking Age finds from Viborg and the finds from Löddeköpinge in west Skåne, a possible seasonal market. A single pit-
house, also from west Skåne (Oxie), has a higher percentage of
cattle/pigs than any of the towns, but the deviation here is probably
due to the uncertainties of the limited excavation. The Trelleborg
fortress in western Sjælland has percentages of 71 and 29 for the two
sets, the horse fragments amounting to as much as 14 per cent.
Another fortress, Lembecksburg, on the island of Föhr, off the coast
of southernmost Jylland, has a cow/pig percentage of 44, less than any
village, but a sheep percentage amounting to as much as 55. This site
may constitute a third category of consumption, having also an
unusual (but still modest) percentage of wild mammals, and many
wild birds too. The Slavonian town fortresses in east Holstein, and
further to the east, fit into the town cluster of Denmark, perhaps not
unexpectedly.

The reason for the distinction between towns and rural settlements
seems to be that the meat animals (cattle/pigs) were delivered in the
towns (and fortresses), which were not able to meet their demand for
food locally. At Hedeby, for instance, only one house has traces of a
stall. The percentages of the same animals would then drop in the
villages, which kept horses and sheep (but not the wool). It is
noteworthy that much the same picture occurs if we omit horses;
these, like sheep, are also more difficult to keep in towns than pigs or
even cows.

These observations are important, since they link up towns and
countryside in the sphere of food output and consumption. The towns
were not merely centres of luxury production and trade but were fully
integrated on all levels with their surroundings. This is apparent from
geographical data as well.

The basic 'parish division' of Denmark probably took place in the
eleventh century. The size of the parishes, as measured by the spread
of churches, varies with the quality of the soil, since they tend to
comprise the same number of souls whether the churches are situated
on poor west Jylland soils, with a low population density, or on
Sjælland, with a high one. The first borders of the parishes are not
known, but we can create hypothetical, and fairly accurate, boundaries
by drawing lines, in a right angle, through the mid-points of the lines
of sightings between the early medieval churches.

Looking at the homogeneous province in terms of soil around the
city of Århus in Jylland, it appears that the size of the Århus parish,
comprising both agrarians and townsmen, is the same as the other
parishes in the area (Fig. 14). This shows that the population in the
parish has simply not been able to feed itself from its agricultural area
and must have received supplies from the whole province. An identical
result is obtained from the city of Ribe.

In the Hedeby area, studies of animal bone fragments from the town and from a rural settlement, Elisenhof, less than fifty kilometres to the west, on the coast, have further exemplified these findings.[23] It is seen, for instance, that the fleshy parts of the limbs of cattle especially, and to some degree of pigs, are under-represented at Elisenhof, if we apply the minimum numbers of individuals (as estimated from the number

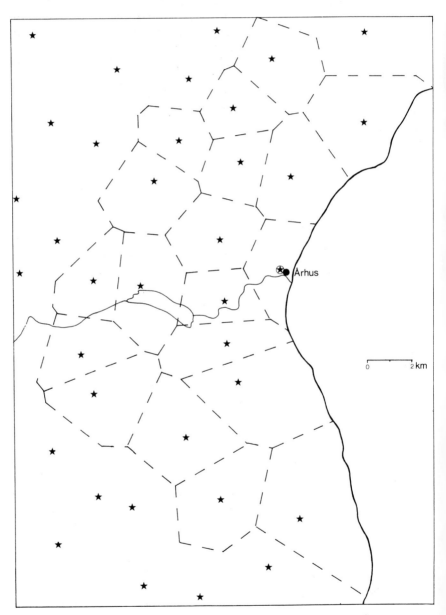

Figure 14 The spread of early medieval churches in the vicinity of Århus (Jylland) with hypothetical 'parish-borders'

of jaws). At Hedeby the same bones are over-represented, as a result apparently of the import of meat from the rural settlements. The lack of jaws at Hedeby indicates that the killing of the animals took place away from the town. If we look, in the same way, at an early Iron Age settlement at Feddersen Wierde on the Weser estuary, some 70 kilometres to the south of Elisenhof, there is no imbalance between the number of jaws and other bones. In this period only small amounts of foodstuffs would be meant for use outside the villages, the units of production; this lack of surplus, incidentally, made the societies more vulnerable to crises. Consequently the early Iron Age settlements cover also the 'town-range' of the above percentages of cattle and pig bones versus fragments of sheep/goat and horses (Appendix VII E). The cattle/pig percentage varies between about 50 to over 80. Indeed with a sufficient number of samples from the centuries between, say, the beginning and end of the first millennium A.D. the coming of towns could be precisely detected on the basis of the meat con-sumption alone, or, by the onset of cereal-agriculture, directed at feeding larger populations, including towns.

Finally, if we study the sex-ratios and the ages of slaughter of the Viking Age animals, we note that the cattle have varying killing ages, the adults being mainly cows (for the sake of the milk and the reproduction). Pigs are often killed young, though at Hedeby many appear to have been kept till they were old.[24] The same distinction is noted for the Hedeby sheep (the old animals being kept for the wool). In Århus and Lund the majority of both pigs and sheep were young, and mostly male.[25]

It is probably too early to comment on these differences, but it is worth remembering that Hedeby had the largest and ethnically most diverse concentration of population in Scandinavia. Furthermore, it was apparently also the most complex and stratified society. This may mean that Hedeby saw greater differences in the access to meat of high quality than the other cities and towns.

D. Rural settlements

The settlement system that formed the basis of Viking Age subsistence is difficult to grasp. We lack a coherent geographical picture, and we have only a modest knowledge of the single sites, except, perhaps, from a few recent excavations.

To judge from the size and plan of the major houses, the basic subsistence units in the early Iron Age were the family and the group of families inhabiting the villages that archaeologists have revealed. The integration on a higher level is more difficult to establish but must have been in existence, since the sites vary, even in the same province, with respect to type and quality of land, for instance, and

accessibility of fishing and of bog-iron for smelting. Some villages
have a single large farm, probably belonging to the chief, others do
not; and this picture is mirrored in the clustering spreads, also within
areas homogeneous in terms of land, of wealthy burials. A fine
example of a village with a chiefly compound is Hodde in west Jylland
from centuries B.C.[26] A village a little earlier in date is Grøntoft, also
in west Jylland, lacking the single, large farmstead but with a clear
tripartite division of the dwelling-houses in terms of size and number
of stalled animals.[27]

   The early Iron Age did not have towns and permanently manned
fortresses; the whole society was rurally-based, and there was no
apparent social stratification within the population. The control of
wealth, both in terms of cattle and land and in terms of luxury objects
like the fine Roman glasses or bronze vessels from wealthy graves,
differed between the social segments; but the leaders did not set
themselves apart from the rest. They lived in a village comprising
commoners also. Only from the so-called Roman Iron Age do we see
indications of a more developed system from the fact that the eastern
Danish islands have a few rich graveyards predominantly for leaders.[28]
Unfortunately, there is very little settlement data from the province;
most of it comes from territories like west Jylland, today marginal
lands, where prehistoric villages are preserved better and are easier to
find because of the light soil (as compared with the clay of the islands).
To judge from the graves only, we may have a slightly different
settlement system in east-central Denmark in the centuries A.D., with
chiefs living in more isolated circumstances. A fifth-century settlement
at Dankirke near the later town of Ribe in Jylland has been found to be
very rich in imports and with a possible 'hall'; it varies so much from
other sites that we may have an early chiefly (or royal) compound
here.[29] Otherwise, such a settlement is not met again until the tenth
century, and at this date both the economic structure of the magnate-
farm and the quality of its central habitation separates it from the village.

   The centuries after the close of the early Iron Age in 400 A.D. are
relatively poor in the archaeological record of settlements, owing to
the abandonment of the marginal lands in the climatic minimum
phase. It is not until shortly before 800 that we again have data of some
size. This is unfortunate since the first townships, Ribe and Hedeby in
Jylland, go back to the eighth century and we should expect the rural
production to respond to this. We have mentioned above the absence
of rich graves and offerings of wealthy objects from the centuries
preceding the Viking Age and have related this to the coming of a
different social system. In the Roman Iron Age the markets of the
so-called civilised world were far away, and international trade was
only occasional. Furthermore, the family bonds of inheritance were
weaker and collective pressures on the chiefs stronger (as the rich
graves and the bog-offerings show); in short, redistribution of the

valuables in society was functioning efficiently, and we may suppose that other resources followed the same channels of internal exchange. In the Viking Age wealth was constantly kept circulating under the impact of the 'rationality' of a market system and a market mentality; valuables could be invested, not only in social status, but also in far more entrepreneurial activities, and ultimately even in land.

In Sweden and Norway rich burials continue into the Viking period, demonstrating the survival here of archaic social structures.[30] The many wealthy burials at the port of Birka (near present-day Stockholm) are a strong supporting point, since the proximity of even a centre of trading did not alter the relationships with wealth. Moreover it shows that Birka must have been a large market for luxury products, rather than a 'town', meaning a centre with several functions. Indeed already in the early Iron Age, and before the start of Birka in about 800, the Stockholm area had another centre of exchange (and – like Dankirke – a chiefly, or royal, site?): Helgö, which was booming in about 500 A.D. While Birka was strongly connected with the eastern trade, resulting in the important influx of Arab silver in the Viking age, Helgö was serving as a market for a few western European products, and especially for locally made trinkets, exchanged for iron and other items from, for instance, northern Sweden.

To return to the scarce Danish settlement data from the centuries preceding the Viking Age, the traditional 'long-house' farmstead of the early Iron Age, with living quarters to the west and a stable to the east, was still in existence in about 400. At Vorbasse in mid-west Jylland a planned village consisted of large, well-built long-houses up to 44 metres in length and divided into several rooms, including a living-room, a stall and possibly a barn (Figs 15-16).[32] Each long-house lies next to one or two minor buildings, normally without a stable, and the whole group is surrounded by fences bordering the square croft. The crofts are in rows (usually two farmsteads share a fence) with village streets, or rather open spaces, in between. The village is followed through four stages, beginning with a few farmsteads (inside heavy fences and perhaps even galleries for protection) and ending with a settlement of twenty to thirty farms before the sudden interruption in the fifth century. In the last phase, lines of pit-houses, probably workshops, accompany the rows of farmsteads (Fig. 16). For the village as a whole there is no decisive distinction in size between the farms, but a few groups of buildings are clearly more important than the rest. Two of these have at one stage some iron-smelting ovens lying next to them, and a smithy among the minor buildings within the fenced enclosure (Fig. 15).

The pit-houses are of the usual type, occurring from this period onwards, about three metres in length and normally with only a couple of posts supporting the roof. The huts are only rarely heated, and their appearance is probably due to increased craft specialisation. It

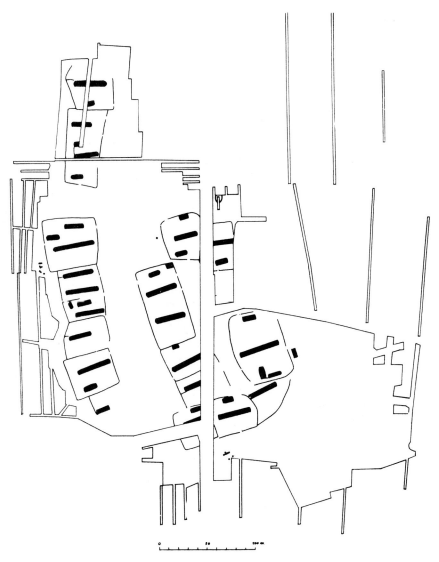

Figure 15 The Vorbasse settlement (mid-Jylland) in the fourth century A.D. North is
    up. (After Hvass)

must have been easier to provide light for artisans working in these
pit-houses than in the main buildings. The Vorbasse huts were used
for making pottery and for weaving (on the usual vertical loom);
weaving, incidentally, is the most common activity associated with
this kind of construction.

The Vorbasse village is situated on poor soils but with access to large
meadow areas; the cattle bones from these excavations reveal larger

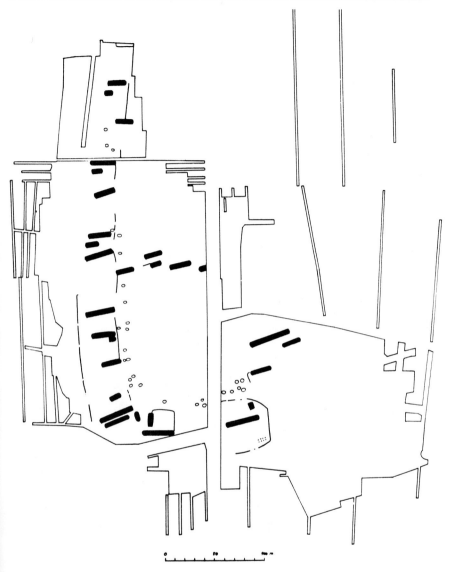

Figure 16 The Vorbasse settlement (mid-Jylland) in the fifth century A.D. North is up. (After Hvass)

animals than are usual for the period. In sum, the crafts comprise iron-working, weaving, potting and the making of grinding stones. Furthermore, gold has at least been polished in one of these huts, but there are no traces of imported luxuries, in spite of the rich assemblage of west European glasses from the contemporary settlement at Dankirke, near the west coast of Jylland, less than 50 kms from Vorbasse.[33] A few more sites of the same character, and from this

Figure 17 A-B. The Vorbasse settlement (mid-Jylland) in the tenth to eleventh
   centuries. Note the three magnate farm enclosures to the west. North is up. B
   represents the latest phase of the magnate farms (fully drawn lines). (After Hvass)

period and province too, have yielded no imports either, and
Dankirke is probably – despite the absence, so far, of craft production
– a chiefly or royal centre (and node in an exchange system). This
interpretation is supported by the discovery of a powerful 'hall', a
single posthole of which held more glass than the entire site of Helgö.
   From the centuries immediately before the Viking Age the data on

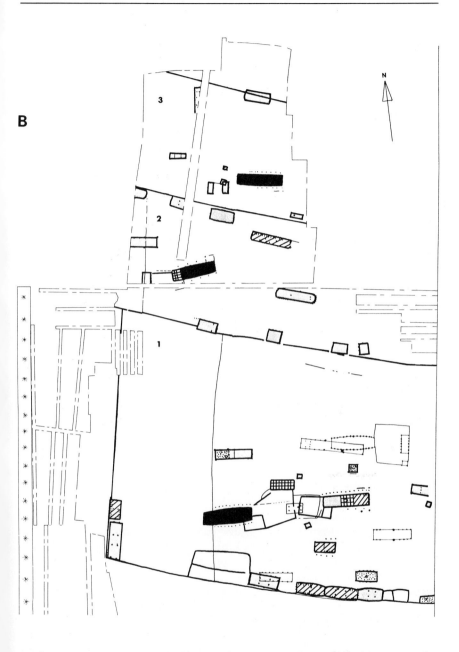

settlement are even rarer. From Skåne a number of pit-houses and a few long-houses extend back to the eighth century at least, but we have almost nothing else to bridge the gap in 600, at the very start of the late Iron to Viking Age expansion in settlement.[34]

The Viking period long-houses often display a 'boat-shaped' form with curved long walls. A classical example is the elegant 'Trelleborg' type hall, up to thirty metres long, which lacks the line of roof-supporting posts down the aisle of the house. Instead, the walls are strengthened by oblique posts along the outer side (cf. Figs 28-9). This gives a large middle room, with space for a central fireplace and two antechambers, each one-third of the length of the main room. Such houses do not have stables, and it is generally characteristic of Viking Age buildings that they show a stronger tendency towards functional specialisation than earlier ones, being also more alike. The lavish use of wood, connected with the short life span of the buildings, must have put great pressure on the forests.

As their name suggests, the conspicuous halls are found in the famous Trelleborg-type fortresses which date to the tenth century, but recently they have occurred also in a new type of rural settlement, the magnate farm. After the abandonment of the west Jylland Vorbasse village in the fifth century, the site was unoccupied until the early Viking Age, where a new village was founded, with long-houses and pit-houses. In the late tenth century this settlement was extended and, we believe, at least partly replaced by three gigantic farms, or rather 'estates', surrounded by fences, framing large crofts (the largest is 120m by about 200m) and, as in the fifth-century village, shared with the neighbouring compound (Fig. 17).[35] At the centre of the croft stands a Trelleborg-type hall and, adjoined to this by smaller fences are buildings comprising a smithy and a bronze founder's workshop. Other buildings follow the periphery along the fence, of which they are part; they include large and smaller stables or stalls, other smithies and dwelling-houses; pit-houses, however, are unknown.

The magnate farms at Vorbasse have several phases, but they do not continue long into the Middle Ages, though we expect such units to have existed later too. We should not underestimate the importance of these discoveries. The size alone – but also the structure of the farms – gives the owner command over more resources and more assistants or servants than any earlier holder of a farmstead possessed. Furthermore, the fact that a 'normal' settlement gave way to the magnate farms indicates a new kind of land-holding, probably of a more dominant kind than is found in the earlier village with its restrictions and co-operation, exemplified by the lay-out of the sites. There is also a village beneath the tenth-century royal fortress of Aggersborg in north Jylland, while the contemporary Trelleborg fortress (on west Sjælland) is perhaps built on the site of an early magnate farm.[36]

Vorbasse is situated only some 25 kilometres to the west of the Jelling centre, and it is difficult to understand the magnate farms without reference to the wider social and political development which was taking place in west Denmark during the tenth and eleventh centuries. We have already referred to the runestones as documents of succession to new rights and to new kinds of ownership of property, and the Vorbasse estates constitute exactly such new rights to land.

Furthermore, the runestones of the contemporary Jelling and 'After Jelling' groups are largely connected with the high kings of Jelling, whose home province comprises the magnate farms of Vorbasse, and are thus intimately related to the political centre.

The position of Vorbasse in the west Jylland landscape, near large meadows, suggests that the raising of animals was the prime activity of the magnate farms. The same holds true of another contemporary group of estates, at Omgård, some 70 kilometres further to the north, which were also constructed over the crofts of a ninth-century Viking village with 'normal' long-houses and pit-houses.[37] At Omgård more finds of artefacts have been made than at Vorbasse. These include ceramics of high quality in the central halls and of a more modest type in the smaller houses along the fences; Norwegian soap-stone vessels are also found and quern-stones imported from the Rhinelands. This shows that the long-distance trade of the Viking Age was not only concerned with luxuries, but also had direct economic significance for subsistence. Near the site are found cross-country fences, roads and apparently a corn-mill, perhaps grinding oats for the plentiful horses of the farms.

The traditional Viking Age villages covering the entire period are also found in the same provinces as the magnate farms. As already shown, the settlements present different types of well-built long-houses (up to about 40m long), with curved or straight long walls and usually with two rows of roof-supporting posts down the aisle, supplemented not infrequently with wall-supporting posts too, especially when the interior posts are missing. The orientation is still often east-west, but stables are no longer so common in the dwelling-houses. In addition, we have a number of smaller buildings, including the many pit-houses. Also on these farms we find pottery of foreign character, soap-stone vessels (from Norway) and the Rhienish quern-stones.[38]

The lay-out of the settlements is designed so that each larger long-house, as in the fifth-century Vorbasse village, lies next to one or two small ones, plus, possibly, some pit-houses. The single farmstead is often surrounded by a fence. At Sædding, near present-day Esbjerg on the west coast of Jylland, the compounds lie around a rectangular open plaza (150m by 30m) remaining in the same place throughout the history of the site, while the orientation of the long-houses changes from east-west to north-south (Fig. 18).[39] This village also has a number of wells.

Many of the settlements show a link back to the eighth century (for instance, in Skåne), but none continues much after the first half of the eleventh century, and so far it is impossible to establish a direct link with present-day villages, of which most go back to the Middle Ages. This discontinuity can hardly be due to climatic circumstances, and is rather a result of the short lifespan of these kinds of buildings

combined with replanning of the entire settlement. Such may have
taken place in connection with the coming of new types of ownerships
or new systems of agriculture (perhaps even the so-called three-field
system) corresponding to the intensification of cereal growing
(compared with the extension of pastures), noted from the pollen
diagrams. The stress on cereals may have been most marked in the

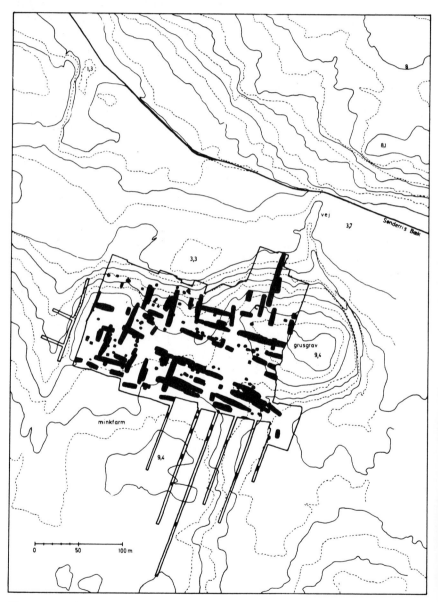

Figure 18 The Sædding settlement (west Jylland) from the tenth to eleventh
centuries. (After Stoumann)

forested central Danish provinces with, as we have seen above, many pigs as compared with cattle and probably little pasture. In turn, small pastures mean restricted fallow land and thus a more intensive growing of cereals. A further factor to be taken into consideration is the military organisation of the country, the so-called 'leding', where each 'herred' (territory) has to man one or more warships. The single village and farm contribute according to their size, and it is clearly in the interest of the administration to create standard measures. Such a development is in itself a strong indicator of the coming of the state, in spite of the many problems of the continuation of settlement from the Viking Age to the Middle Ages.

Among the Viking Age place-names, the -by and -toft endings – occurring, for instance, in the Danelaw areas of England in about 900 – are normally thought to imply planned villages.[40] This may create a problem of synchronisation with the local development in Denmark, which apparently was later. On the other hand, it is clear from the archaeological record that even an Iron Age village like Vorbasse in the fifth century, was, to a large extent, planned, though we are poorly informed about the field-system. (At Vorbasse we know of some exits from the compounds in the direction of the meadows, but not of a division of these.) The 'toft' (croft) for a village name meant, in the early medieval law codes, the regulated plot around the farm buildings. The size of this croft determined the size of the field. The -tofts cluster on the marginal lands of Denmark, in west Jylland and in east Skåne, where there is a good possibility of determining the plan of the village, and probably of its fields as well, owing to the Viking Age colonisation in the areas.[41] Other names, like -torp (and also -by), indicate the general expansion of the Viking Age settlement.[42] But we are left with only the towns if we want to study the history of continued habitation from the Viking Age, with its link from ancient to modern Denmark.

Chapter 5

TOWNS AND FORTRESSES

A. Historical sources for the town

Some of the written historical information concerned with the early towns has already been mentioned, such, for example, as the presence of merchants and the establishment of Christian institutions at various dates. In this chapter we shall concentrate on the whole pattern of towns and on the functions of these centres.[1] We include an archaeological investigation of the fortresses, while the institutions and activities of the towns are studied both from the scarce, but important, written sources and from the archaeological record. Only archaeology provides information about buildings and craft production; in addition, it yields most of the comparative data. The historical sources may, on the other hand, supply a survey (in the case of the major towns) on which centres are functioning, and how they function, at a specific period. As before, we shall try to avoid sources written any later than the Viking Age.

Surveying the written sources, Hedeby/Slesvig in south Jylland is first mentioned in 804 as 'Sliesthorp' and (in 808) as a 'portus' (port) and trading centre.[2] The identity of Hedeby and Slesvig is given by an English source from around 1000, which explains that Hedeby is the Danish name for the site, and Slesvig the Saxon (German) name.[3] In about 870 Slesvig (called 'Sliaswich'), in a source referring to events around 850 (including the erection of the first churches), is again mentioned as a 'portus', and in addition as an international trading centre and as a 'vicus' too (cf. the ending of the word 'Sliaswich').[4] ('Vicus' is a Latin term used for a number of early harbour towns in western Europe.) The word 'Hedeby' appears for the first time in an English travelogue (by the Norwegian Ottar) from shortly before 900 as 'aet Haethum' (at the heathers); Hedeby here is mentioned as a port and trading centre.[5] Hedeby appears, incidentally, as 'Hethabyr' on two runestones from the site itself, as well as from one from the town of Århus, all in 1000.[6] In the German sources of the tenth century, including the ones mentioning the bishop of the town, 'Slesvig' seems to have been exclusively in use, as it was in the continental writings of the ninth century.[7]

Medieval Slesvig, beneath the present town, lies on the northern shore at the bottom of the Sli inlet (Fig. 21). The oldest deposits here are from the mid-eleventh century; but by a smaller inlet on the opposite, southern shore of the Sli lies a larged walled site, the Viking Age Slesvig or Hedeby (Fig. 22). This settlement begins in the eighth century, but the regulated central part did not start until about 800; the wall around is still later, from the tenth century, and, incidentally, is connected with the main frontier wall of Danevirke, across Jylland. Hedeby declines at the end of the tenth century, and disappears completely in the first half of the eleventh century.

Ribe in south-west Jylland is mentioned in about 870 in a source referring to its first church in about 860; the town is here called a 'vicus'.[8] Archaeologically Ribe goes back as far as the eighth century. The episcopal nominations of 948 mention Slesvig, Ribe and Århus, on the east coast of Jylland.[9] The archaeological remains from the latter go back to the beginning of the tenth century and comprise, apart from remnants of pit-houses, an apparently circular wall. The settlement is a planned town, fortified from the start and probably set up by a royal house. The same seems to hold true for Odense on Fyn, which had a nominated bishop by 988,[10] where a tenth-century ringwall is found across the river from the early medieval centre of the present city, starting in the late eleventh century. The ringwall, later 'Nonnebakken', is normally compared with the tenth-century fortresses of Trelleborg type (Section E, below), but the traces of buildings within the wall do not correspond to the regular pattern of the military sites. An almost contemporary parallel to early Århus and Odense is, perhaps, the regulated, and fortified, 'burhs' of the English King Alfred from the close of the ninth century.[11]

According to Adam of Bremen's work from around 1070 a church was built at Roskilde on Sjælland before the death of King Harald, no later than 987.[12] Archaeologically, tenth-century Roskilde is unknown, but access by water, through an inlet, is known to have been carefully blocked by worn-out ships at Skuldelev, twenty kilometres to the north, some time in the early or mid-eleventh century.[13] A better date is given by the remnants from one of the stone churches of the city, extending back to the 1030s, while the first church of stone, on the site of the cathedral, is said to have been begun by the sister of King Knud shortly after 1027.[14] In Adam's work (1070) Roskilde is mentioned as a bishop's seat and as the royal centre of Denmark.[15]

The first Danish coins carrying the name of the mint belong to the reign of King Knud (1018 (in Denmark) – 1035).[16] They comprise Lund (in Skåne, far the largest mint), Roskilde (the second largest) and Hedeby/Slesvig (probably), Ribe, Viborg and Ørbæk, all in Jylland,

Odense on Fyn and also on Sjælland, Ringsted and Slagelse (Fig. 19). The archaeological remains of buildings from the city of Lund go back to about 1020, while a large graveyard, belonging – to judge by its character – to an urban settlement, not yet found, starts before 1000.[17] Also to be mentioned are the many 'After Jelling' runestones (dating to about 1000) from around and inside the town (Chapter 3). The plots of early Lund seem to have been formally laid out; the city is mentioned in about 1070 by Adam as a bishop's seat.[18] In the Middle Ages Lund, like Ringsted on Sjælland, Odense on Fyn and Viborg in north Jylland, was an important thing-place (court and political meeting-place).

The archaeological remains of Viking Age Viborg, also included by Adam in his list of bishops' seats,[19] go back to the ninth century, but they are clearly of a non-urban kind and may, at most, comprise a larger farm. It is not until the late eleventh century that the medieval (and present-day) street system was laid out. On the other hand, the name 'Viborg', meaning 'Vibjerg (hill)', indicates the presence of a pagan religious centre ('vi') on the site. The thing-function may be of the same date, but we have no clear evidence. That 'things' were in existence in Scandinavia at least in the ninth century is learned from Bishop Ansgar's visit to the port of Birka in mid-Sweden.[20] Moreover Viborg's geographical position in Jylland is central, lying at the northern end of the north-south extending watershed which carried the main road system; the site would easily become a meeting-place. Odense also holds a central position (for Fyn) and a name suggesting a pagan religious centre: 'Odin's vi' (Odense), probably connected with the royal Odin-cult.[21] The nomination of this site for a bishopric in 988 is a useful and illuminating piece of evidence.

Viking Age Ørbæk and Slagelse (a town, in the Middle Ages) are unknown, apart from the royals mints, but it is hardly an accident that the fortresses of Aggersborg, on the Limfjord in northern Jylland, and Trelleborg, at Store Bælt, on the Sjælland side, are only four or five kilometres away. Incidentally, the son of King Knud, Hardeknud (1035–42) had coins struck at Slesvig, Ribe, Århus, Viborg, Ørbæk, Ålborg (north Jylland), Slagelse, Roskilde, Lund and Gori (Fig. 19).[22] Viking Age Ålborg is also unknown, the oldest deposits so far, going back to about 1100. Adam of Bremen, in about 1070, mentions Ålborg as a 'civitas' (city), but not as a bishop's seat.[23] The locality of Gori is unknown, but it was probably located in Skåne, as there is a similarity between coins from there and the numerous Lund coins. The complete list of Adam's 'civitates' runs: Slesvig, Ribe, Århus, Viborg, Ålborg, the otherwise unknown 'Wendila' (a name normally referring to the whole province of Vendsyssel lying to the north of Ålborg), Odense, Roskilde and Lund.[24] When dealing with ninth-century events, Adam does not use the word 'vicus' for Hedeby/Slesvig and Ribe, but 'portus' (port).

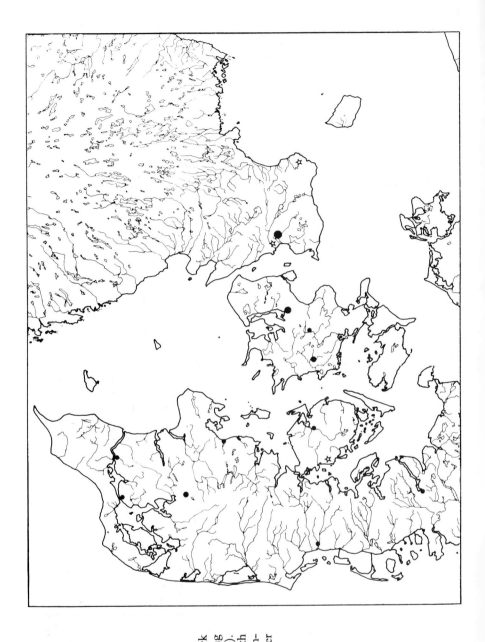

Figure 19 Mints in Denmark 1018 (1014)–1042 (King Knud and King Hardeknud). Size of black dot varies with the number of different coin-types produced. (Stars: other eleventh-century mints)

Before turning to the archaeological data we must try to bring together all the available information on the institutions of the towns, and other centres, in order to form systematic geographical patterns linking up the various types of centres and relating each centre to its rural hinterland.

B. *Geographical patterns and functions of towns*

Town centres are, normally, geographical focal points of a population and production area; they have a surrounding territory which they serve in various ways and which serves and supplies them. Between the towns is often noted an internal ranking, especially in larger and well built-up zones, which participate in the same economic system and employ a developed division of labour and control. On each level of complexity any centre has an unrivalled so-called catchment area, minimising the problems of (land) transportation, whether food, goods, services or control are involved.

A number of models are available for centres and their catchment areas. In those derived from human geography the low-rank centres sit in the corners of hexagons, whose mid-point is occupied by a high-rank centre, itself in a corner of a larger hexagon, and so on, until the highest centres are incorporated too.[25] At the very lowest level are petty centres surrounded by six standard units. The hexagon is used instead of the more natural circle in the homogeneous space, covered by the model, since circles cannot be 'packed'. A prerequisite for the application of these models is that the centre on a higher level fulfils both the obligations of the lower-level centres and those that make it a higher-ranking centre. Another condition, finally, is that the highest centres gather all types of services and control. In Viking Age Denmark this point does not hold true, because the important royal political control is exercised from a variety of smaller and larger sites. Throughout most of the Middle Ages the king and his followers, as well as the central administration, were travelling at regular intervals to carry out their tasks and, literally, to eat up some of the taxes. A true capital (Copenhagen) was not set up until the close of the Middle Ages. An early royal centre, or rather, farmstead, like Jelling, did not lie in, or near, a town; on the contrary as we shall see later, it was situated in between the major towns. The impression of decentralisation is also strengthened by the fact that some of the main 'things', and from time to time even a few of the bishops, were seated outside the towns. For the Viking Age proper, the large fortresses built by kings, such as Trelleborg, Aggersborg and Fyrkat were also set up in the countryside, and not near the towns.

Although the models described above cannot be used for the formation of the Danish state, as they might be used for the

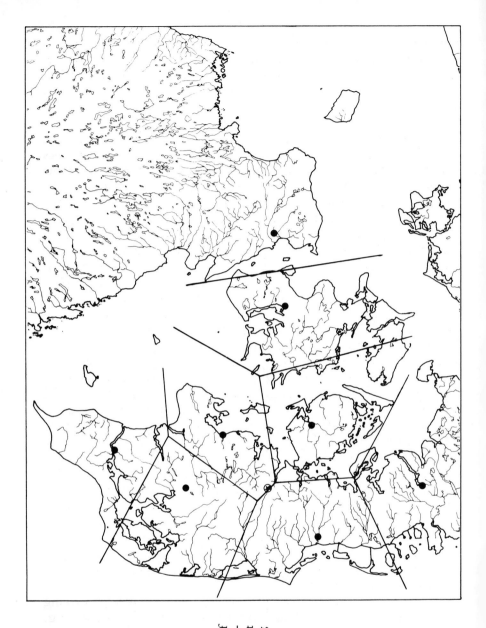

Figure 20 'Civitates' (cities) of mid-eleventh-century Denmark (dots) with catchment territories. Black star: Jelling

civilisations of ancient Mesopotamia or Mesoamerica, for instance, similar methods are applicable when outlining the unspecified complexity of the town-centres and their rank according to such measures.

In the eighth century only two townships ('vicus'/'portus') are known, Hedeby and Ribe, both in southern Jylland. Along with the possible west Skåne market-site at Löddeköpinge,[26] if in fact it does not start a little later, they are the only non-agricultural settlements known, and no certain pattern is established; moreover no written sources mention the localities. In the ninth century Hedeby and Ribe, but no other towns, are referred to in the written sources, and not until the tenth century are the data applicable for geographical analyses of the kind we have outlined above. Among the towns we are hardly wrong in attributing Hedeby first rank and Ribe and Odense, on Fyn, second (Oldenburg, in the Slavonian Holstein to the east of Hedeby, may belong to the same group).[27] Århus should also be mentioned here, but it lies so far away from Hedeby, with the Ribe-Odense-Oldenburg belt in between, that it constitutes a potential major centre. These towns are all tenth-century seats of bishops, and Hedeby in addition was probably the seat of petty kings of the so-called 'Swedish' dynasty and an international port of transit. Århus, and the smaller Odense, were possibly royal planned towns, perhaps with a special reference to the early Jelling-dynasty, to judge from their location. The same applies to Ribe, which in some instances may substitute for Hedeby, especially if aided by Århus for the transit-traffic. Such a route passes through Jelling, and was eased, in the late tenth century, by the construction of the almost one-kilometre-long two-lane bridge across Vejle river-valley at Ravninge.[28] At the same time the importance of Århus is underlined by the cluster of 'After Jelling'-type runestones from the city and its vicinity, indicating a new royal settlement (cf. above). To the north in Jylland the route from Hedeby, over Ravninge, leads to Viborg, which, although not yet a town, may initially have had a central function as a pagan cult-site and a meeting (thing) and market place.

If we outline the catchment territories of the major sites, a striking junction is seen a couple of kilometres from Jelling in mid-Jylland (Fig. 20). (The technique is simply to draw straight borderlines in a right angle across the line of sighting between the towns, etc., and through the mid-point of the line). Jelling is optimally situated for command and control of the highest possible number of other centres, a position which was critically located with the tenth-century political development in mind. Hedeby and the fortifications and fortresses at Danevirke, Trelleborg, Fyrkat and Aggersborg lie in a ring further away (cf. Fig. 1). In addition, they are situated close to some of the most important transportation routes in western Denmark, and we are reminded that state control is very much a question of overcoming problems of transportation, especially over land where roads and the inception of bridges in the Viking Age are important elements. Finally, if the Urnehoved thing in south Jylland (at later Åbenrå) was already functioning in the tenth century, the border between this and the Viborg and the Odense things also ran through Jelling.

In terms of agriculture and basic subsistence materials, Jelling may have used two different resource environments simultaneously; to the west the open pastures of mid and west Jylland, and to the east the forested and rich clay-lands. However, no Viking Age remains, apart from the ones connected with the mounds, runestones and early churches, are as yet known in Jelling. Were a sufficient area archaeologically investigated, we might expect one or more large magnate farms, as at Vorbasse, to appear, perhaps covering the entire present-day village.

In the decades around 1000 we must include Roskilde and Lund in our analysis, of which the last, along with Århus, has a royal settlement, to judge from the runestones, and was therefore of special importance. The same may be attributed to Hedeby/Slesvig. Using the hexagon models, we see Hedeby, Århus and Lund surrounded by the minor centres Ribe, Viborg, Odense and Roskilde.

For the close of the Viking Age and the start of the Middle Ages, we must use the information from Adam of Bremen collected in about 1070, as well as the data on the mints, which give us more levels of centres, instead of the two we detect for the period around 1000 (Fig. 20). To set up a scale we tentatively give one point for each of the following functions: bishop's seat, royal mint of King Knud or Hardeknud or of other kings before about 1070, the period of Adam,[29] a major 'thing' and the attribute 'civitas' (by Adam) which is taken to include some craft, market and trade activity. In this way Viborg, Odense and Lund have four points, Århus, Ribe and Roskilde three points, Ålborg and Ringsted two points, 'Wendila', Ørbæk, Toftum, Slagelse, Thumatorp, Borgeby, Gori and Dalby one point, and Helsingborg zero.[30] The low level is represented by the sites having zero or one point, while the higher levels comprise the towns with respectively three and four points. Of the two-point locations, Ålborg, a 'civitas', may join the high group and Ringsted the low one.

To judge by their place-name endings, Ålborg and Helsingborg have fortresses (Viborg was originally 'Vi-bjerg' not '-borg'), but we cannot include this aspect because of our imperfect knowledge of the rest of the sites. The highest centres, defined especially with respect to the regional situation, are thus Viborg, Odense and Lund, surrounded, in hexagons, by Ålborg, Århus, Ribe and Roskilde, while the rest of the sites make up still smaller hexagons around the two-, three- and four-point localities.

If we stress the external aspects of these sites (only leaving out the 'things') including harbours on the open sea or on inlets, the highest

Table

	Bishop	Mint	Lands thing	'Civitas'	Harbour (open sea and inlets)
Hedeby/Slesvig	x	x		x	x
Ribe	x	x		x	
Århus	x	x		x	x
Viborg	x	x	x	x	
Ørbæk		x			
Ålborg		x		x	x
'Wendila'	x			(?)	
Odense	x	x	x	x	
Toftum		x			
Slagelse		x			
Ringsted		x	x		
Roskilde	x	x		x	x
Helsingborg					x
Borgeby		x			
Lund	x	x	x	x	
Dalby	x				
Thumathorp		x			
Gori		x			?

centres become Hedeby/Slesvig, Århus and Roskilde, while Ribe, Viborg, Ålborg, Odense and Lund are next. This only underlines the spaced-out character of urban activities in Denmark and the lack of true centralisation. The major centres in the eleventh century are, basically, functioning as local 'service-stations' for a province, while the links to other centres are less prominent. On the other hand, at least two clear local levels emerge. The first comprises centres with four points, if we base our study on the already cited indices: bishop, mint, major thing, the 'civitas' attribute and harbour. These include Hedeby/Slesvig, Århus, Viborg, Odense, Roskilde and Lund. A low level of one point is made up of sites like Ørbæk, 'Wendila', Toftum, Slagelse, Helsingborg, Borgeby, Thumatorp, Dalby and Gori. Only one locality, Ringsted, has two points, and two, Ribe and Ålborg, have three.

By the mid-eleventh century the entire country is thus served by major and minor town centres, taking on various activities, while the supreme political power is exercised by a travelling king, supported by vassals and royal farmsteads all over the area. To judge by the extent of the mints, the east may, at the end of the Viking Age, have been valuably regulated by the kings, and it may be no coincidence that Adam of Bremen, in about 1070, places the royal centre at Roskilde.[31] Incidentally, we note that the distribution of good harbours on the sea and inlets, being mainly western, do not correspond to the mints. This would indicate that the coins of King Knud, for example, were not meant primarily for trade, but were used rather as some kind of salary and as a piece of royal propaganda in the new eastern provinces.

A group of small centres, or rather, major farmsteads, belonging to the Viking period is only known from the place-name 'Husby'.[32] The Husbys are, according to medieval sources, royal farmsteads with some military duties. When we include these uncertain localities here, it is due to their striking geographical distribution, which may relate them to the tenth-century early Jelling dynasty.

Apart from a north-eastern Blekinge specimen, hardly Danish in the narrow sense of the word, and a single Husby from north Sjælland, the rest are western, clustering in a narrow zone between Jelling and Hedeby, where they are frequently found on the coast. In addition, we have a Husby a few kilometres from the royal fortress of Aggersborg on the Limfjord, and a similar locality behind the main wall of Danevirke in south Jylland. The Husby in Sjælland and one on the north-west coast of Jylland are lying in the outer, 'defensive' circle of the tenth-century west Danish state.

It is striking that the distribution in no way corresponds to the runestones, and we may have here yet another system of royal dependence. But these are only hypotheses, and the problem of dating prevents their further use. Instead we must draw on the rich archaeological data from the towns and other non-agricultural centres.

C. Population

In terms of population, the towns have undoubtedly been larger and more densely occupied that any other type of settlement. For instance, the number of burials at Hedeby amounts to ten thousand or more, which would give an average population size, throughout the town's 250 or more years of history, of at least 1000 (adult) persons, using the following formula:[33]

$$\frac{\text{Population}}{\text{size}} = \frac{\text{No. of graves (10,000)} \times \text{average life expectancy (30, or, perhaps 40 years)}}{\text{Period of occupation (250-300 years)}}$$

The earliest occupation of the town of Lund comprises a cemetery with over 250 graves from about 50 years, corresponding to a population of 200 persons, and most probably more.[34] Other graveyards in Denmark are much smaller. At Löddeköpinge in west Skåne, a market-centre in the ninth century, about 2000 graves have been found dating from the eleventh and the beginning of the twelfth century, and representing at least five hundred persons.[35] Because of the late date, we are here probably dealing with the cemetery of a whole parish, whose church is nearby. Six hundred burials from Lindholm Høje near Ålborg in north Jylland correspond to a group of only forty persons as an average, since the graveyard is occupied for

500 years from about 500 A.D. to 1000.[36] (This site has often been thought of as a town, because of the large amount of graves, without regard to the long period of occupation.) From the fortress of Trelleborg on west Sjælland come more than 150 graves, corresponding to an average population of about one hundred persons with a period of occupation of fifty years.[37] The similar, but smaller, Fyrkat fortress in north-east Jylland, which existed for only a short period, has about 30 graves.[38] From Ris Fattiggård in north Jylland come more than 100 interments, covering at least one hundred years of occupation, and representing a group of less than 40 persons.[39] Other Viking Age sites have less than 100 burials and they all seem to represent populations of the size of a village, or less. For instance, at Stengade on the island of Langeland a well-excavated cemetery of 83 graves spanning about a century, or perhaps less, implies 30 or 40 persons in the original social group.[40]

For the sake of comparison, it should be mentioned that a very large, and well-documented, cemetery from the centuries before the turn of the first millennium B.C. at Årupgård in south Jylland has yielded more than 1,400 graves; and, although the site is divided into two parts, the total number of persons represented is high, about 100 to 150.[41] A contemporary village site, with a chiefly compound, from Hodde, also in southern Jylland in its major phase, is made up of 53 buildings and 27 farmsteads.[42] This is the largest early Iron Age settlement known and may have held 100-200 persons, about the same as the Årupgård group. Vorbasse of the fifth century, with 30 farms, is perhaps even slightly larger.[43] Møllegårdsmarken on Fyn, the largest non-town cemetery in Denmark, and dating to the first four centuries A.D., has at least 2,000 graves, corresponding to 150 or 200 persons.[44] The Møllegårdsmarken society, because of its size and the many wealthy graves, had a central function on Fyn, especially in the third century, and may, with the other sources already quoted, set the upper limit for population conglomerations in the pre-urban era. It is clear from the above that the establishment of several settlements of even larger size, and with no or little immediate agricultural support, in the Viking Age implied serious problems of supply.

From Hedeby a random sample of 100 skeletons has revealed that 62 per cent (47) of the adult dead were men, and 38 per cent (29) women.[45] Apparently women did not live in Hedeby unless their workpower could be used; their involvement was rarer in the milieu of crafts and trade than in agricultural production. Moreover the Hedeby sample reveals the common lower life-expectancy for women than for men in pre-industrial societies, probably due to the dangers of childbearing, which meant that the majority of females did not survive their twenties. At the Trelleborg fortresses a distinction in numbers of adult men and women has also been noted.[46] The few women of the cemetery are equal to the number of men over forty, amounting to

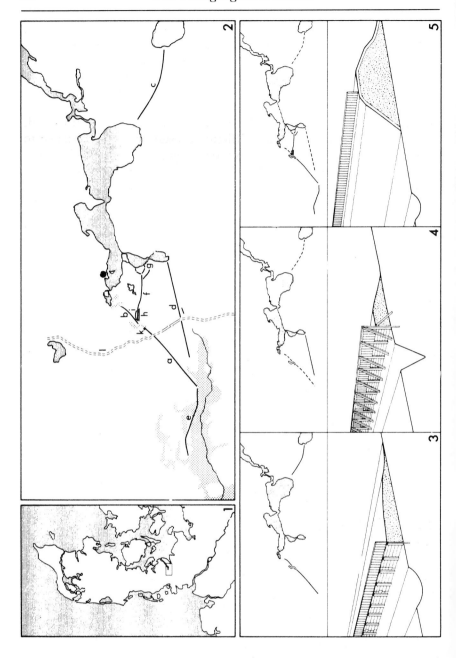

Figure 21 The Hedeby-Danevirke area, southernmost Jylland. Hedeby at (g) (black
   dot: Slesvig city). Letters indicate parts of the Danevirke wall system except 1: the
   main north-south road through Jylland. The illustrations at the bottom show the
   development of Danevirke from the eighth century (left) to the tenth century
   (right) with the early ninth century (Kovirke) phase in the middle. (After H. H.
   Andersen)

only nine, while the males total 31.

It is only at the agricultural sites that we note a normal distribution of men and women; for instance, at Stengade on the island of Langeland we have 12 adult men and 16 women, still counting only those graves where the skeletons can be identified as of one or the other sex.[47]

The areas needed to supply Hedeby for instance with food, workpower and services, are difficult to establish. The distance to other towns, like Ribe, may allow for the entire area from the Ejder river to beyond the present Danish-German border. However, other activities may have competed with Hedeby for the southern Jylland resources, In England, the 'burhs', or planned towns and communal

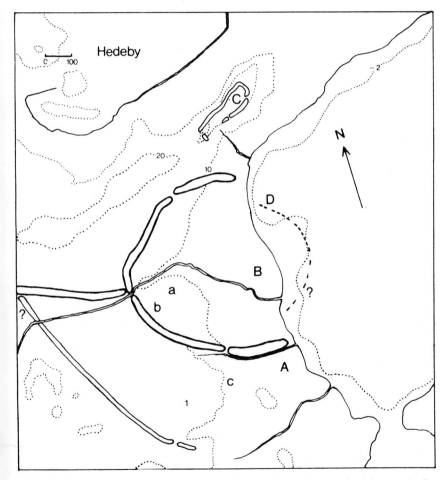

Figure 22 Hedeby. A = the (early) south settlement. B = the central settlement (early ninth century onwards). C = the Fortress. D = Palisade or pier. (a) = the common graveyard in the central settlement, (b) = chamber graves, (c) = the south graveyard (the boat–chamber grave at 1)

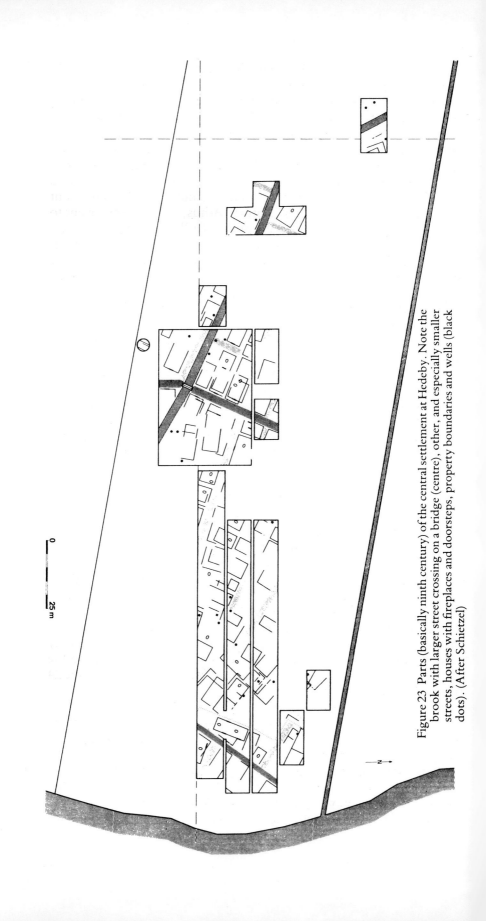

0
25 m

Figure 23 Parts (basically ninth century) of the central settlement at Hedeby. Note the brook with larger street crossing on a bridge (centre), other, and especially smaller streets, houses with fireplaces and doorsteps, property boundaries and wells (black dots). (After Schietzel)

fortresses of King Alfred in the late ninth century occur in a list giving the area (in number of 'hides') of provision and support of manpower for the defence of the sites against, among others, the Danes.[48] If these numbers are applied to Danish conditions, the environment and agrarian systems not being too different, the following appears. The central settlement of Hedeby, covering some 24 hectares, would need about 600 square kilometres if the 'hide' around 900 A.D. is of about the same size as in the eleventh century. Århus, roughly equivalent to the area of Aggersborg, the largest of the 'Trelleborg'-type fortresses would have needed up to 250 square kilometres for support with its less than ten hectares. The figures are uncertain, but it is striking how well the 600 square kilometres for Hedeby correspond to the area, north-east of the town, most densely settled according to the distribution of graves.[49] But in addition, the upkeep and defence of the Danevirke walls would require more land in the same area, beyond the 600 square kilometres for the town itself. Besides, Hedeby may have received supplies by sea.

The findings are in accordance with notions about the population spread round Århus, for instance, and the size of the early parishes, showing that the towns received supplies from very wide areas and were fully integrated with the surrounding province (Chapter 4 C). We have also noted town products and trade goods to be distributed among the rural settlements in return for supplies (Chapter 4 D).

D. Archaeology and the town

Hedeby has a central role in the study of Viking Age towns, their economy and social development.[50] Relatively large areas have been excavated, although they only make up five or ten per cent of the total settlement. The eighth-century site, continuing into the ninth, lies to the south of the later walled area, which was unoccupied until about 810, at the time of King Godfred (according to dendrochronological dating) (Figs 22-3). In the tenth century the south settlement ('Südsiedlung') gave way to graveyards and ditches, probably connected with the construction of the semicircular wall around the central area to the north. The earthen town-rampart, framing some 24 hectares, 550 and 600 metres wide in respectively east-west and north-south, is today between five and ten metres high and displays several phases of construction. Entrances with gate-towers were in the north and south, and possibly in the south-west too, where a brook enters the settlement, bringing sweet-water and carrying refuse to the harbour basin and the small inlet. The wall is difficult to date exactly, but at some stage it is linked with the Danevirke main wall by the so-called connection wall, no later than mid-tenth century, according to dendrochronology (cf. Fig. 21). The latter rampart has also provided C[14]-dates of the same century. Outside the town wall were several ditches, one of which continues to the north of the connection wall, showing this to be later than the first town rampart. Towards the south-west an additional outer wall is found, while towards the sea a semicircular submerged palisade framed the central harbour basin.

To the north of the walled area is a small and relatively early settlement, and above this, on a steep hill, an undated wall system with a number of late Iron Age or even Viking Age burial mounds. Before the construction of other defences, the hill may have served as a refuge, in the same way as the 'stronghold' at Birka, the port in mid-Sweden.[51] Other early cemeteries lie immediately to the west of the northern, the southern and the central settlement. The southern cemetery expanded after 900 towards the east and covers, as noted, the site of the early settlement. The central cemetery also continues into the tenth century, but on the other hand is superimposed in part by the expanding settlement around the brook. But before this happens, we record a division by 900 of the graves into a large group of simple east-west skeleton graves, few of which contain artefacts, though more frequently in a coffin, and a small group of uncremated chamber tombs further to the south-west, near the edge of the semicircular wall, possibly contemporary in date or slightly later. The chamber tombs are more richly furnished and have parallels in the later part of the southern graveyard – immediately to the south of which, incidentally, is found the well-known 'Ship-chamber Tomb' ('Bootkammergrab') also from the beginning of the tenth century.[52] Here a ship has been laid on top of the rich chamber. The early part of the southern graveyard comprises cremations, including urn graves, dating back to the eighth century; but here too the east-west skeleton grave is the rule and is followed in frequency by some older north-south orientated inhumations. In general, the spread of graves is irregular, but the central graveyard of east-west burials had very little space for use and gave the interments a minimum of room, rather like a town burial ground in early Lund.[53] The central chamber grave group lies in parallel rows and may have followed a street. It is obvious, seen from the settlement itself, that the land in the central area was scarce and regulated.

The graves outside the wall do not exceed the tenth century, while some of the interments of the common central burial ground, superseding, incidentally, a shrinking settlement area in the final phase of the history of the town, belong to the eleventh century. Dendrochronologically no constructions on the site are later than 1020. This corresponds with the fact that at least some of the craft activities of the town seem to have ceased at around the close of the tenth century. For instance, no eleventh-century moulds for jewellery have been found.

The excavated area of the early south settlement consists of a single long-house (probably like the ones on the central site) and a rather large number of pit-houses, almost all, unlike the pit-houses in the villages, rectangular and each with a fireplace.[54] In several of these buildings the manufacture of amber beads has taken place, while near one was found a mould for the casting of bronze jewellery. In addition, iron has been extracted, or worked, on the site. The imports comprise a west European 'Sceatta' coin and fragments of Rhinish millstones and pottery. Although the finds are few, we already have some of the facets of the later Hedeby, such for example as the manufacture of luxuries and long-distance trade, even to procure day-to-day articles important for the subsistence economy. On the other hand, there are no definite traces of a regular laying out of the site suggesting its possible use by both local and foreign groups. Many agrarian sites of the same age – like, for instance, Valleberga in Skåne[55] – actually fulfil almost all the criteria set by the south settlement; the absence of long-houses on the Skåne site, however, is probably caused by the excavation technique. The important difference is the fireplaces in the corners of the Hedeby pit-houses, indicating, along with the regular construction, their use all the year round as practically the sole dwellings, and workshops too on the site. In addition, almost no other settlement had such a strategic position as Hedeby between the North Sea and the Baltic. Only fifteen kilometres to the west, by following the Trene and Ejder rivers, it was possible to reach western Europe in a sea-going ship. Reloading at Hedeby would have avoided the hazardous navigation around Jylland and left the traffic on the Baltic, as far as Russia or beyond, (to the Islamic and Byzantine worlds), to sailors with local knowledge of this sea; while at the same time the west Europeans would have been restricted to the North Sea and adjoining waters. The Danes, finally, could benefit from knowledge of the navigation on both the eastern and the western seas.

At the lower end of the Hedeby brook, the central settlement, from its initial foundation shortly after 800, according to the dendro-chronological datings, presents a very different lay-out.[56] A number of rectangular houses have been found belonging to successive phases (Fig. 24). The buildings stand in rows on narrow plots whose fences remain in the same place over time, suggesting that the site was regulated from the beginning of its history and the plots subordinated to a general plan. These houses measure on average about ten by five metres and they almost never have inner posts. They were lightly built with only the wall to support the roof; this was made of wickerwork, or, more rarely, of planks. Doors were usually at the end of the houses, facing the larger and minor plank-covered and permanent, straight streets, from which they were separated by a small court with an entrance mat. As a result of the excellent preservation of the organic material and the recovery of parts of the superstructure, it has been possible to reconstruct the houses fully. In several cases inner divisions are recorded and fireplaces are usually situated in the larger central

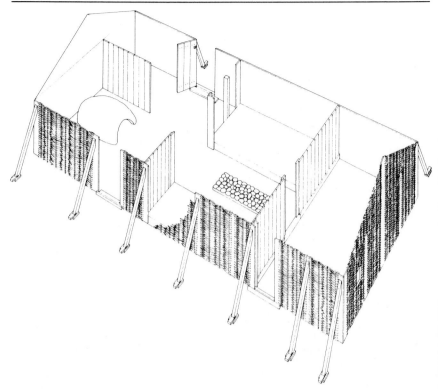

Figure 24   Reconstruction of ninth-century house from the central settlement at
   Hedeby. (After Schietzel)

room. Ovens have also been found, but only in one case is there
accommodation for animals. Unlike the south settlement, pit-houses
are extremely few, and they are lightly-built structures.

The houses have no parallels in the rural settlements, although they
may vaguely resemble the Trelleborg-type halls. It is tempting to see a
connection between the light cheap construction and the specialised
and, above all, more transient functions of this site vis-à-vis the rural
settlements. Furthermore it is clear that space was limited on the site,
the brook was lined with planks, a street is carried across a bridge and
the houses stand close to each other, while garbage is piling up in the
brook, between the fences and in the wells.

Unfortunately it is only in the ninth century that we are able to
discern such a detailed picture; the later deposits are less well
preserved. Studying the spread of artefacts, however, especially
ceramics and metal objects, it is clear that the early settlement located
by the brook only extended roughly as far as the later wall to the
south-west, near the graveyard of chamber tombs.[57] In the tenth
century the settlement obviously filled out the entire space within the
wall. The chamber tombs, for example, are superimposed by

rectangular pit-houses, perhaps on the same streets that divide the rows of tombs. The pit-houses are well-built. They have posts in the corners too, unlike almost every rural pit-house, and are mostly supplied with fireplaces like the similar constructions on the somewhat earlier south settlement.[58] The buildings have been re-newed several times, in each case on the same plot, which, in spite of the lack of fences here, reveals some planning of this peripheral area too.

Looking into the functions of the buildings, especially with an eye to craft production, there is no correlation between any variant of house, or any plot, and any specific activity.[59] Nor has any craft apparently been carried out only in a special part of the town; and the usual idea of a 'craftsman's district' is therefore due to the limited size of the early excavations. Small local clusters of refuse from specific activities do occur, but they move over time – as, for instance, the iron slag in the lower brook area. Surface registration of iron slag, however, all over the central site area, has revealed major concen-trations over about half a hectare or more, in some spaces next to the inner side of the town wall, where the settlement may have been less built-up. On the 'macro-level' too, we should note, there is no such thing as a specific craftsman's quarter, as in some later medieval towns.

Iron-working has already been mentioned among the basic activities. Pottery-making is also recorded, for at least during the tenth century there were wheel-made vessels of a special Hedeby variant.[60] The bone industry is common, especially the rich production of combs of antler; but weaving and working of leather were also substantial crafts. In addition, wood-working must have been an important activity, and on a smaller scale we may mention the dressing of Rhinish quern-stones.

The luxury production of Hedeby comprises bronze and tin jewellery. For the ninth century most of the types were western, belonging to west Denmark and Norway, while in the tenth century south Scandinavian forms are common. During this century gold filigree working was also carried out, and the most costly trinkets of the age were made. Occasionally bronze-decorated weapons were made too. Glass and amber beads were also produced.

In itself the craft production indicates exchange and trade, and to that end a number of weights have been recorded. Local minting is known from the beginning of the ninth century onwards, but especially from the mid to late tenth century. The number of coins from the settlement, however, is very low, and by 1966 the local types were only represented by eight to ten specimens from the habitation deposits, while seven came from the graves.[61] The coin-series imitate Frankish and English motifs, especially the Dorestad coins of Charlemagne, but the Hedeby coins, at least in the ninth century, may only have circulated as coins at Hedeby, and not in the rest of Denmark or Scandinavia, where they usually occur as amulets. The minting ceases at Hedeby in about 980, at the same time as the production of jewellery. Indeed it is an unanswered question to what extent craft activities survived the turn of the millennium and the decline in settlement area.

Among foreign imports, iron also occurs, in spite of the availability of local bog-ore; apparently the Hedeby iron is Swedish in origin and of a high quality due to the low content of phosphoric acid.[62] Soapstone vessels, excellent for cooking, are derived from Norway; from the Rhineland came ceramics and lava quernstones, finished on the site and in need of no further trimming. By the tenth century, only certain types of western pots appear, in particular those that might merely be containers for other goods, perhaps wine. Western Europe also supplied weapons, glass and jewellery, much of it of Frankish origin, while insular trinkets are rare.

Raw materials other than iron must also have been imported to Hedeby – for example, gold, silver, bronze and tin – but not necessarily in the shape of ingots. One ninth-century written source (Ottar) refers to furs and other products of Scandinavia,[63] while the high-quality 'Frisian' cloth, along with silk, occurring in the Viking Age graves of Denmark, are also likely commodities. In another ninth-century source a market for slaves is mentioned at Hedeby.[64]

The important 'imports' comprised food, salt, hides, wool, antler and wood; in addition, the inhabitants of the province probably supplied workpower for various activities. The planned lay-out and defence of the site were in the hands of petty kings, as in the case of the Swedish dynasty, and the king's representative, the 'comes' (count) of the ninth-century written sources. These persons connect the town with its wider social and economic environment for special supplies and protection in return for tribute, and tax and toll on the activities. Whether the officials were residents of Hedeby proper is unknown, but it is not likely. The excavations have not revealed larger and more substantial buildings for such use. The same goes for the Christian officials and institutions, including, incidentally, the tenth-century bishop who temporarily left his seat in 1000 A.D., at the time of the decline of the site, owing to 'unrest'.[65]

To the north of the bottom of the Sli inlet lies the medieval, and modern, city of Slesvig. Recent excavations have uncovered a mid-eleventh century settlement on the waterfront including a wharf and some traces of buildings.[66] One of the stone churches of the city also dates back to this period, and we may have a continuity between Hedeby and Slesvig, though it is important to remember that the hey-day of Hedeby ended at least fifty years before the settlement of Slesvig.

Compared with Hedeby the archaeological remains from Ribe are scarce.[67] On the Ribe river, opposite the medieval city centre round the cathedral, are found substantial deposits of the eighth and ninth centuries. The excavated areas are small, and so structures are few, amounting to pieces of walls, in right angles to each other and made of light posts and planks with wickerwork, like the houses of the central Hedeby site. A well and parts of a pit-house are also recorded, in addition to fireplaces and floors of stamped clay, reflecting a permanent settlement. The deposits are thick by Danish standards, measuring more than one metre, and have given a large number of finds, including many west European imports, ceramics, lava quern-stones of the Rhineland, whetstones, glass, coins (eighteen specimens (Sceatta), from various parts of the habitation deposits, probably indicating a regular use of coins). Other imports are limited to a fragment of a soap-stone vessel from Norway. In addition, there is good evidence of iron-working, bronze-casting of jewellery, some of it even gilded, production of beads of glass and amber, the making of shoes, combs and other objects of bone and antler, weaving and, perhaps, potting too. A large assemblage of animal bones clearly fits Ribe into the town spectrum of Viking Age settlements, along with Hedeby, Århus and Lund, all having a high percentage of the meat animals cattle and pigs.

The parallel to the central site of Hedeby is striking, and with the contemporary eighth-century south settlement in mind, Ribe is the most organised township of its period. The reason may be the direct access to western Europe at a time when the local trade in Scandinavia still took a traditional form and was on a small scale. Already by 400 the Dankirke settlement, a few kilometres to the south-west of Ribe, has strong western connections.[68] In this light, it is the transit traffic between the North Sea and the Baltic which makes Hedeby the largest town in Scandinavia in the Viking period. The many visitors would also be important buyers of the local craft production and add to the size of the market. A recent geological survey in the centre of Århus has shown that the shape of the peninsula, carrying the first town, was roundish, suggesting a circular wall with protection from both land and the open sea.[69] Only minor sections through the rampart, raised round the very first settlement, has been excavated; it enclosed a small number of pit-houses.

Århus was apparently a planned township from the start in the early tenth century with the building of the wall, which had a diameter, like the later Aggersborg fortress, of about 250 metres.[70] The buildings (Fig. 25), however, behind the plank-covered street, following the inner side of the wall, are not laid out according to a strict plan. The basic element seems to be a solid, rectangular pit-house of the 'town-type' with posts in the corners, earth benches and a fireplace. Next to this is a rectangular and lighter pit-house with stave-walls, but without a fireplace, or, a similar roundish building with wickerwork walls, of the same type as the normal pit-house in rural settlements. The solid house has good parallels in the Hedeby south settlement and

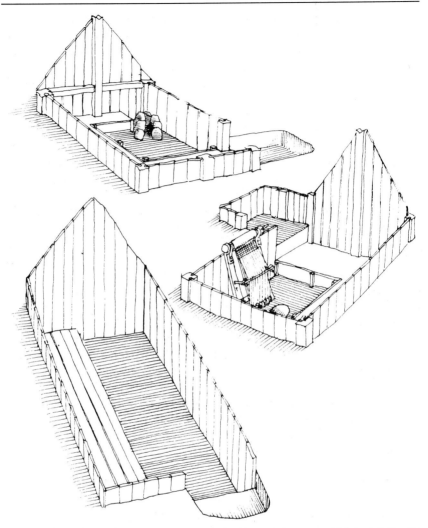

Figure 25 Reconstructed tenth-century pit-houses of the town of Århus (Jylland).
   (After Madsen)

in the quarter above the chamber tombs in the central town. One of
the lightly built houses at Århus contained, among other things,
quern-stones, while one of the solid ones, along with habitation, had
been used for weaving. Apparently we are dealing with sets of
dwellings and warehouses. The light pit-house next to the weaving
one, for instance, contained tools for wood-working and textile-
working and fragments of riding equipment, bronze jewellery, keys, a
comb with a runic inscription, bowls of wood, ceramics and
foodstuffs like cereals. It is clear that the relatively modest buildings
housed persons of some social standing.

Other crafts, reflected in the material, include the casting of metal artefacts, comb-production and, perhaps, the working of gold. The imports comprise whetstones and soap-stone vessels from Norway, pottery of Slavonian type, Rhinish lava quern-stones and a little glass, etc., but, apparently no western ceramics. In addition, there is a scale and a single weight.

With Århus in mind, we may conceive of Odense, being identical with the tenth-century settlement inside the ring wall of Nonne-bakken, as a town of the same character and also with minor buildings.[71] The plans, however, like most of the archaeological data on the town, are unpublished; but the rampart had about the same diameter as the small Fyrkat fortress.

Viborg is already mentioned as being a rural settlement in the Viking Age proper lacking the characteristics, in terms of food supply, buildings and activities, otherwise connected with the towns.[72] The long-houses, for instance, making up the excavated settlements, are otherwise known solely from the town of Lund, where there is only one specimen. In addition, very little evidence of craft production, and few, if any, imports are recorded.

Ålborg, as noted, remains archaeologically enigmatic before about 1100. From Roskilde the earliest remains, of a stone church, go back to the first half of the eleventh century.[73] Other historically named sites, like Ørbæk, 'Wendila', Toftum, Slagelse, Ringsted, Helsingborg, Borgeby, Thumatorp, Dalby and Gori have no Viking Age arch-aeological data, or are unknown except for Dalby, where a stone cathedral was built in the eleventh century. In addition, some of the localities are probably not towns.

Only from Lund do we still have a substantial amount of data on an early town.[74] It is worth noting that the wickerwork fences of the first settlements seem to remain in the same place over time, indicating a lay-out, as in the case of the central site at Hedeby. A street system is known, in addition to a number of wells. The lightly built structures, including a hall, in plan resembling the Trelleborg type, have wickerwork walls, and only later are stave walls seen, as in the churches (Figs 26-7).

Imports are surprisingly few, while craft activities comprise the production of bronze and tin jewellery, working in bone and antler (especially combs), the making of ceramics, shoes, and also wood-working and weaving. In spite of the large areas excavated, the material spectrum is not much differentiated, and we are seeing a kind of site functionally different from the international ports of Hedeby and Ribe. Lund is the only inland town we know of archaeologically; but because of its late date, a reliable comparison with, say, Hedeby is impossible, and the lack of imports – apart, apparently, from some Slavonian and a little English pottery and a little soap-stone – might be due to a shrinking of the international trade in craft products after the

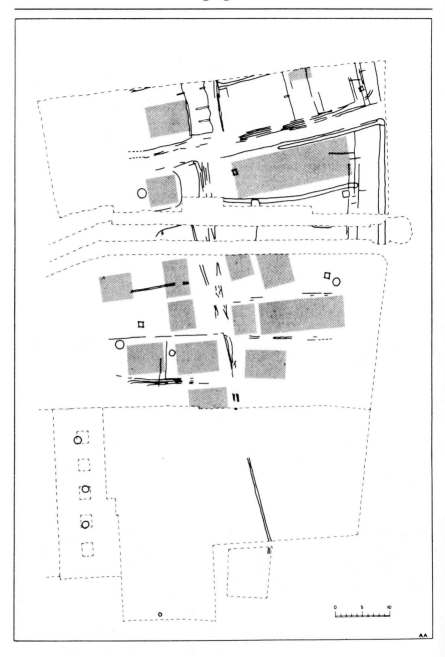

Figure 26 Part of the city of Lund (Skåne) at the beginning of the eleventh century. (After Andrén)

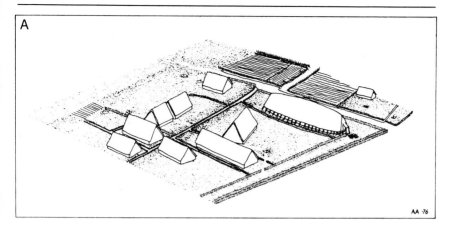

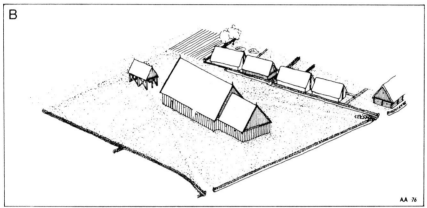

Figure 27 Reconstructions of a part of the city of Lund. A: at the beginning of the eleventh century (cf. Fig. 26), B: in the second half of the eleventh century. (After Andrén)

Viking Age. In any case, the function of Lund is basically directed at the local province, and it is in this context that we see the mint, which in the eleventh century was the largest in Denmark. In 1104 the first Scandinavian archbishop was seated in Lund.

One, or perhaps two, sites are known with town-like functions, but with a rural structure in terms of food supply and constructions. At Löddeköpinge in west Skåne a large walled area on the navigable Lödde river, leading into Øresund, contained an oblong cluster of simple pit-houses, almost all without fireplaces, but no other type of house.[75] Apparently the settlement was seasonal; it covered the ninth century, but it may already have started in the eighth century. The structures were in use at intervals for weaving, iron-working and probably the casting of precious metals and the making of pottery. For a rural settlement there is an unusually high amount of high-quality

'Slavonian' pottery, made however with local clay. In addition, a single coin and a couple of weights have been found, while a few pieces of jewellery and some glass beads ultimately point to western Europe. The site might be interpreted as a market place with some craft production and be seen as an eastern Danish equivalent of the permanent and regulated towns of Hedeby and Ribe. The low wall is a fencing of the territory – which was more than twice the size of the central settlement at Hedeby – rather than a means of defence.

A possibly similar site lies at Lynæs in north Sjælland.[76] In addition, many of the craft and even trading activities of the towns also took place in the large Trelleborg fortresses of the tenth century, but probably on a more exclusive basis.

E. Fortresses and fortifications

The impressive Trelleborg-type fortresses of the tenth century, with their strict plan, ring walls and blocks of identical halls, are traditionally considered to have served only military purposes (Pl. I and Fig. 28).[77] A careful investigation of the Fyrkat site, in north Jylland, however, has revealed that this is only part of the picture.[78] Rather, the fortresses were planned military sites, perhaps not dissimilar in function to the fortresses of 'burh'-type of King Alfred's England in the late ninth century.[79] In shape, the Danish sites have striking parallels among the south-west Holland ring walls, like Oost-Souburg; its date, unfortunately, is unclear but it seems to have been in existence at least by 1000, though it was without houses until the eleventh century.[80] The structures of the Dutch site differ from the Danish ones, but the symmetrical lay-out is also characterised here by straight, plank-covered axis streets, crossing each other at right angles, and leading through four gates in the rampart. Earlier ring forts in Denmark are but poor 'proto-types' for the Trelleborg-type, as for example the ninth-century Lembecksburg on the Föhr island, off the west coast of south Jylland.[81] The rampart of Lembecksburg is ten metres high, the diameter 100 metres, making the site rather similar in size to a Frankish fort of the same period, with parallels, for instance, in Holstein. It may perhaps have been connected with the mid-ninth-century Danish fief of Rurik, an exiled pretender to royal power in Denmark, backed by the Franks (Chapter 2 B). Other more modest sites may also date from the early Viking Age, but none display the symmetry of the Trelleborg-type.

In terms of the ring wall alone, the Trelleborg fortresses, Aggersborg on the northern shore of the Limfjord in north Jylland, Fyrkat in north-east Jylland, near present-day Hobro, and Trelleborg itself, on west Sjælland, have contemporary parallels in the Nonnebakken rampart at Odense and probably at Århus too. The Århus

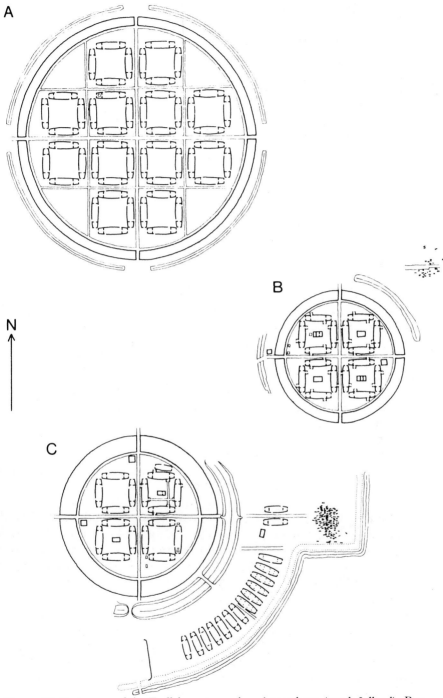

Figure 28 Fortresses of the Trelleborg-type. A = Aggersborg (north Jylland). B = Fyrkat (north Jylland). C = Trelleborg (west Sjælland). Note cemeteries. Scale 1:4000. (After Olsen et al.)

wall is of about the same size as the one at Aggersborg, measuring 240 metres, while Fyrkat measures 120 metres at the innerside and Nonnebakken probably the same. Trelleborg's diameter is 15 metres longer (and of the same size as Oost-Souburg), but here we also have a lower fortress circle wall on one side.

The circle area of the three fortresses is divided by streets, running north–south and east–west through the gates; in addition, a plank-covered street runs along the innerside of the wall, as in Århus. The wall itself is strengthened by palisades, galleries and ditches. At Aggersborg an additional four streets are known, dividing the space into twelve, instead of the usual four, blocks. The blocks are filled in with a square of four halls of the Trelleborg-type with one major room, and two smaller ones at the ends. The long walls are curved and supported by oblique outer posts. In addition, minor, almost all rectangular, constructions are found, including a 'town-type' pit-house, at Fyrkat, with parallels in Århus and Hedeby. The small buildings lie in the middle of the blocks, at the gates, etc. (Fig. 29). The lower fortress at Trelleborg is made up of halls and other long-houses lying in a semicircle from the east to the south gates, outside the main ditch. A bend of the outer wall and ditch leaves room for the cemetery. Also at Fyrkat a cemetery was found outside the main fortress.

The large Aggersborg fortress is situated at a crossing by a narrow part of the middle Limfjord inlet.[82] In the Viking Age the Limfjord was open to the west, constituting a protected sea-route which was probably preferred to the navigation around Jylland. Fyrkat is in the river valley leading into the Mariager inlet, a few kilometres from the

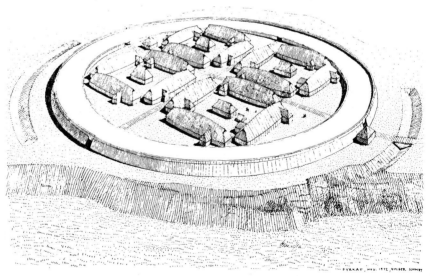

Figure 29 Reconstruction of the Fyrkat fortress (north Jylland). (After Olsen et al.)

open water. The wet areas helped to protect the fortress, controlling also the several fords and bridges in the area. Trelleborg lies in the fork between the confluence of two streams a few kilometres from the Store Bælt. This site has by far the strongest ramparts and the broadest ditch, which powerfully reflects the need for protection. All the fortresses seem to lie at important routes of transportation, and especially at junctions. Odense also, incidentally, has such a position.

Traditional historiography has connected the fortresses with King Sven and his son Knud, in about 1000, and their campaigns and sway over England. In this context the barracks would be winter quarters and training camps for the Danish army. This preconception has hampered an objective dating of the artefacts from Trelleborg, which was the first to be excavated, and Aggersborg. The investigation of Fyrkat has shown that it was in use only for a short period, since repairs to it are few. It was apparently not rebuilt after a fire and has therefore given all the sites an unequivocal tenth-century date, and, in addition, demands a new view of the function of the fortresses.

C[14]-dates, and especially a detailed analysis of the objects from Fyrkat, point to a construction at the mid-tenth century, before the campaigns in England, and a short-lived period of occupation in the second half of the tenth century. At Trelleborg there are traces of a smaller, 'civil', tenth-century settlement, perhaps a magnate farm to judge from a hall, prior to the fortress.[83] The artefacts have good parallels on Fyrkat and in other tenth-century finds, while they clearly differ from the picture at Lund at the beginning of the eleventh century. Furthermore the period in which it was functioning must have covered at least the last quarter of the tenth century, while it is unlikely that it goes back to the first half of the century. This is in accordance with dendrochronological data suggesting a date around 980 for at least repairs of the site.

Aggersborg is preceded by a rural settlement of the eighth and ninth centuries, continuing into the tenth century. Dating the fortress is difficult, but it should be noted that clear eleventh-century artefacts are unknown within the rampart. On the other hand, the structures of Fyrkat and Aggersborg are so similar in detail that we expect contemporeneity between the two fortresses. All three sites are most probably constructed by the same architect and owner, the Jelling King Harald, and at approximately the same date.

The fortresses are at almost the same distance from the Jelling centre and form, with the Danevirke walls to the south, the mentioned belt of defences around the centre of the state (Fig. 1). As noted below, the same belt contains a number of cavalry graves belonging in general to the same settlement (Chapter 6). In this context, the heavily defended walls find an explanation, and the fortresses a function, not as training camps, but small royal 'burhs' at the perimeter of the readily defined realm of the kingdom, controlling the border provinces and regulating the traffic, perhaps including the collection of tolls of passage.

In terms of ideology, as an explanation of the society, the royal power and control are expressed materially in the extremely strict architectural planning and execution of the fortresses. The four gates, lying along compass lines to the north, south, east and west, do not take into consideration the properties of the surrounding landscape, the master plan being more important than any rationalisation. On the other hand, the four gates allow for easy counter-attacks, while the round shape gives the largest possible inner space compared with the length of the rampart. The thirty-metre-long halls are the most impressive houses of their age, but the overall plan is quite 'democratic', lacking a central focus or a large construction. The halls, on the other hand, have had different functions, which brings us back to the irrationality of the master plan; however, they may not have housed the leaders of the society, who in all likelihood were living on their farms.

A detailed study of the spread of artefacts and fireplaces on Fyrkat has served to clarify what activities took place in the buildings.[84] Traditionally, each hall was thought to house the crew of one longship, but at Fyrkat only some of the halls contained hearths, for heating and cooking, and a few wall benches for bedsteads. Apparently only a quarter of the halls were ordinary dwellings, or banquet rooms, with a fine fireplace but no benches. The rest were stores or stables (one-third), smithies (one-sixth) and workshops for the making of artefacts of costly metals (one-sixth?). The latter activity took place also in one of the minor houses.

Studying the lay-out, it is apparent that the dwellings and the banqueting hall all lie on the east-west street – the main street – as shown by the guard-house at the west gate. The workshops are on the north-south street, while smithies and stores lie close to the rampart, so that a smithy is not next to an ordinary dwelling hall.

Stores are characterised by the absence of hearths and other factors. One of these buildings contained in a small end-room a large amount of high-quality rye, imported from Poland or the Ukraine, probably seed corn.[85] Smithies are defined by concentrations of slag, forge stones, whetstones, and workshops by, among other things, crucibles and moulds for ingots of costly metals. Sherds of cooking-vessels made of soap-stone are notably plentiful in the dwellings. In sum, the crafts of Fyrkat comprise ironworking and work in gold and silver and probably in bronze too, as well as weaving. No agricultural tools were found, and only a few weapons. Like manpower for construction, for defence and for the production of materials, food must have been supplied by outside labour.

Apart from the soap-stone vessels and whetstones from Norway, the imports are a few pieces of jewellery from the Baltic and perhaps a few Slavonian ceramics (as well as the rye); and glass beads originally came from western Europe. A coin and a few weights point to some trade or other commercial transactions.

This picture replaces the 'barracks' of earlier research. Rather, Fyrkat has been a royal stronghold with storage for commodities, which were perhaps collected through taxation or toll, and had sufficient room for the production of iron articles and costly ornaments, which played a role in the social exchanges. In sum, Fyrkat is directed at regulating the province, economically and socially, at the same time as it is extracting products from it and relating to the supra-regional trade, even in subsistence goods, probably through status as a toll-station and perhaps even as a mint.

Trelleborg also, in spite of the poorer excavation, shows traces of a functional division of the halls.[86] For instance, the buildings without fireplaces similar to the stores of Fyrkat are known at Trelleborg on the rampart side of the blocks. They make up a quarter of the halls in the central fortress, but in the lower fortress, to the south-east, only two out of fifteen halls have hearths, raising the possible number of magazines to more than half the constructions. In the centre the stores are in the two southern blocks only, which indicates perhaps that the main gate is to the north (with a guard-house). The other two halls in the south-western block and the southern house in the north-western block may have been smithies. In the northern half of the site we have halls displaying a higher quality of housing. For instance, the two northernmost houses have traces of wooden floors in the main rooms, and the eastern hall in the north-west block has a limestone framing of the hearth, like the 'banqueting hall' at Fyrkat. At least these buildings were dwellings. From the north-eastern block come a few tools reflecting work in precious metals, and the southern house here may have been a workshop.

Weapons are more plentiful than on Fyrkat. For instance, a substantial number of arrow-heads are recorded from the gates, also showing traces of fire. Several burials in the cemetery point to violent deaths. In addition, agricultural implements are frequent, especially short scythes, for hay-making, absent at Fyrkat. The female presence is represented by tools for weaving and some bronze jewellery. Exchange is witnessed by scales, weights and a single coin. Among the imports are quality ceramics of west European and Slavonian type, soap-stone vessels from Norway, Rhinish lava quern-stones and a few Baltic bronzes and some glass beads.

In general, Trelleborg is seen as a close parallel to Fyrkat, and the same applies to Aggersborg, but the survival circumstances are so poor here that activity studies are impossible.

Finally, it should be mentioned that Trelleborg, in terms of meat-consumption, differs from the normal rural settlements, having more cows and pigs compared with sheep and horses, but the percentage of these animals, on the other hand, is not so high as in the towns, owing to the relatively substantial ratio of horses, which are rare in towns. This is in accordance with the idea that the fortresses received supplies from a wider province. In terms of craft activities, the diversification is also higher than in the rural settlements, but we lack the differentiation of, say, Hedeby. As the unequal distribution of the sexes on the cemetery shows, military duties have played an important role too, and via the fortresses the king might have exercised power, when required, in a rather thorough and direct way.

Other defensive systems of the Viking Age, apart from the town walls and fortresses, comprise a number of sea-blockades, especially in inlets, and at least one major cross-country wall system, the famous Danevirke at Hedeby, which protected the country from the south and, like other strongholds, was a potential frontier at which tolls might be collected (Fig. 21).

The main wall of Danevirke (and the northern wall), as far as their initial phase is concerned, are constructed in the first half of the eighth century; dendrochronology focuses on a date about 730.[87] The same date perhaps also applies to the wall across the Svansen peninsula to the east, making up the major part of the southern shore of the Sli inlet. The western extension of the main wall may be later, but hardly much later. In about 800 the Kovirke wall was constructed, which also protected Hedeby (Pl. VIII). This rampart shows few traces of repair, and its entire length was constructed at the same time; but probably it was not effective for defence after about 900. The early main wall may also have been in a poor condition at the time when the Kovirke wall was constructed. A third phase, of which we have relatively little dating when it comes to details, belongs to the tenth century. This phase comprises a renewal of the main wall, perhaps its western extension too, the town ramparts around Hedeby plus the connection walls between the two. The latter are dated dendrochronologically to about 955 and 968.

As we have noted above, Jylland was threatened at the beginning of the ninth century and indeed suffered from Frankish attacks. The Kovirke, belonging to this period, is most probably the wall of King Godfred of 808, constructed by his army and, according to the Frankish Annals, with only one gate perhaps, among other things, for toll purposes. The political events leading to the construction of the first main wall, however, are obscure, but cross-country wall systems in Denmark go back to the beginning of the first millennium A.D., as Olmer's Dyke in southern Jylland shows.[88]

The written sources speak of a renewed southern attack in 934, followed by a breakthrough of Danevirke in 974, and a Danish military movement in 983, overrunning a German border fort. The third phase of Danevirke is most probably connected with these offensives, and it may have been initiated under the impression of the 934 attack. The construction is contemporary with the building of the

Trelleborg fortresses, and together these fortifications all protect the core of the west Danish state, regulating traffic towards and away from this, probably including the collecting of tolls. The later Danevirkes, the last from 1945, are of little interest in this context.

In terms of its physical features, the early wall system comprises a ditch, four to five metres wide and one and a half metres deep, with a rounded bottom and a wall ten metres broad and two metres high and equipped with a wooden palisade front. The engineer designed the Kovirke wall to be about two metres high, but narrower, only six or seven metres. The ditch is V-shaped and more prominent, being four metres broad and originally almost three metres deep. The Kovirke also has a wooden front, very homogeneously executed. The third phase comprises a smaller, rounded ditch, but a stronger earthen wall, up to twenty metres broad and four or five metres high, probably surmounted by a palisade.

A number of roads and bridges also of this period are probably connected with the royal power. The tenth century was an especially crucial period in which the Jelling dynasty expanded the road system and, in order to secure easy and rapid transportation, built bridges (which, furthermore, may have yielded tolls). It is hardly a coincidence that an almost one-kilometre-long, two-lane bridge was constructed at Ravninge in about 980 (according to dendrochronological datings) ten kilometres to the south of Jelling.[89] The bridge would have carried a load of five tons and was part of the main north-south-going road system through Jylland. Other bridges have also come to light from the period, but they are smaller. Together these constituted a great step forward from the cobbled fords of the Iron Age.

On Samsø in the southern Kattegat Sea, a plank-lined channel, going one kilometre east-west through the island and dating from the Viking Age, perhaps the tenth century, has been found.[90] This is probably the most surprising construction of its kind, connected with the control of the central Danish waters, including the northern end of the Store Bælt and the bay of Århus. It allows for ships to move fast in the direction either of Jylland (through the channel) or of Sjælland from the protected Stavnsfjord inlet. In addition, it constitutes a final example of the mobilisation of resources possible in the Viking Age, referring to the organisation of the countryside. It is to these social and political structures that we now turn, with the aid of the burials in conjunction with these findings, and also to individuals.

Plates

Plate I. The tenth-century Fyrkat fortress, north Jylland, from the air

Plate II. The tenth-century Ladby ship-burial, Fyn

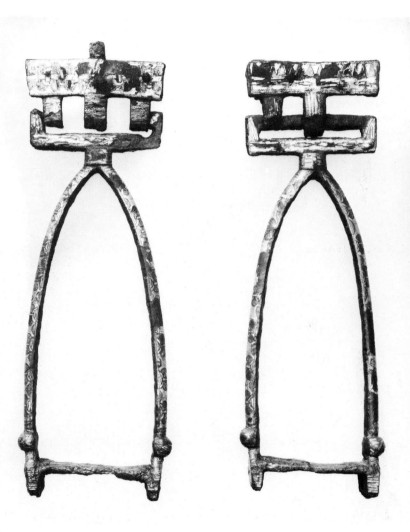

Plate III. Silver and copper decorated stirrups, length 35 cms, from tenth-century cavalry grave at Nr. Longelse, island of Langeland

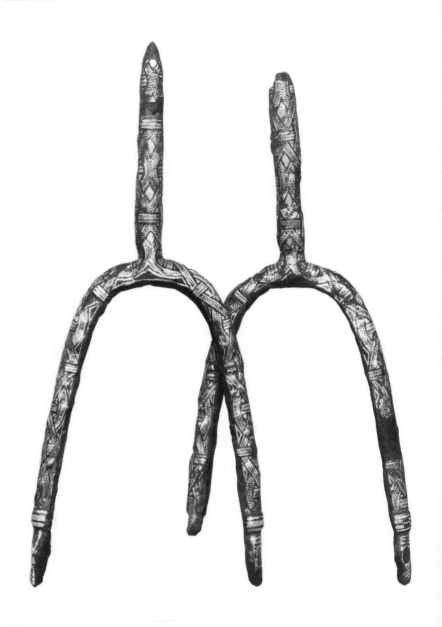

Plate IV. Silver and copper decorated spurs, length about 21 cms, from tenth-century cavalry grave at Nr. Longelse, island of Langeland

Plate V. Brooches of bronze (the small one gilted) from tenth-century female
interment at Ladby, Fyn. Length of tortoise buckles 10.5 cms

Plate VI. Sample from late tenth-century silver-hoard at Tarup, Fyn. Note Arabic coins

Plate VII. Buckles of gold from tenth-century hoard at Hornelund, west Jylland.
   Diametres 8.5 cms

Plate VIII The Kovirke frontier-wall, southernmost Jylland, seen from the west; ditch to the

Plate IX. Sword from a bog at Bjørnsholm, north Jylland. Early ninth century. Length of handle 16.9 cms

Plate X. Ship-setting and runestone (on small mound) at Glavendrup, Fyn. About 900 A.D.

Plate XI. Iron-axe (with silver inlays) from burial chamber in Bjerringhøj (Mammen), north Jylland. Late tenth century. Length 17.6 cms.

Plate XII Aerial View of Long Melford, Suffolk (1930s): 'old Hall' and 'The Bury' greens clearly visible, with the cricket-pitch in the middle.

Plate XIII. The runestones at Jelling church, mid-Jylland. King Gorm's stone to the left, King Harald's to the right. Tenth century. (Cf. Fig. 3)

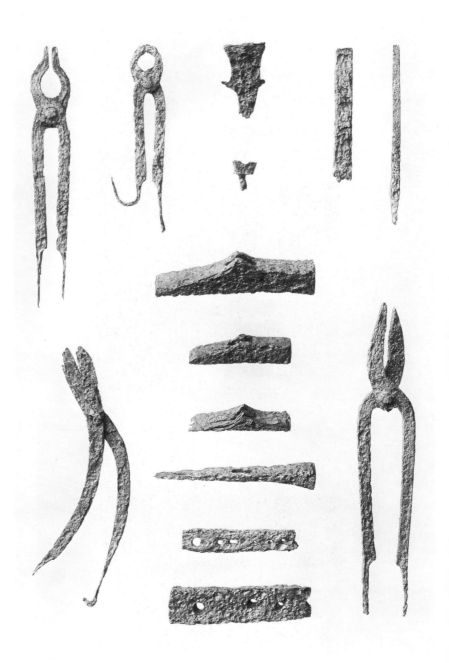

Plate XIV. Iron tools from a tenth-century hoard at Tjele, north Jylland. Biggest pair
of tongs (to the right) 30 cms long

Plate XV. Soap-stone mould from Trendgård, Overlade, north Jylland for crosses, a
Thor's hammer (pagan symbol) and ingots. Tenth century. Length 9.2 cms

Plate XVI Page with illustration of an English manuscript from the early eleventh
century showing King Knud (Canute) and queen at Winchester

Chapter 6

SOCIAL AND POLITICAL
IMPLICATIONS OF THE BURIALS

A. *Viking Age graves*

The type and content of the Viking Age graves in Denmark tell us in symbolic language much about the social position of individuals. Often the person himself is no longer present, usually because the skeleton has decayed; furthermore, a number of cemeteries are composed of cremations. Nevertheless in some cases it has been possible, as mentioned above, to study sex ratios and age profiles, and we have noted that the number of women in the towns, and especially in the fortresses, is low compared with the number of men, while the two sexes are equal in the rural cemeteries.

In terms of the types of grave, the cremations, sometimes in urns, but usually surviving as a patch in the ground of burned bones and ashes, disappear with the tenth century, this being clearly a pagan rite.[1] Most cremations are from Jylland. To the south-west cemeteries of urn-graves occur, while to the north of the Limfjord inlet we have cemeteries of cremation patches, covered by small barrows of various shapes and often set in a stone frame or surrounded by stone-settings shaped, for instance, in ship form. The burial goods, as expected, are few, but the cremations do not seem to be any poorer than the average Viking Age inhumation, if we omit the number of tenth-century graves which are particularly richly furnished (Fig. 30). Most of the cremations on the Ris Fattiggård cemetery in northernmost Jylland, for instance, hold zero to two artefacts. The burials with a few artefacts, however, more often contain nails from a wooden coffin, showing a correlation between a modest, and seemingly fortuitous, furnishing and the quality of the container of the body. The usual grave-goods in the village cemeteries and other graves are knives, petty jewellery and native pots, but even these may be lacking, as in the cemetery of inhumations on the Trelleborg fortress, where only a few burials have

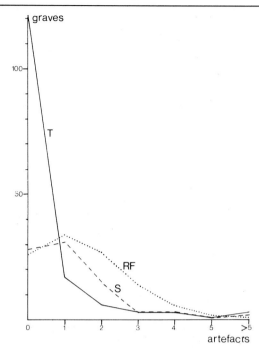

Figure 30 Distribution of wealth in three cemeteries as measured by the number of
   different artefacts in the graves. RF = Ris Fattiggård, north Jylland, basically ninth
   century (Ramskou 1950, 144f.). S = Stengade, island of Langeland, tenth century
   (Skaarup 1976). T = Trelleborg, west Sjælland, tenth century (Nørlund 1948)

even a single artefact.

Apart from the provinces in Jylland mentioned already, cremations
occur rarely. Inhumations are found all over the country, but they are
few in northernmost Jylland. The north Jylland cremations may well
correlate with a tribal area, geographically well circumscribed.

Traditionally, furnished graves are considered pagan; but it is a fact
that a number of interments with Christian crosses of the tenth
century contain other grave-goods too.[2] Not until the close of the
tenth century do furnishings actually disappear, perhaps in connection
with the establishment of burial grounds around churches. On the
other hand, the majority of inhumations are poor anyway, and in
addition they usually follow the 'Christian' east-west orientation
(though not rigorously), with the head to the west, and a supine
position of the body.[3] Few graves have the head to the east or the body
in a crouched position. A prominent group of burials, almost all from
Skåne and Bornholm, however, lie north-south. Mounds, some of
them old Bronze Age mounds, are relatively rare, but they occur
frequently on the island of Bornholm, which, incidentally, has most
of the north-south and crouched graves. Bornholm may also be seen

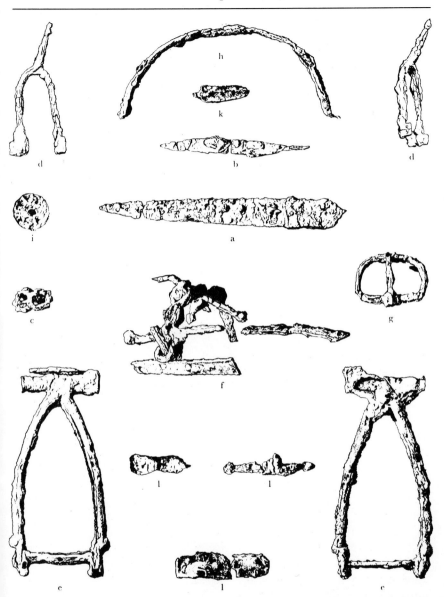

Figure 31   Tenth-century cavalry grave from Kasmusmølle, south Jylland. Note spurs
(d), handle for wooden bucket (h), spearhead (a), heavy bit (f), stirrups (e), etc.
(Height of stirrups circa 26 cms). (After Brøndsted)

as a separate 'tribal' area.

A tenth-century cemetery from Stengade on Langeland[4] (cf. Fig.
30) displays the different types of cover for the body in use in Viking
Age Denmark: a simple wrapping, a wooden coffin, or a chamber.
The chambers are all from about 900 or the tenth century[5] and, apart

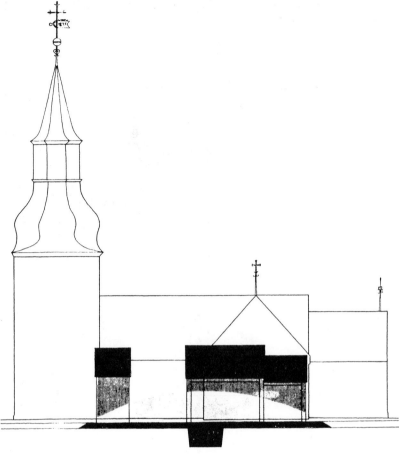

Figure 32 Stave-church and tenth-century chamber grave beneath the medieval church at Hørning, east Jylland. (After Krogh et al.)

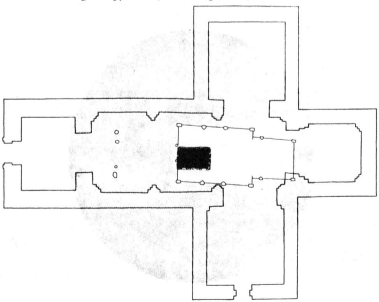

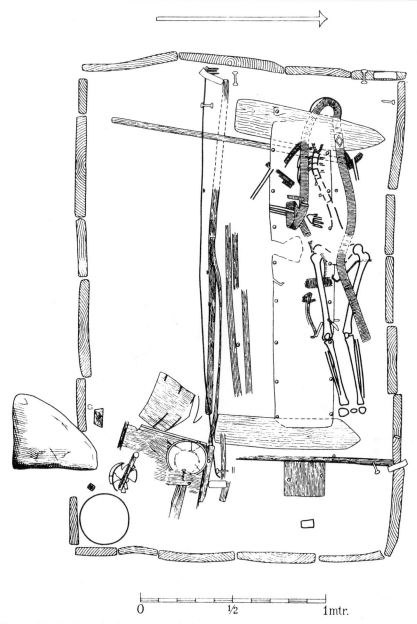

Figure 33 Carriage-body grave in chamber from Hørning (cf. Fig. 32). (After Krogh et al.)

from a small chamber on Bornholm[6] stemming perhaps from a local tradition, are found in west Denmark, most probably connected with the prominent personages of the Jelling dynasty. The chamber is meant for display at the interment. Finally, a number of highly interesting female graves, where the dead rest in the body of a carriage, have been found (Figs 32-3).[7] They stem from the same province as the chambers, and sometimes lie in such.

As to the burial goods, weapons occur rarely, except for a group of cavalry interments and other warrior interments dating from tenth-century west Denmark (Fig. 31).[8] Jewellery is more common, probably because it belongs to the dress. This means that women's graves are easier to determine than men's, which lack trinkets, and generally weapons too. In addition, rules of inheritance may vary. Weapons have usually been passed on to the younger generation, who assume the obligations, and though the jewellery may belong to the personal garments there are indications that ornaments are inherited too. On Bornholm, for instance, the ninth-century graves are quite often furnished with jewellery, while it seems to be missing in the tenth century. Moreover silver ornaments, found in treasure hoards, are practically never recorded from graves, and must have constituted the family fortune of wealthy groups. In general, the lack of furnishings from prominent burials correlates negatively with the degree of social development. West Danish tenth-century burials, for instance, are found with costly garments but with only a few grave goods. The rich ninth-century Bornholm burials cluster round a traditional chiefly centre of four to five hundred years on the north coast.[9] The tenth century, however, witnesses a transformation of this society and a concomitant spreading out of prominent personages on farms all over the island; as a result the graves are poor. On the other hand, the new social positions emerging in the society may still be marked by lavish furnishings and burials, in the same way that the runestones, supposedly, mark the transition of newly won rights. The return of weapon graves to west Denmark in the tenth century, after having been rare for seven or nine hundred years, must be seen in this light.

In sum, the burials can only be used for social studies if we take a wide number of aspects into consideration, such as the character of the traditional rites, patterns of inheritance and the political and ideological development. A serious error, for instance, is to rank the burials according to wealth if it cannot be demonstrated that they hold the same positions with respect to these other factors.

B. *Warriors of the tenth century*

As noted, Danish male burials of the first millennium A.D. rarely contain weapons except during the tenth century, while by contrast Norwegian and Swedish graves are fairly well equipped throughout the period. We attribute this to a firmer and a less firm rule of succession respectively. Graves with tools are also rare in Denmark, though a few contain iron-smiths' equipment (cf. also Pl. XIV).[10]

There are no indications that the lack of grave goods is a certain sign of poverty. The centuries around 500, for instance, see rich hoards of gold, and the 'empty' phase before the Viking Age proper is a period of agricultural expansion as well as the foundation of the ports of Ribe and Hedeby.

In the ninth century the few weapon graves are poorly furnished, while the tenth-century cavalry graves, not infrequently in chambers, contain swords, lances and riding equipment, such as powerful bits and stirrups designed for cavalry combat in formations – pieces that are unknown in the previous periods. They often contain a horse too (Appendix VIII, Pl. II-IV, Figs 31 & 34). In addition, bronze-plates and wooden buckets are also a feature of these graves.[11] The tenth century also has graves with rich riding equipment, but as a rule with no weapon, or just one humble weapon, such as an axe; it also has burials on a lower level with poor riding gear: just spurs and a modest spear or an axe. Simple weapon graves occur also, having no trappings or the like, and usually just a single weapon. Some of these burials, however, do belong to the highest social echelons, as the Bjerringhøj chamber grave in north-east Jylland shows,[12] containing exquisite garments and an axe, lavishly decorated with silver-inlaid work (Pl. XI). Practically all these burials are inhumations. The distributions, especially of the cavalry graves, must be considered reliable, since such burials are difficult to overlook in fieldwork.

Most of the weapon graves, and especially the heavy cavalry interments with stirrups, etc., are found in a belt around the Jelling province, corresponding to the fortresses of Trelleborg type and the Danevirke walls, and thus marking the borderlands of the state (Fig. 34).[13] It is natural to see this novel group of graves as representing persons with military obligations, perhaps in return for land; a parallel might be drawn with the runestones of Jelling type, reflecting the establishment of new rights of property. A closer look at the distributions, however, reveals differences between the spread of runestones and cavalry graves in north Jylland. The stones of the Jelling type – and, for that matter, the 'After Jelling' type too – cluster in the eastern part of north Jylland, while most of the heavy cavalry graves are found exactly to the west of this group, and also to the west and south of the fortresses at Fyrkat and Aggersborg.

The simple weapon graves of north Jylland (without riding equipment) apparently lie in marginal areas compared with the heavy cavalry graves. They also appear on cemeteries, for instance at Fyrkat,[14] while the cavalry interments are solitary, and often in earlier barrows, perhaps to give the burials a local status. In southern Denmark, however, the heavy cavalry graves are found in cemeteries and not infrequently together with burials accompanied by poorer riding outfits and less conspicuous weapons. Here the simple weapon graves without trappings, etc., also lie in cemeteries, for instance at

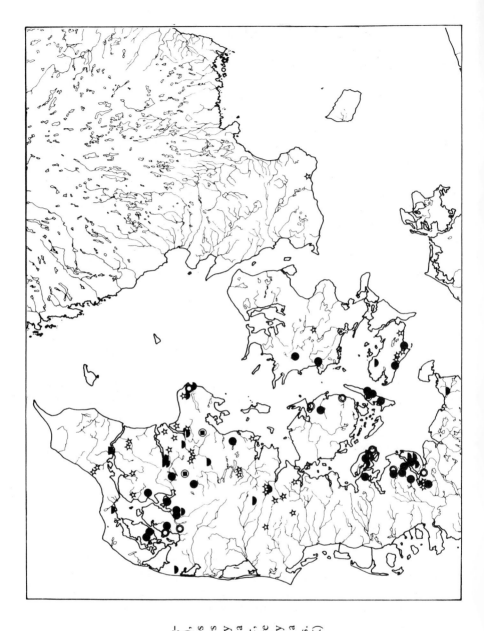

Figure 34 Distribution of Jelling-type runestones (stars), cavalry graves with stirrups and body of carriage graves (crescents). For the cavalry graves a black dot indicates a burial with a sword or spear, a ring with a black square that an axe is the only weapon and a double ring a grave without weapons. (Appendices IV, VIII & IX)

Hedeby and Trelleborg,[15] and in the same areas as the other weapon graves. At Trelleborg, incidentally, a grave with a bronze plate and an axe, decorated in silver, lies at the centre of the cemetery next to one of the wealthiest female interments of the site.[16] In the south the weapon burials and cavalry burials altogether cover a belt from south-east Jylland and the island of Als across the island of Langeland and the shores of Store Bælt to the island of Lolland. Apart from a few specimens on the island of Lolland, and at Hedeby, this province too is devoid of contemporary runestones, which, as has been indicated above, show very little overlap with the heavy cavalry graves and other burials with riding equipment. It should be mentioned too that the heavy cavalry graves in general are found fairly close to the coast, which might correspond to the military duties of the buried per-sonages. Furthermore, two of the burials are connected with ships: the rich Ladby burial on east Fyn (Pl. II),[17] with, among other things, eleven horses, and the wealthy so-called 'Ship-chamber grave' at Hedeby.[18] In the latter the chamber is covered by a ship, while in the former the dead man was laid in the warship itself. Otherwise chambers are found with a number of other heavy cavalry graves, especially from the southern cluster.

To the east in Denmark almost no weapon graves occur, and the area has no heavy cavalry burials. The situation here is similar to the ninth-century circumstances in the whole country. To conclude, the interments already mentioned practically all relate to the early west Danish Jelling state. A number of social positions were created here, unknown to the earlier society, and not transferable in the usual way, since weapons were deposited with the dead person.

C. Female graves

As mentioned, the women's graves of the Viking period are generally recognised by their jewellery of bronze and beads; very rarely do silver trinkets or other costly artefacts occur, although the garments sometimes are excellent. In addition to the artefacts, and a possible female skeleton, some graves are recognised by a special type of coffin, the body of a carriage, or, in a few cases, a complete carriage.

The traditional and optimal female dress of the Viking Age consists of a slip extending to below the knees, like a long shirt without sleeves and with an opening at the neck, closed by a small fibula.[19] Over this is worn a shorter woollen 'spencer', the shoulder-straps of which are fastened by the well-known, richly ornamented, pair of tortoise buckles. The dressing is finished by a long cloak, closed by a larger buckle. Even if all women may have been in possession of the full dress, though of differing quality, only a few were buried with the buckles (Fig. V). We therefore expect the burials with, for instance, two tortoise buckles to represent women of high standing, their day-to-day jewellery not being inherited by the next generation, like the silver trinkets. More emphasis is sometimes put on the quality of the coffin, perhaps the body of a carriage, or the burial chamber itself, as in a number of unusually rich graves, from the Hedeby area. In addition, two Fyn persons, apparently women, are buried in full carriages with, among other things, horse-collars, beautifully decorated with gilded bronze-fittings.[20] At least one waggon is from a large chamber 30 metres square. A possible third, but poorer, waggon grave comes from west Sjælland.[21]

The most prominent specimen of the body-of-a-carriage grave is from the chamber of the Northmound at Jelling (Fig. 2), probably containing Queen Thyra.[22] In the same chamber, apparently, also lay the widower, King Gorm, until their son, King Harald, had them both moved to the chamber beneath the first wooden church between the mounds at Jelling. The rest of these burials are, as indicated, also west Danish (Figs 32-3), apart from a single example from the Oldenburg town-fortress in Slavonian east Holstein, perhaps a Dane married to a local lord.[23] (Both King Harald and his son married Slavonian women, and we expect their relatives to have participated in political marriage alliances too.) The Oldenburg and the Jelling graves underline the connection of this type of grave with the establishment of tenth-century west Denmark.

A closer look at the carriage-body graves reveals that they are situated in the same belt around Jelling as the fortresses, and the weapon graves, including the heavy cavalry burials (Appendix IX, Fig. 34). In north Jylland, however, they tend to avoid the cluster of cavalry graves with weapons in the west-central part of the zone, being more frequent to the east. Indeed, they are often found in localities with male graves containing an axe, for instance in the Fyrkat graveyard, and even at Lindholm Høje, basically a cremation cemetery.[24] A fine burial chamber with a body-of-carriage coffin beneath an early wooden church at Hørning, near the town of Randers,[25] may be a female parallel to the Bjerringhøj chamber with the conspicuous axe with an ornamented silver inlaying.[26] In south Jylland the carriage-body graves in chambers are found on the cemetery at Thumby-Bienebek, to the east of Hedeby, along with heavy cavalry graves containing weapons, also in chambers.[27] Likewise at Ketting on the island of Als,[28] the same two types of graves, but not in chambers, are combined. On the island of Lolland to the east a solitary specimen is found in a cemetery with an axe-grave.[29] A final example worth mentioning is from the Jelling area itself, otherwise poor in burials.[30]

The better equipped carriage-body graves sometimes have fine garments, interwoven with gold and silver threads, and even lined with silk, but not the traditional buckles of tortoise shape.[31] Apparently the dress is different from the traditional one in being more flowing, like the contemporary upper-class dress worn in western Europe, inspired by Byzantium. Though we do not know much about male dress – only that it probably comprised trousers, a short coat and mantle (cf. Pl. XVI) – the information on female dress is important, demonstrating that the Jelling rulers also differed in appearance from both their predecessors and the contemporary leaders in eastern Denmark adapting to west European norms. In the tenth century very few tortoise buckles are found in west Danish graves, while they are common to the east.[32] Incidentally, a flowing male dress which also begins to appear on the Continent in the tenth century, may have been introduced, but the evidence is uncertain. The other grave goods accompanying the carriage-body graves comprise silver fibulae, bronze vessels, chests, etc.

The symbolism implied in the use of a waggon for a coffin is difficult to grasp. We might see these as a means of transport to the hereafter, but then we would expect them to have been spread evenly throughout the area, and to correspond with the cavalry graves of the men. Furthermore, the bodies in the carriage graves hold both Christian and pagan symbols, like Thor's hammer (cf. Pl. XV).[33] Rather, the symbolism appears to be social, reflecting the interest of the state in easy transportation, facilitated by roads and bridges built and maintained by the royal vassals, who also themselves travel in style by waggon and horse. In terms of vassalage, it is significant that the body of carriage graves in north Jylland corresponds to the male graves with just an axe.

As we have seen, the female graves of the tenth century connect various types of male graves with each other and constitute an important direct link with the Jelling centre. They originate from the time shortly before when the Christian burial rites eliminate much of the traditional potential for social studies, previously held by the graves.

D. Men and women, rank and affiliation

We have attempted to classify the major groups of graves, especially for the tenth century. We must now try to summarise the picture and to relate it more fully to other aspects of society (cf. Fig. 34).

In terms of the type of burial we take the chamber to be of a higher rank than the coffin, since it indicates a display at the interment, the dead lying in state in the chamber. But chambers also occur in village cemeteries, as at Stengade on the island of Langeland and at Esbjerg in west Jylland, and may disclose local leaders.[34] At Stengade the graveyard seems to be divided into six clusters, perhaps representing farmsteads. One of the clusters is made up of chamber tombs, while a single chamber tomb lies in one of the other clusters, containing a slave as a form of 'burial goods'. Chambers of higher rank may contain heavy cavalry burials, finer weapon graves of the simple type, carriage body graves (Figs 32-3) including the Jelling chamber in the Northmound,[35] and other prominent female burials with, for instance, tortoise buckles.

Another problem is the chronological differences. At Hedeby we have chambers that are apparently earlier than the horizon of carriage body graves, since they contain women still wearing the tortoise buckle-dress,[36] and relatively early weapons, horse-bits, etc.[37] The same may hold true for other chamber graves in the south, like the Ladby ship grave (Pl. II),[38] in many respects a parallel to the 'Boat chamber grave' at Hedeby.[39] The Boat chamber, however, held a person commanding only one-third of the Ladby military unit, to judge from the accountable pieces of horse trappings. In addition, the Ladby ship lies next to a wealthy woman's grave with tortoise buckles (Pl. V). The two ship graves reflect a kind of 'naturalism' in the make-up of the grave which was later unknown. There is on Fyn a parallel in the two, apparently female, burials with full waggons, also from relatively early in the tenth century.[40]

At the city of Hedeby no chamber graves or other types of burial with riding equipment have occurred, apart from the 'Boat chamber grave'. As noted, such graves are otherwise well-known in the southern Danish countryside, where cavalry interments with bits, stirrups and weapons occur in cemeteries. Associated graves probably held the family members and followers of the mounted lords, the women resting in, for instance, the carriage body graves and the other men in graves with less costly equipments.

Already in the ninth century, corresponding to the early runestones marking new lines of succession to position and property, the southern Danish area saw the establishment of rights to land, apparently not inherent in the traditional society. The same area is almost devoid of tenth-century stones, although the cavalry and carriage body graves reflect royal vassals who might have been granted land. Apparently such transfer either took place earlier or local lords by the tenth century accepted the military duties of this vassalage. In a sense this is the same thing. What is clear is that the ruling families set themselves apart from the rest of the society, in life and in death. For instance, at Stengade, on the island of Langeland, the village cemetery is located a few hundred metres from a smaller cavalry graveyard.[41]

In north Jylland the Jelling-type runestones of the tenth century clearly avoid the cluster of cavalry graves with heavy weapons, lying in the area to the west of the stones. Because of the missing stones we might also in this case favour the idea of local leaders taking on the military duties, but the lack of a family context whereby these interments never lie in graveyards is strange. This could perhaps be explained by insufficient research, but only in regard to poorly equipped graves which are easily overlooked. Significant too is the practical absence of carriage body graves within the cluster. A possible parallel to the north Jylland case is the phenomenon unveiled in connection with the western part of the south Skåne cluster of runestones in 1000 of a transfer of rights to persons of the same age (Chapter 3 C). The underlying factor is a military duty, lasting for more than one generation, but not giving the family as such a special status (cf. the absence of carriage body graves in the north Jylland group of heavy cavalry graves). One of the burials contains a thin golden neck ring, a most uncommon feature in the Viking Age, which may have symbolic significance.[42] A runestone from about 1000 mentions a high-ranking slave given gold and, probably, a 'free neck', i.e. his freedom.[43] Symbols denoting freed slaves are known from Europe, and we may have the same in the north Jylland case, suggesting, along with the mentioned runestones, the employment of such personages for the royal machinery of power. This has parallels, incidentally, in other early states where the kings try to exempt themselves from as many traditional bonds as possible, using only 'foreigners' devoted to them.

The north Jylland runestones correspond, however, at least in part, to the spread of the carriage body graves and the simple male graves with just an axe, represented, for instance, at the cemetery pertaining to the royal fortress of Fyrkat.[44] A single axe grave even comes from a chamber, at Bjerringhøj (Pl. IX),[45] as do a few of the north-eastern body-of-carriage burials. Two heavy cavalry graves in chambers come, significantly enough, from the western fringes of the runestone belt, perhaps indicating the same sort of tenure as in the south, but in distribution relating to the poorer cavalry burials immediately to the west. All in all, the runestones and the axe burials are, with the fortresses, situated closer to the border of the west Danish Jelling state than the cavalry graves. We have a division of duties, perhaps between forces at the frontier and in the fortresses, and those which were 'tactical' units, probably the navy. It is also at the border that land would most easily become available for vassals, using the stones to mark their rights.

The axe graves are few in the south, but a couple come from the Trelleborg cemetery in western Sjælland[46] and from Lolland;[47] Lolland also has a single carriage body grave, a type perhaps occurring also on the island of Langeland.[48] The rarity of carriage body interments from the Trelleborg cemetery may reflect the status of the personages buried, but may equally be a chronological problem related to the late date of the fortress.

E. Slaves

From the Danish Viking Age we have a few examples of slaves being sacrificed at the burial of their master. For instance, in a tenth-century cemetery at Lejre on Sjælland a decapitated and tied man was lying in a grave over another male person equipped with grave goods.[49] On the contemporary Stengade cemetery, on the island of Langeland, a chamber grave held a man with a silver-ornamented spear.[50] Partly on top of him was a second man, handcuffed and decapitated. From the archaeological literature comes the famous Norwegian ship burial at Oseberg where an elder female slave accompanied the queen.[51] Also well-known is the Arabic account, from Russia, describing, most probably, Scandinavians sacrificing a young girl at the death of her master.[52]

Unfortunately, the slave question has not been given enough attention, though slave labour is often thought to have constituted an important part of the work force. In terms of burials we must allow for normal double graves, and possibly for suttee too. In the latter case, however, we may also deal with a kind of slave burial, namely of a woman, perhaps even richly furnished, not considered a member of her husband's family, and therefore with no rights of inheritance, although with a possible claim.

We chose to identify 'slave burials' as graves where a person with very few or no grave goods is lying on top of another with possible richer furnishings. In addition, slaves may have been buried in separate graves, as horses were sometimes, and such cases inevitably evade classification.

In pre-Viking Age Denmark, slave burials are apparently known from the rich Bornholm data.[53] From the ninth century a couple of instances are known from Sjælland, where burials were lying on top of each other, the person underneath being in at least one case a woman with grave goods.[54] More examples come from the tenth-century cemetery at Lejre,[55] a slave also having a female master, and others are known from the Sjælland and Skåne localities. On the other hand, it is significant that no slaves are known from the numerous well-documented tenth-century graves of west Denmark.[56] The picture of the graveyard of the Trelleborg fortress in western Sjælland is somewhat unclear. It comprises among other things 'mass graves', but in at least one case, and probably two or more, we seem to have true burials with slaves.[57] This brings us back to the name Trelleborg, perhaps 'Slave stronghold' which is difficult to interpret but perhaps refers to the application of slave labour at the site.[58] Another possibility is that the garrison was made up of freed slaves and other 'marginal' persons in the society. This might, for instance, be in accordance with the absence of the high female status in the graves compared with the carriage body graves, found at Fyrkat,[59] though of course it may just be a chronological problem. The grave goods are very poor but do comprise weapons with silver inlays and scales, otherwise belonging to the upper social echelons. This, however, could still be in accordance with the slave hypothesis. We have mentioned the possibility of freed slaves serving in the army of the Jelling kings, and we know for certain that persons of this status raised runestones over prominent officials.[60]

Apparently traditional Viking, and pre-Viking, societies knew of slaves in some numbers. This accords not only with the Sagas, basically dealing with the old-fashioned Norwegian and Icelandic countries, but also with the ninth-century description of slave gangs at Hedeby.[61] In the same societies slaves were sometimes sacrificed at the burial of their master. In addition, slaves were apparently killed in connection with pagan rites.[62] In the west Danish Jelling state we know that slaves were not treated in this way. The only evidence we have for the Danish state society in the Viking Age is of freed slaves, although slavery did exist as a social status in Denmark for another two hundred years.[63] In the pre-state societies the slave may have been an important status object and a domestic help, but he required constant feeding, often in times of need, as well as surveillance, and his economic importance, except for special tasks, was limited in Denmark. It may have been more profitable for the lords to exempt taxes from a class of copy-holders, who, however, might stem from freemen. The coming of a market and the urban economy also favoured a flow of goods and labour, which was not possible in the previous society founded rather on kinship relations and some slave work. As an object of trade the slave was more important, especially when sold to the Arabs (cf. Chapter 7 D), who used slave work to a large extent for agricultural and industrial activities.[64]

The coming of Christianity put restrictions on the trade in slaves, especially Christian slaves, but the Church itself used slaves for labour. The only sphere where a European impact may be seen in the tenth century is in the lack of sacrifices in west Danish burials; but these, to judge from the symbols used, are both pagan and Christian graves. In other words, the questions of slavery are economic and social rather than ideological.

We have traced a number of economic and social institutions, and their geographical settings, and have delineated the flow of goods and services. However, we have dealt very little with the links to the wider European environment, except in terms of some historical events. Only thus can we fully understand the properties of the Danish institutions and estimate to what extent economic success or failure were a result of local or foreign circumstances.

Chapter 7

SILVER HOARDS AND ECONOMIC SURPLUS

A. Changing amounts of silver

The hoards of silver jewellery, coins, etc., of the Viking Age are a rich source of information about a wide range of phenomena, from patterns of warfare and regional and social distribution of wealth to fluctuations of the amount of silver, coinage, exchange and international connections. In this chapter we employ the finds from before 1040, the approximate end-date of the North Sea empire and the close of the Viking period soon after the death of King Knud. Most silver-hoards were found before the First World War, a fact which gives the sample a high degree of stability.[1]

The hoards of the ninth century are few and light in weight, only one or two being above 500 grammes of silver; only half a dozen, at most, contain coins. Moreover almost all the artefacts contained in them are complete, and 'hack-silver', used for balancing exchanges and as small change, does not amount to much. All hoards, except one, are found less than four or five kilometres from the coast (Appendix X, Fig. 35).

In the tenth century and early eleventh century the finds are plentiful. They are often rich, especially in some areas, and they usually contain both coins and hack-silver, and sometimes also silver ingots, though a number of hoards are made up of unbroken artefacts, often including gold (cf. Pl. VI and VII). (In the following the few objects of gold are converted to silver value by multiplying by eight. This ratio is perhaps too small, but at least it does not overestimate the gold.) The later the find, however, the more coins dominate the hack-silver (Fig. 53). Several of the hoards, especially from the last quarter of the tenth century, are from inland areas, but coastal finds are still common (Appendices XI and XII, Fig. 36).

The change in distance to the coast from the ninth to the tenth

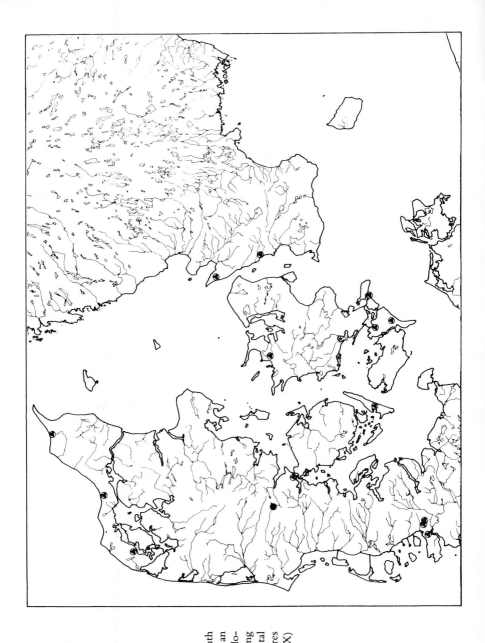

Figure 35 Silver hoards of the ninth century. A black dot marks an inland find (five or more kilometres from open water), a ring with a black triangle a coastal find (four or less kilometres from open water. (Appendix X)

century is taken to imply a shift in the patterns of warfare from mere piracy to penetrating expeditions.[2] The rationale is that there is a greater chance that people, in times of warfare, bury their valuables, and indeed are killed and are therefore prevented from retrieving the silver. The idea that the owners of the hoards died abroad, the finds tending not to reflect local circumstances, is refuted on grounds of the change in distribution vis-à-vis the coast. We cannot believe, for instance, that the ninth-century Danish raiders in western Europe had their homelands only on the coasts of Denmark, nor is it likely that only people in these areas possessed silver. Moreover the inland finds of the eleventh and twelfth centuries are again relatively few, probably as a consequence of the integration of the country. Periods of unrest clearly known from history, as for example the mid-eleventh century or the mid-seventeenth century, also correspond to an increase in the deposition of hoards of valuables.[3]

Nor does another proposal gain support – that the hoards are offerings. The number of finds, or the amount of silver found, do not correspond to the relative population sizes of the various provinces as measured by the agricultural potential, calculated from the so-called 'barrels of hard corn'-values and comparable units. (In pre-industrial Denmark the spread of the population correlates strongly with the subsistence potential measured this way.)[4] This would imply that the offerings were carried out to very different degrees in the various areas. Nor is it any support for the theory that many of the silver-hoards come from bogs. A high proportion of the seventeenth-century finds are also from bogs, and it is hardly possible to ascribe them to Danish pagan rites at that period.[5] On the contrary, historical sources from the seventeenth century tell us of people hiding their silverware in a bag, tied to a tree, and then dropping it into a lake or bog. Furthermore, none of the Viking Age finds were made together with animal bones or other indicators of offerings; nor do the depositions cease at the general acceptance of Christianity in 1000.

This is not to deny that factors other than warfare had an impact on the picture of the finds. The spread of silver also plays a role, and the same is true of the social distribution patterns. In the following discussion, concerned with the entire area in successive periods, the amount of silver throughout the Viking Age is in focus. The size of the silver stock must have been important to the societies under the impact of a growing market economy and valuable for securing alliances and service, including protection.

Since the degree of warfare combined with the silver importation are the main variables of the find-picture, we set up a degree of aggression (K) to isolate the size of the stock of silver. We use twenty-year periods for the era 900 to 1040, but fifty-year periods for the ninth century, where the number of finds is small. The dating of the finds is based on the earliest possible date of the latest coin in the hoard, the

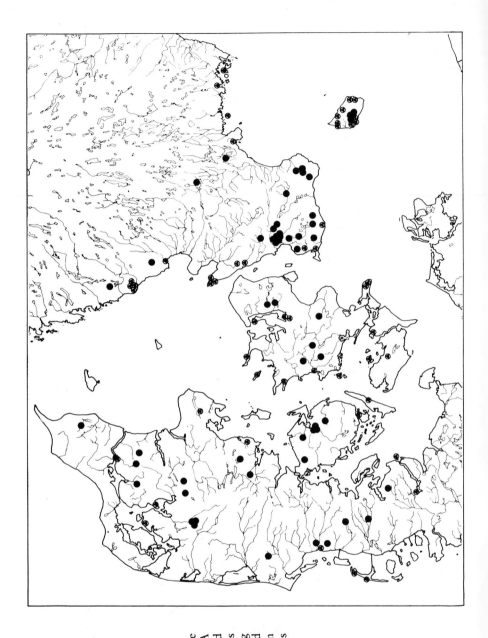

Figure 36 Silver hoards of the period c. 900 to 1040 A.D. A black dot marks an inland find (five or more kilometres from open water), a ring with a triangle a coastal find (four or less kilometres from open water). (Appendices XI & XII)

'terminus post quem' of the find. This seems to be practically identical with the date of the deposition of the hoard, since coins, stemming from different sources, like the English, German and Arabic specimens, tend to have the same end-dates when occurring together in Danish finds.[6] Operating with samples of hoards, the dating should be no major problem, and except for some special difficulties of the ninth century only hoards containing coins are included. For the ninth century the relative number of coin-hoards is much smaller than for the tenth century, and for the sake of comparison the first-mentioned sample is standardised accordingly.

The degree of aggression (K) is based on the ratio between the inland finds (five or more kilometres from the coast) and all finds; consequently the more inland finds, the higher the degree of aggression. The relative size of the silver stock is determined by dividing the total number of finds (N) for each time period by the concomitant K-value, $\frac{N}{K}$, or:

$$\text{Amount of silver} = N \div (N_{inland} \div N) = \frac{N^2}{N_{inland}}$$

For the ninth century we use a standard K-value for both periods, calculated from all finds owing to the small number of hoards. The resulting curve of the amount of silver shows a moderate stock for the first half of the ninth century, diminishing in the second half (Fig. 37). At the beginning of the tenth century the silver rises drastically, dropping to its lowest value in about 950. (The peak in 900, made up entirely of eastern (Arabic) silver, corresponds strikingly to the tradition of a presence of Swedish lords at Hedeby in the same period.) A new, but much lower, peak lies in about 1000 A.D., at the time of the large English payments of silver to King Sven and his son Knud; this peak also is followed by a decline. It is significant that the early west European payments to the Danish Vikings, especially in the late ninth century, have little or no impact on the size of the stock. Apparently the means were spent abroad, as have been suggested on other grounds.[7]

It should be added that exactly the same results are obtained by using the grammes of silver instead of the number of finds for the N-values of the N÷K formula (K still calculated on the basis of number of finds), as is shown by a study of the tenth and early eleventh century alone (Fig. 37 B). More interesting is the fact that another study, for the period 900 to 1040, showed that the average weight of the hoards follows the same main trends as above, except that the drop after 1000 is lacking (Fig. 38). In the periods of depression the silver stock of each individual gets smaller, and so concomitantly do the hoards. The observation concerning the early eleventh century implies that the silver was concentrated into fewer hands than previously.

As noted, the late ninth-century payments to Danish Vikings do not

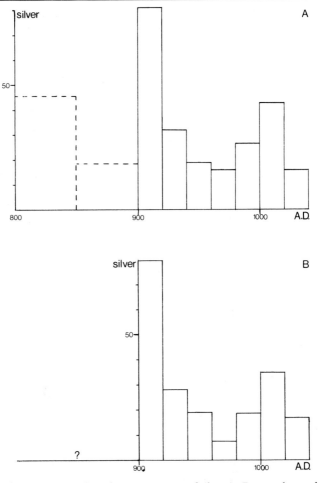

Figure 37 Fluctuations in the relative amounts of silver in Denmark as calculated on the basis of respectively the find-numbers (A) and the silver weights (B). For the ninth century the results are somewhat uncertain

show in the finds, which is in accordance with the lack of contemporary west European coins in Denmark. On the other hand, the early ninth-century peak corresponds to a group of mainly Arabic, but also some Frankish, coins of that date. The early tenth-century peak is parallel to a high number of Arabic coins, and a few west European coins, from those same years. The influx in 1000, however, consists mainly of English and German coins, the decline of the Arabic specimens being paralleled by the mid-tenth century depression (Fig. 43). The German coins start soon thereafter, while the English influx is a little later and mainly connected with the campaigns around 1000. Furthermore, the English coins decline after the breakdown of the North Sea empire, while the German coins, probably obtained by regular trade, continue to flow into Denmark. The western imports altogether make up the peak in about 1000. As we shall see below, a correspondence exists between the degree of influx of silver from various areas; trade and exchange in one direction stimulated the activities in another and led to a larger silver stock in Denmark. On the contrary, the crisis in the importation of silver in the second half of the ninth century, for instance, caused an increase in the raids and attacks on western Europe. But it is important to note that the serious problems of the mid-tenth century did not result in a similar pattern; instead, the society was transformed into a state, which fifty years later was strong enough to control England for some length of time. The late 'Viking Age' in England differs in many respects from the early one of the ninth century.

In Denmark the 'cash problems' in about 950 were solved, for instance, by grants of land and by expansion of the local economy, which, unlike the international economy, may well have functioned with little silver at hand. The arrival of the German coins, however, and a strong increase in the minting of local coins, of a very low weight, in the second half of the tenth century, also stimulated the internal exchange. But the silver stock had not recovered at the beginning of the tenth century.

B. Distribution of wealth

The silver hoards are the best way of studying the distribution of wealth among the higher social echelons of Viking society. The K-value measured above the degree of conflict for various periods, but it is also applicable to the different provinces. The N÷K values thus give the size of the silver stock of the geographical areas. (To be accurate, we use in the following only the grammes of silver for the N-values in the N÷K formula – K still calculated on the basis of number of finds, not the number of hoards; we also include the finds without coins.) One problem is that we must deal with large areas to obtain significant results of the time series and long periods of time to produce reliable outcomes for the various provinces. Another difficulty, resulting from the small number of finds, is that the very mid-Jylland Jelling province in the tenth century is almost completely devoid of hoards of silver.

For the period 900 to 1010 we note that the silver is spread quite unevenly throughout Denmark (Appendix XIV). We have stan-dardised the amounts by dividing them by the size of the agricultural potential, taken, as measured in the so-called 'barrels of hard corn' and comparable units, to reflect the relative population sizes, demon-strable for later periods of pre-industrial Denmark.[8] Bornholm, for instance, has an extremely high amount of silver compared with the

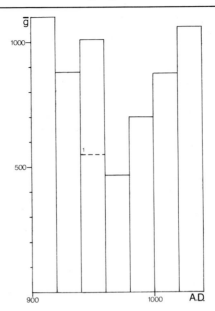

Figure 38 Average weight of the silver-hoards of the period 900 to 1040 A.D. (1) gives
the average if the Terslev-find (Appendix XI) is omitted, the largest of the period

population of the island (2.01). This could stem from geographical
conditions, the inland area being relatively small, but even with a
K-value like that held by nearby Skåne, Bornholm holds the highest
amount of silver in Denmark (0.84, or, with the K-value for only
south Skåne, 0.88). This, incidentally, makes the suggested riches of
another island of the Baltic, Gotland, more credible and not merely a
result of the exposure to piracy with an accompanying high frequency
of deposition (cf. below). Northern Jylland (silver amount 0.05) and
Fyn plus the surrounding islands (0.09) have very little silver. South
Jylland, including the Jelling province, is relatively rich (0.16),
especially if southern Slesvig is excluded (0.20). (Fyn together with the
latter area make 0.07.) Sjælland and surrounding islands come next to
Bornholm in their riches (silver amount 0.70), while Skåne is more on
the level of south Jylland, having 0.19 as index. South-western Skåne
alone is 0.22, while north-eastern Skåne, together with the neighbouring provinces of Halland and Blekinge, makes 0.13 (Fig. 39).

Leaving Bornholm aside, Sjælland is, perhaps unexpectedly, the
wealthiest zone in the tenth to early eleventh century (most finds
stemming from the second half of the tenth century). On the other
hand, Sjælland and surrounding islands make up the largest area of
high-quality soils in Denmark and must have been quite densely
populated, though with much forest. To the west of Sjælland, the
border areas of the early Jelling state, characterised by their fortifications, cavalry graves and weapon graves, etc., are poor in silver

in spite of the presence of dependants of the centre. But here we have suggested that grants of land, and not cash payments, were used as compensations for military and other obligations. The land may have been taken from rebel groups, for instance, and the grants augmented by the silver decline around 950. The province housing Jelling was in possession of more silver. Apart from sheer poverty, which we may detect in the marginal provinces of Halland, north-eastern Skåne and Blekinge, the little silver in western Denmark is most probably due to investments in various enterprises, like the fortresses, and the buying, for instance, of luxuries or even food-stuffs, such as the Slavonian rye found at the Fyrkat fortress.[9] It is obviously important to look further into the social aspects of the distribution of silver.

The average weight of the hoards also has a significance, indicating much in a different and independent way about the size of the silver stock, as measured against the division of wealth among the higher echelons. We expect the amount of silver in an area to correlate with the average weight, as was the case in the above study of the time trends (Appendix XIV). Bornholm, however, has a very low value, only 365g, in spite of the large stock of silver. The social conditions were probably quite equal on the isolated and rather small island. For south Jylland the average is relatively high, 1155g, and, excluding southern Slesvig, 1422g. Still higher comes the Sjælland island group with 2001g, while north Jylland and Fyn have, respectively, 339g and 488g. Skåne makes 688g, or, without the north-eastern part, 743g. Halland, Blekinge and north-eastern Skåne amount to 394g. Apart from the deviating result on Bornholm, the picture corresponds well, as expected, with the above calculations of the size of the silver stock.

In the ninth century, southern Jylland may have been the wealthiest area, the hoards having an average weight of 1033g with 192g only for the rest of Denmark. Only three ninth-century finds above 500g are made, all from south Jylland (Appendix XIII).

A preliminary 'degree of social stratification', built on the ratio of silver hoards, respectively above and below 500g, can be established for the finds from the period 900 to 1010. The picture corresponds, as expected, to the above scatter of the average weight. The more finds over 500g in an area, as compared with the number of finds below 500g, the higher the average weight of silver hoards, and the higher the preliminary degree of social stratification. To arrive at the true degree of stratification we must divide the preliminary values by the corresponding measures for the amounts of silver in the various areas, since the latter distort the picture of the social division of wealth, when using a fixed intersection, the 500g.

The preliminary degree of social stratification for the ninth century is 0.30 (three finds above 500g divided by ten below; cf. Appendix XIII). The observed amount of silver is 6705g and the K-value 0.08 (one inland find divided by thirteen in all); the standardised amount is 6705

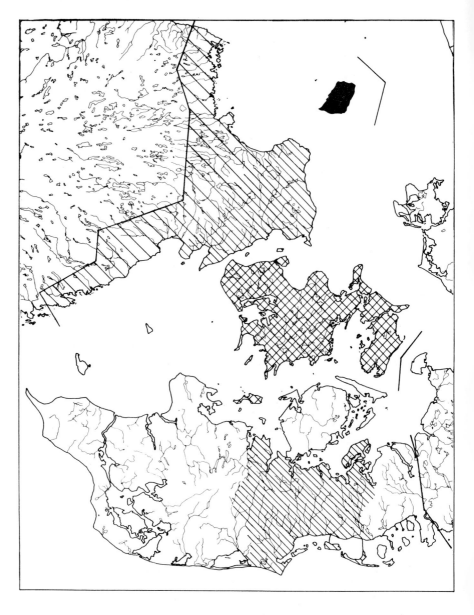

Figure 39 The geographical distribution of silver in Denmark for the period 900 to 1010 A.D. (The shading varies with the amount of silver per capita.) (Cf. Appendix XIV)

divided by 0.08 and by the about 500,000 (or rather more) barrels of hard corn, making up the entire area, or about 0.15. The true degree of stratification is thus 0.30 divided by 0.15 or *2.00*, a value very different from the preliminary one, but low compared with the figures for the following period calculated in the same way (cf. Appendix XIV).

In the picture of preliminary degrees of social stratification, for the tenth and early eleventh century, Sjælland and surrounding islands have the highest value, but the true degree gives only 2.38 to this area. Indeed, only Bornholm is lower (0.21), while neighbouring south and west Skåne makes 5.84, Fyn, etc., 3.75. North Jylland has the value 5.66 and south Jylland, the most stratified zone, 6.94 or, without south Slesvig, even 8.27. The marginal areas Halland, north-east Skåne and Blekinge makes 3.82 (Fig. 40).

This adds a great deal to our picture of the spread of silver. Bornholm was a well-adapted chiefdom, or petty kingdom, where wealth, in spite of the riches, was evenly distributed among the higher social echelons. The leaders must have been relatively powerless and probably more occupied with checking each other and with securing the income from the Baltic trade and piracy than with competing with other societies, for which a more stratified social structure would have been needed with a concentration of wealth in fewer hands. A different society existed in Skåne and especially in south Jylland, including the Jelling province, with a high degree of stratification but a moderate silver stock, notably in south Jylland. Here one looks for competition between the provinces, especially between west and east as we have often noted above. The frontiers of the west Danish state see less stress, although they hold important institutions like the fortresses.

As to the limited amount of silver in the west, in spite of a more developed economy, and in spite of taxation of the towns and collection of tolls, it is possible that the initial economic integration of the country took place as a result of the state of west Denmark acquiring goods and labour from their neighbours. In this way silver may have moved to less stratified societies like Sjælland. In addition, such processes, in west Denmark, would have speeded up the granting of land, instead of valuables, as compensation for services. The situation, however, is precarious, and we expect the better organised societies eventually to expand into the other areas to gain direct control over the resources. This is in accordance with the expansion of the Jelling state towards the east, where the relatively stratified Skåne may have constituted the only serious obstacle to the hegemony of, for instance, King Harald. It is also significant that the expansion includes the establishment of west Danish institutions like towns, mints and bishop-seats in the east, and we must not rule out the settling of royal vassals, as reflected by the runestones, in about 1000.

It is dangerous, however, to study this development in isolation from the wider political and economic environment. Notwithstanding

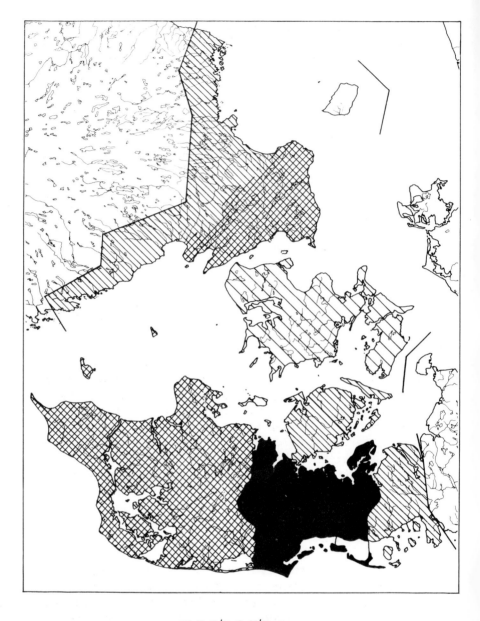

Figure 40 The degree of social stratification for various Danish provinces as measured by the division of silver for the period 900 to 1010 A.D. (The shading varies with the degree of social stratification.) (Cf. Appendix XIV)

the importance of the internal structures, no social system is fully understood from this perspective alone.

C. Nordic coinage

As noted, the silver, including the thousands of foreign coins, was normally used for making ornaments of local forms and decorated in the characteristic Nordic styles. Ultimately, most of the jewellery was cut to pieces and along with coins employed in exchanges, to which the scales and weights, especially of the tenth and eleventh centuries, bear witness. A small amount of the silver, however, was used for the early local minting, and even if many Danish and foreign coins were pierced, or otherwise treated, and used as ornaments, some true coin transactions must have taken place, at least at Hedeby.

The Nordic coins of the ninth century seem to have been struck at Hedeby (Fig. 41).[10] They imitate Frankish coins of Charlemagne from Dorestad in the Netherlands and a number of other Frankish coins, especially the types with ships of Louis the Pious. The Nordic coins do not carry the name of the mint, nor of any Danish lord, so we do not know if local kings were involved, though it is likely. Another model for the Nordic coins is Frisian (and English) 'Sceattas' with face masks and animals. The imitations of these are minted from about 825 and until about 850, while the 'Charlemagne' series belongs to about 825.

In contemporary finds these Nordic coins occur only at the ports of Hedeby,[11] Kaupang in southern Norway[12] and Birka in mid–Sweden,[13] in a solitary Norwegian grave[14] plus, possibly, a Danish burial, and on a market settlement (Löddeköpinge in Skåne).[15] Almost all the specimens from Birka are found in women's graves and have, except for a single coin from a purse, been pierced or equipped with a suspension. The coin from the above settlement is pierced; so too were the coins from the Norwegian burial which were worn as trinkets. These early Nordic coins may have been in use as a means of exchange at Hedeby only; the specimens from Kaupang and the Danish grave are fragmentary and perhaps also trinkets. Not until the tenth century are Nordic coins spread widely outside the towns and perhaps accepted as a general means of payment without being constantly weighed. At Hedeby the ninth–century coins may have been sent into circulation as some kind of payment, serving as a status symbol for the persons using them and thereby also facilitating minor transactions. Obviously the rare early coins were not meant for the population at large, and apparently they were not given a generalised political value for propaganda purposes.

The ninth–century coins come from about forty localities in a total of only 69 specimens, according to a stocktaking in 1966.[16] This is in strong contrast with the Nordic coins of the tenth century, stemming

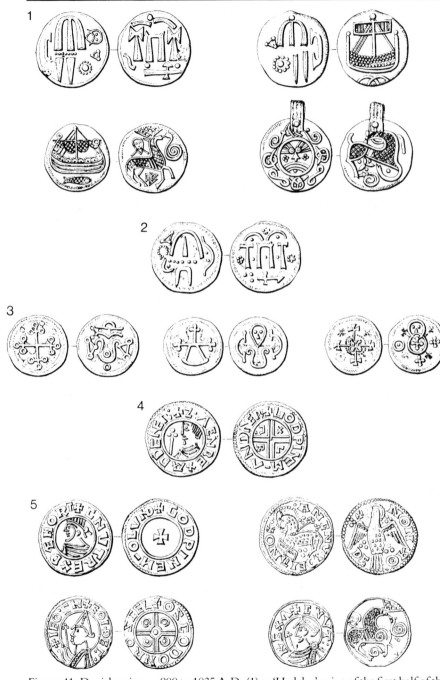

Figure 41 Danish coins, c. 800 to 1035 A.D. (1) = 'Hedeby' coins of the first half of the ninth century. (2) = a 'Hedeby' coin of the first half of the tenth century. (3) = coins of about 975 A.D. ('cross-types'); (2) and especially (3) are demi-bracteates. (4) = coin of King Sven (c. 987-1014). (5) = coins of King Knud (1018(1014)-1035) from Lund (first row), Roskilde and (probably) Hedeby. (Coins after Hauberg)

from 173 sites in, especially, Denmark, Sweden and Poland holding 858 specimens. The late coins are divided into a number of types, of which the early ones, dating from 900/950 to about 985, are still vaguely imitating the late eighth-century coins of Charlemagne. The Nordic types, however, were now of only half or one-third the weight of the prototypes of 1.1g (Fig. 41). Another group of coins, the so-called 'cross-types', from about 975 to 990, are also very light and devoid of name of mint and lord. The cross-types derived their motifs partly from the common west European coins with a cross, and partly from the Byzantine series with Christ sitting on a throne. Moreover some of the crosses have specific parallels among the eastern coins. The cross-types are minted during the reign of King Harald, 'who made the Danes Christian', and the symbolism is chosen accordingly. It is interesting that these types are absent in the southernmost part of Jylland, including Hedeby, which suggests the establishment of a second mint in Denmark.[17] The cross-types are unknown from towns, but occur, for instance, at Trelleborg, which was perhaps the mint. Furthermore, these series have been mass-produced, since we have at least 392 specimens from 75 localities. The contemporary 'Hedeby' types, of the same weight, dating from about 975 to 985, are also struck in larger numbers; we have 348 coins from 41 sites, while the types of the first two-thirds of the tenth century occur in 48 localities, but only in 98 specimens.

Apart from Denmark, and especially Gotland, with many hoards, the tenth-century types, especially the cross-series, have also made their way to the early Polish state, the homeland of the wife of King Sven.[18] The spread hither of Nordic coins witnesses the close economic contacts, reflected in Denmark in a number of imports ranging from weapons, jewellery and pottery to the high-quality rye at the fortress of Fyrkat.[19]

The disappearance of minting at Hedeby in about 980 corresponds well with the decline of the city, but it should be mentioned that coins resembling the Danish series were struck in mid-Sweden at the close of the tenth century.[20] At Birka, however, the latest Nordic coins found come from the first half of the tenth century, the town having been abandoned shortly after 950.

The latest cross-types may have been minted during the reign of King Sven, but the only certain coins of this period are modelled on English ones, bearing a cross and, on the obverse, a picture of the ruler, King Sven of Denmark, according to the inscription (Fig. 41).[21] From now on the coins have a clear political propaganda value for the kings and reflect their hegemonic rule. They carry, along with the name of the lord, the name of the mint, and, as a guarantee of the quality of silver and of the weight, the name of the moneyer too. Particularly during his later years, King Knud (d. 1035), the son of Sven, expanded his minting, first of all to the east, where Lund and

Roskilde, in the newly won provinces, were the most important localities. A monopoly silver coinage, however, was not established until the end of the eleventh century, while many foreign coins of small denomination were still circulating widely. The number of Sven's coins is very small, and at the beginning of this century only four were known, from four localities, as compared with 32 ninth-century and 588 tenth-century coins of the earlier types.[21] In this survey the number of Knud coins was 492 (from 59 localities), while the number of coins of Hardeknud, the son of King Knud, was 633, from 36 finds.

By this period the coins were probably serving as an all-purpose means of exchange, though they may still have been put into circulation on special occasions, for instance as payments to the army. Considering their propaganda value, it is hardly coincidence that most of the coins were struck to the east of Store Bælt, and not in the Jelling homelands to the west.

D. Trade and imported silver: the Arab connection

In the Danish silver hoards of the ninth century we have at least 113 Arabic coins as compared with 33 west European, mainly Frankish coins, and no Nordic ones. The same picture is seen for the port of Kaupang in Norway, and for Birka too. At Kaupang we have 20 Arabic coins, four west European coins and one Nordic coin.[22] From the graves at the mid-Swedish township of Birka come 10 west European, 30 Nordic and 46 Arabic coins, many of them used as trinkets.[23] Only at Hedeby do the Nordic and west European coins, throughout the Viking Age, occur more often than the Arabic ones,[24] which, however, are three or more times as heavy as the European specimens.

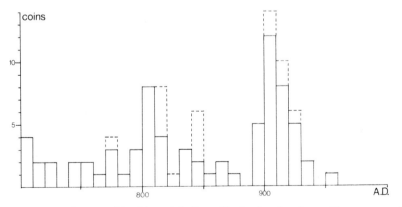

Figure 42 Distribution of Arabic and (indicated by broken lines) west European, and a couple of Byzantine coins of the graves from Birka, mid-Sweden

Studying the dates of the ninth-century coins, the Arabic coins concentrate in the early half of the century. At Birka, for instance, 17 coins are from between 800 and 850 (20 before 800, but probably also belonging to the ninth-century period of importation), while only three stem from 850 to 890 (Fig. 42). The west European coins also cluster in the early half of the century. (The date of the Nordic coins is not commented upon, since it is dependent on the imported ones.) The Kaupang picture is similar, but the number of coins is much smaller. In sum, we observe an early period of the ninth century with international contacts and, as we have seen above, a sizable silver stock, followed by a period of little trade and a shrinking amount of silver. This latter phase corresponds to the major Viking raids in western Europe, which must be viewed in the light of competition for scarce surpluses. (We should also remind ourselves that the ninth century might have witnessed a climatic depression with consequences for the harvest.) Nevertheless, little silver was carried back to the Scandinavian homelands, to judge by the coin dates.

Moving on in time, the Arabic coins become very common from about 890, corresponding to the major peak in the amount of silver at the beginning of the tenth century. Soon after, however, in the middle of the century, the Arabic coins disappear almost completely (Fig. 43). A German[25] and, a little later, an English importation of coin began in the second half of the tenth century, but the west European coins did not make up for the eastern losses, which put the silver stock at its lowest in about 950. Furthermore, at the beginning of the tenth

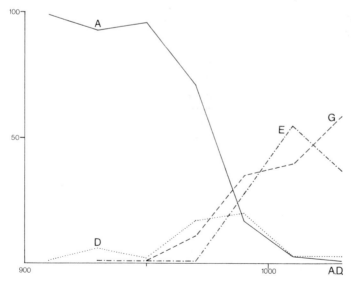

Figure 43 Percentages of respectively Arabic (unbroken lines), German (broken lines), English (broken lines with points) and Nordic, basically Danish (lines of points) coins in the silver-hoards of the period 900 to 1040 A.D.

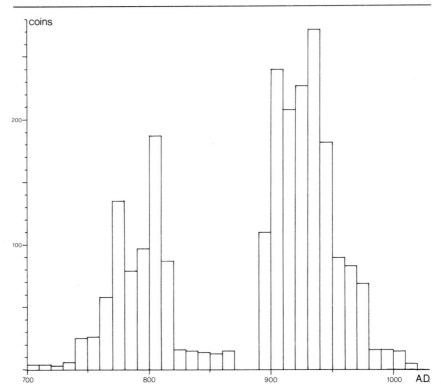

Figure 44 Distribution of Arabic coins in a sample of north-west Russian silver-hoards

century some Arabic coins reached western Europe from Scandinavia, found, for instance, in English silver hoards of the 'Norse' provinces.[26]

The Kaupang harbour apparently did not survive the late ninth-century decline in silver, and Birka certainly did not live out the drastic mid-tenth-century depression.[27] This shows how fragile the Scandinavian townships to the north of Denmark were, and also that they functioned mainly as markets for luxuries, first of all of western origin, in exchange for Arabic and some west European silver too. At Birka a town wall was set up shortly before the site was abandoned in 950-960. The rampart is lying on top of a grave with a coin from about 925 and may reflect an increase of raiding in the Baltic, corresponding to the tenth-century silver decline (cf. the contemporary town wall of Hedeby). The early tenth-century silver peak is reflected in the Birka graves, where 30 Arabic coins are of the period 890 to 930; 20 of these are from 900 to 920, while only three later, from 930 to 950 (Fig. 42). The corresponding western coins are only five in number, but date from the period 900 to 930 and are parallel to the major Arabic importation. Eight Nordic coins of the tenth century have also been found, all of which were struck at Hedeby, where minting was resumed in the early tenth century after a cessation of about fifty years.

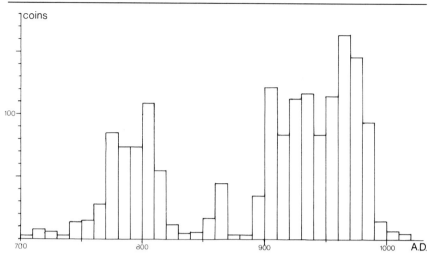

Figure 45 Distribution of Arabic coins in a sample of south-west Russian silver-hoards

As in the ninth century, we note a correlation between the periods of international trade and coin importation from both the east and the west and the size of the silver stock, as established for Denmark. This is not to deny that most of the silver was eastern; from western Europe came more goods.

The pattern of imported Arabic silver directs our attention to Russia. From there we have a sample of 42 hoards, with Arabic coins covering the whole Viking period from 780 to 1040 without intervals and spread geographically from the Finnish Bay to the old provinces of Kiev and Poltava and, to the east, from the area at Kazan on the middle Volga to the lower Don.[28] Fifteen of the finds are from before 900, 17 from the tenth century, and the rest later. The Arabic coins of the sample, from 700 onwards, totalling five thousand, display a clear two-peak distribution with a deep depression between the periods of intensive import (Figs. 44–6). The first concentration, as in the Birka graves, lies around 800 – in Russia perhaps a little earlier than at Birka. The second, and strongest, peak comes after 890, ending in the tenth century, while very few coins stem from the period 870 to 890. Indeed, after 820 the number of coins is already declining in Russia. To the east, in the Kazan area, the tenth-century depression takes place as early as the second quarter of the century, while in north-west Russia, closer to eastern Scandinavia (and Birka), a more gradual decline is seen by 950. In the south-west, however, Arabic coins still arrive in relatively large numbers until the last quarter of the tenth century.[29]

The drastic fluctuations in the flow of Arabic silver into Russia can hardly be explained by shifting intensity of minting in the Islamic world.[30] They must be connected with alterations of the trade patterns and, in the end, of the Arabic demand for, or ability to acquire, those

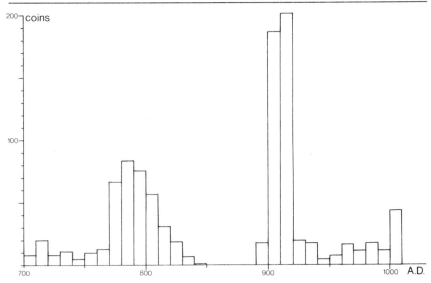

Figure 46 Distribution of Arabic coins in a sample of eastern Russian silver-hoards

slaves, furs and weapons that were supplied from Russia and other areas. (The Slavonian, Finnish and Scandinavian populations received very few Islamic products apart from the silver coins.) Warfare, of course, may also have interrupted the connection but, with the Scandinavian experiences in mind, we tend to see fighting and decline in trade as connected factors, each spurring the other in a negative direction. Moreover the ninth century, especially the latter half, saw much unrest within the Islamic world, such as the long and terrible Zanj slave revolt in southern Mesopotamia.

The problem of alternative markets must also be taken into consideration. During the ninth century the Arabs came into control of some southern French and Italian towns, as well as the island of Sicily, for instance, through which slaves may have been acquired. The Franks participated in this trade, exchanging non-Christian slaves. Even earlier, Muslim Spain had established close connections with the Frankish and other slave markets in western Europe. Incidentally, the word 'slave' discloses that many of these persons originated from the Slavonian areas. To the east, furthermore, on the borders of the Turkish peoples, and in Africa, slaves entered the Islamic world. But the general unrest of the latter half of the ninth century seems, all in all, to be a better explanation of the decline of Russian trade than the existence of alternative markets, since these were long established.

The decline of Arabic silver in the tenth century might be explained in the same way, stressing unrest, but a stronger factor is probably the emptying of the silver mines in Transoxania and other areas (near

Samarkand and Bukhara). Indeed, the majority of the tenth–century Arabic coins in Scandinavia are from Samanid dynasty mints in these extremely rich provinces. Under the ruler Naṣr II (913–942) the influence of the emirate stretched as far north as Bulghar on the Middle Volga, where there was an important Muslim settlement. To the west and north only Finnish-speaking tribes, with a language not too unfamiliar to the neighbouring Swedes, separated the Islamic from the Scandinavian world, in spite of the enormous distance between, say, Birka and Baghdad. Furthermore, the large Russian rivers facilitated the communication, and from the beginning of the tenth century we possess written Arabic sources describing the transportation of, among other things, slaves and furs through Russia, commodities which were exchanged for eastern silver, for instance at Bulghar.[31]

Studies of the composition of Arabic coins in the single Russian or Scandinavian silver hoards have revealed some interesting patterns, giving rise to a wide variety of speculation about the trade and exchange.[32] The Russian and Scandinavian finds of the ninth century have long tails of older coins whose distribution may disclose, for instance, an importation peak around 800 (Fig. 47), at the time of Harun-al-Raschid,[33] known to the Franks as the Caliph who sent Charlemagne an elephant, which, incidentally, died during a campaign against the Danish King Godfred in 810 (cf. Translations). Another, and smaller, peak in the imported silver is best seen in the hoards of south-west Russia and of Scandinavia and dates from about 850.

Shortly after 900 the finds were loosing their tails, being a natural consequence of the late ninth-century recession of the silver, together with the powerful flow in the early tenth century and a constant export of the coins and melting down for jewellery (Figs 48-9).[34] The more silver there is, the more will be exported or used for trinkets and, in short, consumed. The later hoards of the tenth century have long tails with a powerful termination, reflecting the heavy importation of the early part of the century and the gradual decline of the Arabic coin stream (Fig. 50).[35] As noted above, the decline took place at different times in different areas. It should also be mentioned that the contemporary hoards of coins within the Islamic world have weak

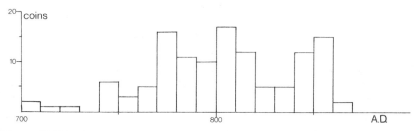

Figure 47 Distribution of Arabic coins in a ninth century mid-Swedish silver-hoard (Fittja)

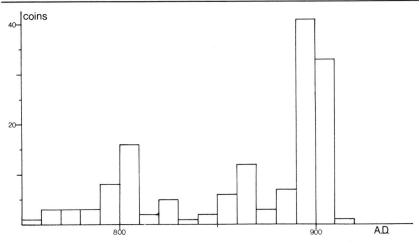

Figure 48 Distribution of Arabic coins in an early tenth–century silver–hoard from
  Over Randlev, east Jylland

tails and are made up almost entirely of new coins (Fig. 52).[36] This
signifies, for instance, that Russia, almost devoid of Arabic coins in the
later ninth century, received a large stock of new coins at the
beginning of the tenth century, which explains why the tenth–century
hoards hold few old Arabic coins as compared with new ones. On the
other hand, the hoards in the Islamic world before 800 often have long,
quite powerful tails, since they are made up of both old and new coins
(Fig. 51).[37] This observation explains the long tails of the Russian and
Scandinavian finds of the ninth century. Furthermore, it demonstrates
that the many solitary eighth–century Arabic coin finds in Scandinavia
were most probably part of the general ninth–century importation and
not a result of pre–Viking Age contacts. This accords with the dates of
the hoards too; in both Russia and Scandinavia the earliest hoards with
Arabic coins stem from the 780s.[38] Incidentally, the composition of the
eighth–century hoards in the Islamic world throws some doubts on the
effect of the famed reform of coinage of 'Abd al–Malik in about 700.[39]

As noted, the composition of the hoards is caused by several factors:
import, export and consumption. But not infrequently the patterns, as
Bolin puts it, are taken to reflect the export flow only.[40] The heavy tails
would thus mean that the old coins were piling up, because of the
decline or absence of exporting, while new ones were still coming in.
But this easily leads to false conclusions. For instance, the powerful
tails of the hoards of the mid–tenth century reflect a period of strong
importation, followed by a decline. The export, and the consumption,
are regarded as merely dependent on the size of the import.

Bolin saw the Arabic silver flowing freely through Scandinavia and
into western Europe from 850 and until the appearance of the tail with
powerful termination in the hoards, before 950. Bolin's reasons for not

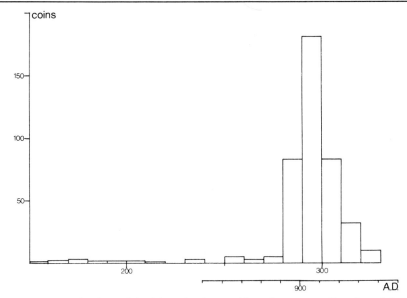

Figure 49 Distribution of Arabic coins in a mid-tenth-century silver-hoard from Terslev, Sjælland

admitting Arabic coins into southern Scandinavia, and from there to the west, before 850 are weak, since we have, among other things, four hoards from Denmark with such coins and a terminus post quem before 850.[41] For the period 800 to 850 Bolin saw a Frankish dominance in coins, reflecting west European purchases of, among other things, slaves and furs for sale to the Islamic world. In about 850 the Scandinavians took over the transactions themselves, using the trade routes through Russia. As a result, Arabic silver now flowed into Scandinavia and gave the Vikings the background for launching their attacks on western Europe. Furthermore, this silver, according to Bolin, should have caused an expansion of the western economy in the same period.

According to our own discoveries, the raids in western Europe correspond to the drastic decline in silver of the later ninth century. This was not noted by Bolin. Furthermore, Arabic coins are extremely rare in the west, though this may be because they were melted down, since the quality of the Arabic silver coins is very fine. Moreover their use as a means of payment, being non-Christian and of another standard, in countries with a more or less controlled coinage, was limited and difficult. In fact, we have little knowledge of the amount of silver flowing from, say, Samarkand to London via Bulghar and Hedeby.[42] But it may have been fairly modest. At Hedeby Arabic coins do not outnumber Danish and west European coins;[43] and while gigantic amounts of silver were involved in single

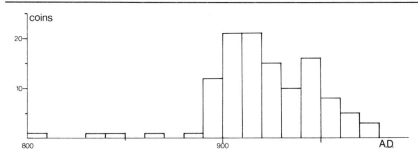

Figure 50 Distribution of Arabic coins in a late tenth-century silver-hoard from Vaalse, island of Falster

transactions within the Islamic world, the largest Russian hoards do not exceed forty kgs, while the Scandinavian finds make up, at most, one-fifth of this, or eight kgs of silver. Furthermore, the few Arabic coins in western Europe almost all stem from the early tenth century, corresponding to the noted peak and subsequent to the raids. Finally, to judge by the number of Arabic coins found in Scandinavia, the ninth-century types make up only 10 per cent of the total amount, and the peak of the early ninth century may have been less prominent here than in Russia.[44] This is seen also from the silver curve above for Denmark, though it should be remembered that the coins were more commonly turned into artefacts in the ninth than in the tenth century.

In Fig. 43 we give the relative percentages of Arabic, German, English and Nordic coins for the Danish hoards of the period 900 to 1040. It clearly shows how drastically the percentages of Arabic coins were dropping in the middle of the tenth century, the period of depression of the silver stock. We have already discussed some of the consequences of this decline, which corresponds well with west, and especially south-west, Russia. Denmark may thus have received the last Arabic coins through Poland, an area with intensive contacts with southernmost Scandinavia by the late tenth century.

The mid-tenth century saw other changes also in the composition of the hoards. In a study of the eastern Danish provinces, and particularly of Skåne, it has been shown that the weight of minted silver in the finds, vis-à-vis jewellery, was rising drastically at this time, to reach almost 100 per cent after 1000 A.D. (Fig. 53).[45] This demonstrates how investment in trinkets gave way to silver cash, a much more flexible means of exchange, and how transactions involving coins were fast becoming a day-to-day phenomenon for still larger parts of the population. The late tenth century also has the first mass-produced local coinage. A parallel, though slightly earlier, development involves hack-silver, the percentage of which, vis-à-vis the unbroken artefacts, is rising at the same time as the single pieces are becoming smaller.[46]

The disappearance of the Arabic flow of silver was also a final

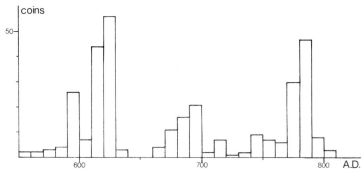

Figure 51 Distribution of (Arabic) coins in an early ninth-century hoard from Umm-Hajarah, north-east Syria

departure from an undeveloped economy, based on barter, where smaller exchanges did not involve coins and where larger transactions were probably often of the nature of gift-exchanges, whole artefacts being used as a means of exchange.[47] It is hardly an accident that the few pure coin hoards of the tenth century cluster in the south-western part of Denmark, with its more developed economic institutions, including towns.[48] On the other hand, finds dominated by whole artefacts, and usually with few or no coins, are most common on the Sjælland island group, a wealthy area, as we have seen, with a low

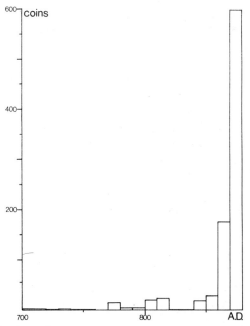

Figure 52 Distribution of (Arabic) coins in a late ninth-century hoard from Susa, south-west Persia

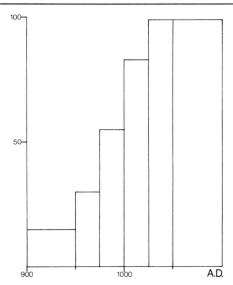

Figure 53 Percentages of minted silver in hoards from eastern Denmark for the period
    900 to 1100 A.D. (Redrawn from Hårdh)

degree of social stratification and, probably, also an old-fashioned
economic system. This type of hoard makes up two-thirds of the finds
from Sjælland, but only one-third of the Jylland hoards; in Skåne,
which was also a relatively stratified society, the hoards of whole
artefacts constitute an even smaller percentage, probably because of
the relatively late date of the finds.[49] The temporal aspects of the
geographical spread of the silver hoards are further developed in the
following section.

E. Silver hoards and political events

We have previously discussed the Viking Age silver hoards as possible
indicators of conflict; and we know of the west Danish expansion
towards the east in the late tenth century and of a number of southern
aggressions against Jylland. The question remains as to whether the
spread of finds corresponds to these events, and if so in what way.

Coin-dated hoards of the first half of the tenth century are few but
become more numerous in the turbulent period up to 1010, especially
in the case of inland finds (Fig. 54; cf. Appendix XI). The hoards
before 960/970 have the following spread: five or six are from south
Jylland, three from north-east Jylland and one from the island of
Langeland, while the Sjælland island group musters three. Bornholm
and southern Skåne have only two hoards, while as many as twelve are
known from north-west Skåne and Halland; finally, there are four

from north-east Skåne and Blekinge. The hoards of the period 970 to 1010 are scarce in south and east Jylland (two finds), while north Jylland and Fyn (and surrounding islands) have respectively seven and six. Sjælland has four, but southern and western Skåne has twelve and Bornholm even has eight. Halland has no finds, and Blekinge just two.

Sjælland and the surrounding islands were affected by some unrest both early and late in the period. To the east, north-west Skåne and Halland underwent disturbance only early on, while the rest of Skåne and Bornholm experienced disturbances in the later part of the period. South Jylland had problems in the early part of the period, north Jylland and Fyn in the later. If we look at the inland finds alone, which reflect more penetrating disturbances, we note early unrest probably in Halland and perhaps in other areas too. However, it is clear that the late troubles are largely concentrated in north Jylland, on Fyn, and in south and west Skåne, the most fertile and densely populated part of the province.

If King Harald's runestone at Jelling, which mentions his hold over 'Denmark all' (and 'Norway'),[50] is erected in the early 960s, it is of special interest to study the distribution of the hoards from the period 940 to 960 (only one find from the 960s is known). These finds are spread relatively evenly throughout the country, though some dominance is seen for the areas to the east of the Store Bælt. Nothing in the picture speaks against the claims of King Harald on the stone; we seem to have a general period of unrest preceding the 'unification' of the country.

Still, the Jelling state proper was a west Danish phenomenon, being bordered, for instance, by the ring of fortresses and cavalry graves. The later disturbances probably reflect attempts to establish a true hegemony over the country (Fig. 55; cf. Appendix XI). The problems start in northern Jylland in the 970s, but are felt most in the 980s, and partly also in the 990s in the mid-southern part of Denmark. In the 990s, but especially in about 1000, the disturbances concentrate on Skåne and Bornholm. This movement corresponds to the eastward spread of the Jelling state system, exemplified by the foundation of towns and by the royal settlement in Skåne, and indicated by the 'After Jelling'-type runestones which date also from about 1000. It should be added that finds from the 1010s are very rare; this means that the country was at rest during the days of the major campaigns in England, which were headed by King Sven and his son Knud (cf. Fig. 56).

A major battle, at 'Svold', probably off the west coast of Skåne, in 1000 left King Sven in a strong position vis-à-vis the neighbouring countries.[51] In the late 980s the same king led a rebellion against Harald, his father,[52] but it is difficult to include this, as well as the former, event in the picture. The same goes for the German attacks on the border, in 934 and 974, the Danish counter-attack in 983, and King Sven's siege of Hedeby in about 1000.[53] Many of the highlights of the

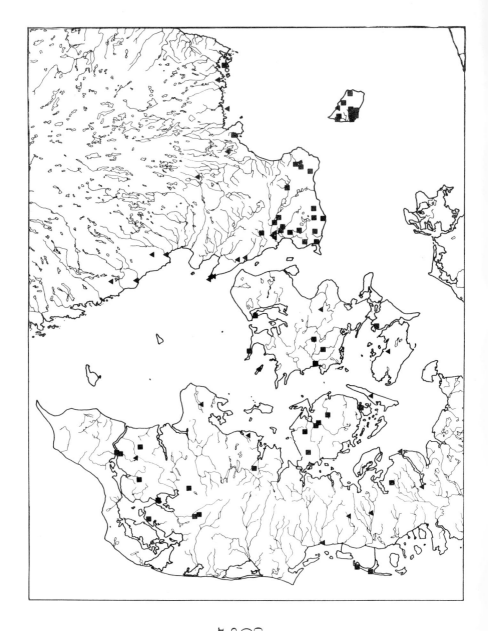

Figure 54 Coin-dated silver hoards of the period 900 to 1040 A.D. before (triangle) and after (square) 960 (Appendix XI)

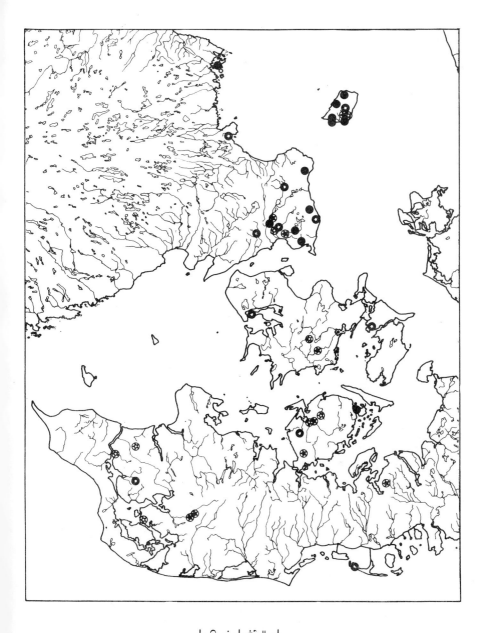

Figure 55 Coin-dated silver-hoards of the period 970 to 1010 A.D. by decades. White star and ring = 970–980; black star = 980–990; white star in black dot = 990–1000; black dot = 1000–1010 (Appendix XI)

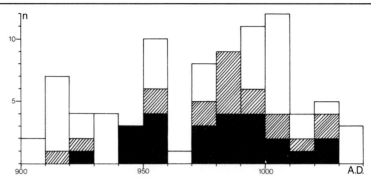

Figure 56 Coin–dated silver hoards of the period 900 to 1040 A.D. by decades and according to distance from open water. White signature = 0–4 kilometres from open water; striated = 5-9 kilometres from open water; and black = 10, or more, kilometres from open water. (Appendix XI)

political/historical record may not have directly affected the population at large.

The southern pressure is more clearly demonstrated in the periods of minting at Hedeby. It is hardly an accident that the first Nordic coins belong to the phase of Frankish interest in Denmark in the first half of the ninth century, corresponding to the early peak in silver and the international contacts with both east and west. The first half of the ninth century also saw the important controlled planning of Hedeby and the establishment of the first churches in the southern Jylland towns.

The late ninth century, the general period of decline, saw the abolition of these relations and institutions. At the beginning of the tenth century the new influx of silver and expansion of trade involved the west too, leading to the German attack of 934 on the riches of Hedeby, where minting was renewed. Further southern pressure is seen in the nomination of the first bishops in 948, but at this time a new depression of silver, among other things, led to a number of changes in Danish society, including King Harald's conversion to Christianity. Shortly afterwards the German emperor sought to emphasise his impact on the Danish bishops, but probably in vain.

A flow of German silver, corresponding to an increase in trade relations, is parallel to the attack in 974, but also to a modernisation of the economy, including a wider use of coins and the first local massminting. In 988 the German nomination of a bishop for Odense took place in a country which now was different in every important institution from the Denmark of King Godfred, two hundred years earlier, though the integration of the east was probably not yet complete.

Although the German impact was now slackening for the time being, and was to some extent substituted for by an English one – for instance, in the case of coins – and Denmark had become a political unity, set apart from its neighbours, the country was also on the way to being transformed into a west European state.

Chapter 8

SUMMARY

In the last half of the first millennium began a period of climatic optimum. This was accompanied by a population growth and a development of the subsistence economy, not only in size but also in kind; the previous stress on the rearing of animals, for instance, was checked by an expansion of cereal-growing, in which rye became more common, though barley was still the major crop. The emphasis on plant protein led to a larger population than ever before, though the ratio between agricultural (open) lands and forest was no larger in 800 than it had been at the beginning of the millennium. That period had been another phase of climatic optimum, whereas the centuries around 500 A.D. suffered severe hardships of cold, wet weather, poor harvests and a relatively small population.

Agricultural expansion was aided also by new tools, such as the wheel-plough, while the settlement pattern remained much the same as before. Villages were apparently regulated, and contained single farmsteads, made up of one or more long-houses on a traditional model, with both living quarters and the stable under the same roof, with associated minor buildings for craft and other activities. Some socio-economic ranking within the villages is seen in a few major farms. But in the tenth century another type of farm develops, the magnate estate, with fine living quarters separated from the rest of the buildings, having special functions and lying along the perimeter of the large courtyard. The magnate farms had so far appeared only in western Denmark, but here we have other reasons to expect clear social divisions of the population in the tenth century. The common villages were also restructured at the end of the Viking Age.

International exchange had already been practised for five thousand years in Denmark, but in the eighth century the ports of Hedeby, and especially of Ribe, were established to facilitate the trade with western Europe. In 800 Hedeby, protected by the Danevirke frontier walls, was laid out as a planned settlement and developed into a major centre of exchange, and of the transit of goods and persons between the

North Sea and the Baltic, and also of craft activities. In these towns the first Christian churches date from some time in the ninth century.

The towns received supplies from the countryside, which became more necessary in the tenth and eleventh centuries, when towns were established further to the north and to the east, and turned into regional centres with institutions such as bishoprics and mints. In the tenth century fortresses of the Trelleborg type were erected; apart from being military strongholds around what we consider to be the west Danish state centred on Jelling in mid-Jylland, they may have served, among other things, as toll-stations and as sites for the manufacture of artefacts of costly metals.

These economic institutions, of course, were not functioning in a social limbo. The early Iron Age societies were apparently chiefdoms, sometimes quite extensive but with limited social stratification, though the magnates held many prerogatives. In 800, in a still more stratified society, the central Danish provinces apparently held the leadership, for instance in the warfare against the Franks. In these areas the germ of land rights is apparent, these no longer being only part of the traditional family structure. For instance, followers may have received grants from the king in return for military services, and a petty system of 'vassalage' was established. Other royal 'officials' comprised the counts of the towns and the commandants of the fortresses.

In the tenth century the system of vassalage was expanding, as is shown by the runestones, which demonstrated publicly the new rights of land; vassalage is also clear from certain types of burials which follow the border around the state in west Denmark with its town economy and magnate farm economy. With the breakdown of traditional leaderships and their economic foundations, caused by the strength of the kingship and its dependents, the stage was set for the old magnates to enter the new social system, turning corporate rights into more private ones. This development may have been facilitated already by the development in the ninth century of the idea of one supreme kingship for the whole country.

The strength of the king of Denmark, of the Jelling dynasty, is demonstrated in 1000 A.D. in the expansion of military settlements towards the eastern provinces. But the apparatus directed itself at even larger enterprises, culminating in the conquest of England, even if this was only an episode. Soon the runestone documents disappear, and rights of land are in the hands of a new establishment, set apart from the rest of the population. In the state, these personages, along with the Christian institutions, themselves major owners of land, kept a check on the royal power.

The regulated village and magnate farm economy was well suited to the development of the towns, with their need both for foodstuffs and for a wealthy outlet for their products. International connections, on the level of international trade, may have played a considerable role here. For instance, crises in the supply of silver, a crucial means of payment for services, may have increased the number of grants of land and have thereby added, albeit unwittingly, to the changes in Danish society that occurred in the Viking Age. The first crisis in the supply corresponds to the raids in western Europe of the late ninth century, and here the social system is attempting to 'export' its problem, perhaps also under pressure of a minor ninth-century climatic recession. The serious crises of the mid-tenth century, however, did not lead to such measures. Instead, a new society was being created based on stable rural institutions and with fortresses and towns serving as centres of control and supply. This society of the tenth century, expanding to all provinces in about 1000 A.D., we call the state of Denmark. The germs of its institutions are already found in the ninth century, and perhaps even earlier, but the system did not function as a whole until a later date.

We have attempted to describe this 'secondary' state development as fully as possible. The available data is measured against a wide array of factors seen in conjunction and in relation to the functions of society. But in spite of all reductions the picture is both complex and open to discussion. Ironically, the Vikings themselves would never have considered their age complex. They seem to have been a practically minded people, though they possessed a strong interest in antagonisms. Their art, or whatever they might have called it, always fills up the whole space available with dynamic shapes (cf. Fig. 57).[1] No room is left for the uncertain, apart from what is really uncertain in the fate of man and of the world. Christianity, however, attempted to close this mental door.

Figure 57 Animal-ornament from whip-shank (silver) in the Ladby ship-burial. Scale 2:1. (After Thorvildsen)

TRANSLATIONS FROM LATIN OF
NINTH-CENTURY CONTINENTAL TEXTS
ON DENMARK
(The Latin syntax is followed closely.)

A. ANNALES FRANCORUM, 808 A.D.

. . . But Godofridus (Godfred), before returning, destroyed the emporium situated on the coast of the sea – which in the Danish language was called Reric and brought great advantages to his kingdom by payment of taxes. He removed the merchants from there and sailed on the fleet to a port, which is called Sliesthorp (Slesvig), with the whole army. There he remained for some days and decided to protect the border of his kingdom on Saxony, in such a way that, from a bay of the eastern sea, which they call Ostarsalt, to the western sea, a defence rampart was placed on the entire northern bank of the Egidora (Ejder) river, interrupted by only one gate, through which carriages and horsemen could be sent out and received. Having divided this work among the commanders of the troops, he returned home.

B. ANNALES FRANCORUM, 810 A.D.

. . . While he (Charlemagne) was dwelling there for some days, the elephant, which the king of the Saracens, Aaron (Harun), had sent him, suddenly died. When finally the troops were gathered, he hastened to the river Alara (Aller) as fast as he could, and after having set up camp near its mouth into the river Wisura (Weser), he awaited the outcome of the threats of King Godofridus (Godfred). For this king, conceited by a vain hope of victory, boasted he would meet the Emperor in pitched battle.

C. VITA ANSGARII, Section 24
(circa 850 A.D.; written around 870 A.D.)

. . . In the port which in his (Horik I) kingdom was the most suitable for the purpose and nearest to this country, called Sliaswich (Slesvig) where the meeting of merchants from all regions was held, he permitted him (Ansgar) to erect a church, assigning also a place where the priest could stay. He gave freedom so that anyone in his kingdom, who wished to, could become a Christian . . .

NOTES AND REFERENCES
(For abbreviations see *Bibliography*)

Chapter 1   THE VIKING AND THE STATE

[1] *DR* 216.

[2] *DR* 330.

[3] *DR* 334.

[4] *KLNM* XX, 20ff.

[5] More recent syntheses comprise Brøndsted 1960[1], and 1960[2], Christensen 1969, Foote & Wilson 1970, Sawyer 1971, and Skovgaard–Petersen 1977; cf. Skovgaard-Petersen 1971.

[6] A classic account of feudalism, focusing on the institutions of vassalage and fief, is Ganshof 1964. The word 'feudal' may also be used to characterise a type of society.

[7] Olsen & Schmidt 1977, Roesdahl 1977.

[8] General survey of the Iron Age, Brøndsted 1960[1]. See, also, below.

[9] General surveys are Stenberger 1964 and Magnus & Myhre 1976.

[10] Cf. Skovgaard-Petersen 1977, with references.

[11] General historical survey, Skovgaard-Petersen 1977.

[12] General works comprise Engels 1884, Balandier 1967, Fried 1967, Flannery 1972, Service 1975, Webb 1975, Webster 1975, Eder 1976, Wright 1977, Cohen & Service 1978 and Claessen & Skalník 1978 (important). (For discussions of urbanism, see e.g. Weber 1958 and Ucko, Tringham & Dimbleby 1972.)

[13] Fried 1967, Sahlins 1968, and Service 1971.

Chapter 2   HISTORICAL SOURCES

[1] Jones 1968 is an example of a rather uncritical use of such sources for historical reconstruction.

[2] For the following, consult the list of written sources and the bibliographies in Christensen 1969 and Skovgaard-Petersen 1977.

[3] Loyn 1962.

[4] *Annales Francorum* for the following.

[5] *Vita Anskarii*. (For the churches, see 24, 31 and 32.)

[6] *Annales Fuldenses*.

[7] *Annales Fuldenses*.

[8] Kendrick 1930.

⁹ Widukind I. 40; cf. Thietmar I, 17, and Adam I, 57.

¹⁰ Christensen & Nielsen 1975 (written sources), 126, 129 and 133.

¹¹ Cf. Christensen 1969, 226f. (Widukind III, 65).

¹² Cf. Christensen 1969, 230f. and Christensen & Nielsen 1975 (written sources), 129 and 133.

¹³ Widukind I, 40; Thietmar I, 17 (a later source) 'Knut'; and Adam I,57 (an even later source) 'Hardeknud Gorm'. Cf. *DR* 2 and 4; Queen Asfrid, the daughter of Odinkar.

¹⁴ *DR* 41 and 42.

¹⁵ Thietmar III, 6 and 24.

¹⁶ *The Anglo-Saxon Chronicle*. Kendrick 1930.

¹⁷ Adam II, 41 and 55.

¹⁸ *Annales Francorum* 817.

¹⁹ *Vita Anskarii* 31f.

²⁰ E.g. Gregorius Turonensis, 515 A.D. (III, 3).

²¹ *Annales Francorum*, also for the following.

²² *DR* 188.

²³ *Vita Anskarii* 32.

²⁴ *Annales Francorum*.

²⁵ *DR* 209.

²⁶ *DR* 230.

²⁷ *DR* 189, 190, 192 and 193.

²⁸ King Alfred 9.

²⁹ King Alfred 10.

³⁰ King Alfred 2.

³¹ Skautrup 1944.

³² *DR* 217.

³³ Adam I, 48f.

³⁴ *DR* 2 and 4, also for the following.

³⁵ *DR* 41 and 42. Dyggve 1942 and 1954 with earlier literature. Excavations are still (1978) in progress in the church; cf. Krogh 1966 (but otherwise unpublished). Various authors in K. M. Nielsen 1974; also Christensen 1975 and Roesdahl 1975.

³⁶ Adam II, 28.

³⁷ Cf. Christensen 1969, 226f. and 230f., and Skovgaard-Petersen 1977, 167f. and 170f. (Widukind III, 65).

³⁸ Hald 1963.

³⁹ E.g. Thietmar VII, 36 and especially Adam II, 27f.

⁴⁰ Adam II, 39 and *DR* 55.

⁴¹ Moltke 1976, 253.

Chapter 3 RUNESTONES AND PEOPLE IN A
         CHANGING SOCIETY

¹ Most recent surveys are *DR* and Moltke 1976; cf. Nielsen 1969 for alphabets and recent datings.

² E.g. Moltke 1976, 108f.

³ *DR* col. 1013ff.

⁴ *DR* 202, 209 (Glavendrup) and 230 (Tryggevælde; also ship-setting).
⁵ *DR* 26 (Læborg) 29 and 34.
⁶ *DR* col. 1013ff.; *DR* 41 (Gorm's stone).
⁷ *DR* 42 (Harald's stone), and *DR* 2 and 4 (the 'Knuba stones').
⁸ *DR* col. 1013ff.; cf. *DR* 1 and 3 (the 'Sven stones') and 345 (probably King Knud).
⁹ Also *DR* 30 (Bække 2, of Jelling-type).
¹⁰ *DR* 143, 264 (post 'After Jelling'?) and 280; cf. the numerous eleventh-century Swedish stones of this kind, Jansson 1976, 93f., and Carlqvist 1977.
¹¹ *DR* col. 1013ff. and Moltke 1976, 269f.
¹² *DR* 209.
¹³ E.g. Loyn 1962, various entries, among others 189.
¹⁴ Discussion e.g. Skovgaard-Petersen 1977, 194f.
¹⁵ *DR* 40.
¹⁶ *DR* 133.
¹⁷ *DR* 106 and 143.
¹⁸ *DR* 339.
¹⁹ *DR* 218 and 363 (province of Blekinge).
²⁰ *DR* 125 and 339.
²¹ *DR* 143.
²² E.g. Aakjær 1928, Nielsen 1945 and Ruprecht 1958. Cf. Ljunggren 1959 and Düwel 1975 (some other titles, 'landmand', 'bomand', 'bonde', 'landhyrde' etc.).
²³ *DR* 109 ('After Jelling'), 110 (Jelling) and 114 (Jelling). Cf. *DR* col. 932.
²⁴ *DR* 91 and 314.
²⁵ *DR* 1 and 3 (Sven), 345 (Knud).
²⁶ Data: *DR*. Cf. descriptions of types of inscriptions, col. 820f.
²⁷ *DR* 345.
²⁸ *DR* 295.
²⁹ *DR* 269.
³⁰ *DR* 280.
³¹ *DR* 279.
³² *DR* 1.
³³ *DR* 291 (bomand); *DR* 338 (bonde); Ljunggren 1959, Düwel 1975.
³⁴ *DR* 277.
³⁵ *DR* 294.
³⁶ *DR* 337.
³⁷ *DR* 314. Cf. *DR* 133 (Jelling-type, north Jylland; this 'landmand' is 'best, and first').
³⁸ *DR* 314 and 315 respectively.
³⁹ *DR* 295-7.
⁴⁰ *DR* 279 ('didn't flee at Uppsala'), 337 ('lie in London').
⁴¹ *DR* 334-5.
⁴² *DR* 330.
⁴³ *DR* 318.
⁴⁴ *DR* 298.
⁴⁵ *DR* 1.
⁴⁶ *DR* 3.
⁴⁷ *DR* 6.
⁴⁸ *DR* 63.

⁴⁹ *DR* 68.

⁵⁰ *DR* 67.

⁵¹ *DR* 108.

⁵² *DR* 107.

⁵³ *DR* 58 and 91 respectively. Cf. 314 (Lund).

⁵⁴ Moltke 1976, 253 ('man of tidings'; quite a recent find, not included in the sample), *DR* 134 (the manager of land), *DR* 58 and 91 (smed).

⁵⁵ *DR* 117. Otherwise see above.

⁵⁶ *DR* 78.

⁵⁷ *DR* 154–5.

⁵⁸ Cf. *DR* 1 and 3, and 295.

⁵⁹ *DR* 81.

⁶⁰ *DR* 213.

⁶¹ *DR* 220.

⁶² *DR* 380, 387, 389 (drengs), 372 (thegn), 402 (bonde).

⁶³ *DR* 379.

⁶⁴ Cf. Moltke 1976, 269f.

⁶⁵ *DR* 405.

Chapter 4 SUBSISTENCE AND RURAL SETTLEMENT

¹ Aaby 1976.

² Dansgaard et al. 1975, Dansgaard 1977.

³ Jelgersma et al. 1969.

⁴ Dansgaard 1977.

⁵ Broholm II (1944), Figs 81-2, and IV (1949), Figs 106, 108, etc. Cf. Randsborg 1974, 41f.

⁶ E.g. Brøndsted 1960¹, 236f.; fields 94f. Brøndsted 1960¹, also for general information.

⁷ Neumann 1977.

⁸ Exhibition at the Viking Ship Museum, Roskilde.

⁹ Brøndsted 1960¹, 209 etc.

¹⁰ Broholm 1943-9 and Brøndsted 1960¹.

¹¹ In general, Iversen 1973.

¹² Brøndsted 1960¹, 105f.

¹³ Brøndsted 1960¹, 243f. (cf. ill.).

¹⁴ Møhl in Klindt-Jensen 1957, e.g. 313.

¹⁵ E.g. Lange 1971 and Jelgersma et al. 1970.

¹⁶ E.g. Hedeby (Schietzel 1969, 53), Archsum (Kossack etc. 1974, 363), Lindholm Høje (Brøndsted 1960¹, 360f. (cf. ill.)) and Löddeköpinge (Ohlsson 1973).

¹⁷ H. Andersen 1958; cf. S. W. Andersen 1977.

¹⁸ Feddersen Wierde (at Bremerhafen), Haarnagel 1975, 26f.

¹⁹ Berglund 1969.

²⁰ Cf. Jankuhn et al. 1952¹ and Jankuhn 1976, 62f.

²¹ Ekman 1973, 10f.

²² Møhl in Klindt-Jensen 1957, e.g. 313; also for below.

²³ Reichstein 1973.

[24] Reichstein etc. 1974; cf. 46.
[25] Møhl in H. H. Andersen et al. 1971; cf. 325, and Ekman 1973; cf. 73f. respectively.
[26] Hvass 1975.
[27] Becker 1965. See also Jankuhn et al. 1977 (various authors; Iron Age and later).
[28] Brøndsted 1960[1] (e.g. Juellinge, 153f., Himlingeøje (more than one site), 189f., etc.).
[29] E. Thorvildsen 1972.
[30] Stenberger 1964; cf. Arbman 1943 (Birka); Magnus & Myhre 1976.
[31] Holmqvist 1976.
[32] Hvass 1976, Hvass 1977[2]. Excavations still (1978) in progress.
[33] E. Thorvildsen 1972.
[34] E.g. Ohlsson 1971, Strömberg 1969-70, Strömberg 1978, etc.
[35] Hvass 1977[1], Hvass 1977[2].
[36] Aggersborg: Olsen et al. 1977, 144f., and Roesdahl 1977[2]. Trelleborg: Nørlund 1948, 44, Fig. 26 (in red). This structure strongly resembles the main building in the first phase of the largest magnate-farm at Vorbasse.
[37] L. C. Nielsen 1976, L. C. Nielsen 1977. Excavations still (1978) in progress.
[38] References in Appendix VII to landed settlements and, in addition to the above titles, e.g. E. L. Nielsen 1968, Vorting 1972, Kossack et al. 1974, Bantelmann 1975, S. W. Andersen 1977; cf. several references in Ohlsson 1975-76, for instance Strömberg 1961.
[39] Stoumann 1977.
[40] Survey Hald 1965; cf. Christensen 1969, 44ff.
[41] Map Skautrup 1944, 42.
[42] Maps Skautrup 1944, 41 and 115.

Chapter 5   TOWNS AND FORTRESSES

[1] General surveys in Jankuhn et al. 1974, Blom 1977 and Barley 1977.
[2] *Annales Francorum.*
[3] *Ethelwerdi Chronicorum* I.
[4] *Vita Ansgarii* 24, 31 and 32.
[5] King Alfred 9; cf. 10 (Wulfstan's journey).
[6] *DR* 1, 3 and 63.
[7] *Diplomatarium Danicum* I, 1, 126, 330f. and 343f.
[8] *Vita Ansgarii* 32.
[9] *Diplomatarium Danicum* I, 1, 126.
[10] *Diplomatarium Danicum* I, 1, 343f.
[11] Biddle 1976.
[12] Adam II, 28.
[13] Olsen et al. 1969.
[14] Olsen 1960.
[15] Adam III, 76 and 77 and IV, 5.
[16] Hauberg 1900, 69.
[17] Andrén 1976.

[18] Adam III, 77; cf. IV, 8 and 9. Nearby Dalby was for some years a second Skåne bishop-seat; cf. Adam, same references.

[19] Adam III, 77.

[20] *Vita Ansgarii* 26f.

[21] Hald 1963.

[22] Hauberg 1900, 69. During the reigns of the kings succeeding Hardeknud, coins were also minted at Toftum (on Fyn) and at Borgeby and Thumatorp in Skåne; Toftum under king Magnus (1042-7), Borgeby and Thumatorp under King Sven (1047-74) and even later rulers. King Sven is a contemporary of Adam of Bremen.

[23] Adam IV, 5.

[24] Adam III, 77; IV, 4 and 5, etc. For 'Wendila' see IV, 5; it is not clear from the syntax whether W. also is a 'civitas'. Other references give W. as a province: Adam IV, 16, etc.

[25] General presentations e.g. Hodder et al. 1976, 53f.

[26] Ohlsson 1975-6.

[27] For this Slavonian 'fortress-town' and bishop-seat in the mid-tenth century; cf. e.g. Adam II, 16.

[28] Ramskou 1977.

[29] Cf. Hauberg 1900, 69 and note 22.

[30] Helsingborg (Adam II, 40) is not mentioned above. For Dalby, cf. note 18.

[31] Adam IV, 5.

[32] E.g. *KLNM* VII col. 94f. (J. Rosén). Data: Weitemayer et al. 1920-30 (and other editions).

[33] Cf. Donat et al. 1971, 237f. Hedeby: Steuer 1974, 19f.

[34] Andrén 1976.

[35] Cf. Ohlsson 1973, Ohlsson 1975-6. The cemetery currently undergoing excavation (1978).

[36] Ramskou 1976.

[37] Nørlund 1948, 105f.

[38] Roesdahl 1977[1], 73f.

[39] Ramskou 1950, 144f.

[40] Skaarup 1976.

[41] Jørgensen 1975.

[42] Hvass 1975.

[43] Hvass 1976, Hvass 1977[2].

[44] Albrectsen 1971.

[45] Schaefer 1963, 211f. See also below.

[46] Nørlund 1948, 112f.

[47] Skaarup 1976, 220f. (R. Gilberg).

[48] Biddle 1976.

[49] Müller-Wille 1976[2], Taf. 1.

[50] Surveys Jankuhn 1976, Schietzel 1968, Schietzel 1969, Schietzel 1975, Steuer 1974; cf. Hübener 1959. See below as well.

[51] E.g. Arbman 1939.

[52] Müller-Wille 1976[1].

[53] Andrén 1976.

[54] Steuer 1974.

[55] Strömberg 1969-70.

[56] Schietzel 1969, Schietzel 1975.

[57] Cf. Hübener 1959, 179f. and e.g. plans 24-5, and Steuer 1974, 154f. The two authors differ somewhat as to the precise extent of the ninth-century settlement.

[58] Jankuhn 1976, 117 (Abb. 30).

[59] Cf. Schietzel 1968 and Schietzel 1975.

[60] For the following see especially Jankuhn 1976, and in addition Schietzel 1968.

[61] Cf. Malmer 1966, 261f.

[62] Cf. Jankuhn 1976, 209f. (Jankuhn 1976 also for the following).

[63] King Alfred 3f.

[64] *Vita Rimberti* 18.

[65] *Vita Bernwardi* for the year 1000.

[66] Vogel 1975.

[67] Bencard 1973.

[68] E. Thorvildsen 1972.

[69] Aalkjær 1976.

[70] H. H. Andersen et al. 1971.

[71] Cf. Olsen et al. 1977, 86f. and Roesdahl 1977[1], 167f.

[72] E. L. Nielsen 1968.

[73] Olsen 1960.

[74] Blomqvist 1974 and Mårtensson 1976 (cf. Andrén 1976).

[75] Ohlsson 1973, Ohlsson 1975-6.

[76] Unpublished; excavation still (1978) in progress.

[77] Cf. Nørlund 1948.

[78] Olsen et al. 1977 and especially Roesdahl 1977[1], (together with Nørlund 1948 the main references for the following); cf. Christiansen 1970.

[79] Biddle 1976.

[80] Trimpe Burger 1973.

[81] Kersten et al. 1958, 90f.

[82] Cf. also Roesdahl 1977[2].

[83] Nørlund 1948, 44 Fig. 26 (in red).

[84] Roesdahl 1977[1], 153f.

[85] Helbæk 1977.

[86] Data in Nørlund 1948; cf. also Roesdahl 1977[1], 164f.

[87] H. H. Andersen et al. 1976.

[88] Neumann 1977.

[89] Ramskou 1977.

[90] Stiesdal 1960.

Chapter 6 SOCIAL AND POLITICAL IMPLICATIONS OF THE BURIALS

[1] Survey Ramskou 1950; cf. Ramskou 1976. Skåne: Strömberg 1961.

[2] E.g. Brøndsted 1936, 119 (grave 56, Jelling) and 131 (grave 3); Müller-Wille 1976[2] (grave 21).

[3] Survey Brøndsted 1936. Skåne: Strömberg 1961.

[4] Skaarup 1976.

[5] Müller-Wille 1976[1], 116f.

[6] Becker 1953.

[7] E.g. Müller-Wille 1976[2], 13f.

[8] Cf. Müller-Wille 1976[1], 125f.

[9] Reallexikon 3 (Bornholm II; C. J. Becker).

[10] Müller-Wille 1977.

[11] Cf. Müller-Wille 1976[1], Müller-Wille 1976[2]. Main data Brøndsted 1936.

[12] Brøndsted 1936, 106f.

[13] Cf. the distribution of the similar graves in northern mid-Sweden, bordering the Uppland central area, map Hyenstrand 1972, 36.

[14] Roesdahl 1977[1], 73f.

[15] E.g. Nørlund 1948 (Trelleborg); Müller-Wille 1976[1], 127f. (with Fig. 54) (Hedeby).

[16] Nørlund 1948, 94, graves 128 and 129 respectively.

[17] K. Thorvildsen 1957.

[18] Müller-Wille 1976[1].

[19] Cf. Munksgaard 1974, 163f.

[20] Brøndsted 1936, 143 (Søllested) and 144 (Møllemosegaard).

[21] Gryderup, Boeslunde parish; National Museum C 24106-12.

[22] Brøndsted 1936, 56f.; cf. Müller-Wille 1976[2], 21f.

[23] Müller-Wille 1976[2], 23f.

[24] Respectively Roesdahl 1977[1], graves 2 and 24 (axes) and Ramskou 1976, e.g. graves 1345, 1739 and 2204 (axes).

[25] Krogh et al. 1961.

[26] Brøndsted 1936, 106f.

[27] Müller-Wille 1976[2].

[28] Brøndsted 1936, 128f.

[29] Brøndsted 1936, 180f.

[30] Brøndsted 1936, 119 (grave 55).

[31] Cf. Munksgaard 1974, 163f.; also for the following.

[32] Sample Brøndsted 1936 and Strömberg 1961.

[33] Brøndsted 1936, 128f. (Ketting) and Müller-Wille 1976[2] (Thumby-Bienebek).

[34] Skaarup 1976 and Vorting 1972 respectively.

[35] Brøndsted 1936, 119 (grave 56); cf. Müller-Wille 1976[2], 21f.

[36] Aner 1952[1] and Steuer 1974, 36 (Kammergrab 5).

[37] Aner 1952[1] and Müller-Wille 1976[1].

[38] K. Thorvildsen 1957.

[39] Müller-Wille 1976[1].

[40] Brøndsted 1936, 143f. (graves 79 and 80).

[41] Brøndsted 1936, 149f. and Skaarup 1976.

[42] Brøndsted 1936, 88 (grave 8).

[43] *DR* 58.

[44] Roesdahl 1977[1].

[45] Brøndsted 1936, 106f.

[46] Nørlund 1948.

[47] Brøndsted 1936, 181f.; (body-of-carriage grave 180).

[48] Skaarup 1976, 185 no 15, (14 too?).

[49] S. W. Andersen 1977.

[50] Skaarup 1976, 56f.

[51] Brøgger etc. 1917-1928; I, 146f. Cf. also several graves at Birka (Arbman 1943).

[52] Ibn Fadlán. Birkeland 1954, 17f. Cf. Ibn Rustah (Birkeland 1954, 14f.).
[53] Vedel 1889, 143f. (i.a. Lousgaard 47).
[54] Ramskou 1963-5.
[55] S. W. Andersen 1977.
[56] At Højstrup, northernmost Jylland (Brøndsted 1936, 85f. and Ramskou 1950, 161f.), tenth-century inhumations, including a carriage-body and two axe graves, in barrows are superseded by cremations. The latter might have been considered slave-burials if it was not for the fact that cremation is the dominant rite of burial in the province. In any case, northernmost Jylland is a marginal part of the country. Other Jylland 'secondary' graves are even less likely 'slave-burials'.
[57] Data Nørlund 1948.
[58] Nørlund 1948, 189f. (G. Knudsen).
[59] Roesdahl 1977[1].
[60] *DR* 58 and 91.
[61] *Vita Rimberti* 18.
[62] Thietmar I. 17.
[63] *KLNM* XIX, col. 13, 'Træl' (slave) (various authors).
[64] Cf. Lombard 1971.

Chapter 7 SILVER HOARDS AND ECONOMIC SURPLUS

[1] Data in Skovmand 1942 and Hårdh 1976, the finds made before 1942.
[2] See e.g. Hatz 1974 for a detailed discussion of the factors normally thought to have produced the picture of find.
[3] Cf. Wilson 1968 for England.
[4] Cf. Randsborg 1974.
[5] Data from Olrik 1909, 112f.
[6] Cf. Sawyer 1971, 104f.
[7] Sawyer 1971, 99f.
[8] Cf. Randsborg 1974.
[9] Helbæk 1977.
[10] See Malmer 1966 for a monograph on this subject.
[11] Malmer 1966, 261f. and 297; cf. Steuer 1974, 42.
[12] Blindheim 1974, Skaare 1976, 139 and Malmer 1966, 283.
[13] Arbman 1939. Data: Arbman 1943 and Malmer 1966, 278f.
[14] Malmer 1966, 283 (find 117).
[15] Malmer 1966, 265 (find 23). The single coin from the Löddeköpinge settlement (Skåne), Malmer 1966, 297; cf. Ohlsson 1975-6, is without doubt contemporary with the early eighth- to ninth-century site.
[16] Malmer 1966. Also for the following.
[17] Malmer 1966, map Pl. 57 (as compared with map Pl. 56).
[18] Malmer 1966, maps Pl. 56 and Pl. 57.
[19] Żak 1975; cf. Helbæk 1977 (rye). See also Herrmann 1968 for East Germany (DDR) etc.
[20] Malmer 1966, 238f.
[21] Hauberg 1900. Also for the following.
[22] Skaare 1976.

[23] Data Arbman 1943. Also for the following.
[24] Cf. Nöbbe 1936. Jankuhn 1943, 72ff. and 203f.
[25] Cf. Hatz 1974.
[26] Dolley 1966.
[27] Blindheim 1974 and Arbman 1939, respectively. Cf. Sawyer 1971, 177f.
[28] Sample by S. Bolin (unpublished), rendered in Sawyer 1971, 219f.; figures converted by the present author.
[29] For the exchange with central Europe: Lewicki 1974.
[30] Economic historical survey of the Islamic world: Lombard 1971.
[31] Birkeland 1954 (cf. *KLNM* I, 'Arabiske kilder til Nordens historie', col. 194f. (Birkeland)). Jacob 1891. Arne 1914, archaeological data.
[32] Especially Bolin 1953.
[33] Sawyer 1971, 226f. (also for the following), Linder 1938 for a mid-Swedish hoard (Fittja).
[34] Compare Galster 1934 (Over Randlev, Skovmand 1942, 66f.) with Hauberg etc. 1914 (Terslev (later in date), Skovmand 1942, 111f.).
[35] Thomsen etc. 1842-3 (Vålse, Skovmand 1942, 95f.).
[36] E.g. Miles 1960 (Susa).
[37] E.g. al-'USH 1972 (Umm-Hajarah).
[38] *KLNM* I, col. 182f. ('Arabiska mynt', U.S.L. Welin, etc.). Cf. the Bolin-sample in Sawyer 1971, 219f.
[39] Cf. Grierson 1960.
[40] Bolin 1953. Also for the following.
[41] Skovmand 1942, find I A 9, I B c, II A 42 and II C 8. The latter two finds were probably not deposited until the early tenth century, however.
[42] Cf. Duplessy 1956, Dolley 1966.
[43] Cf. the samples in Nöbbe 1936 and Jankuhn 1943, 72ff. and 203f.
[44] Cf. figures given in *KLNM* I, col. 182f. ('Arabiska mynt', U.S.L. Welin, etc.).
[45] Hårdh 1976, 128f.; cf. Lundström 1973 for Gotland in the Baltic.
[46] Hårdh 1976, 132f.; cf. Lundström 1973 for Gotland.
[47] Cf. Grierson 1959.
[48] Skovmand 1942, find II A 13, II A 22, II A 27, II A 28a, II B a, II B c and II B d; Jahnkuhn 1952² (Steinfeld). From east Denmark come only Skovmand 1942, find II A 60 and Hårdh 1976, find 90 (both with termini post quos in the 990s). Two more eastern finds are uncertain.
[49] Data Skovmand 1942; cf. Hårdh 1976.
[50] *DR* 42.
[51] Cf. Adam II, 40.
[52] Cf. Adam II, 27f.
[53] Cf. *DR* 1 and 3.

Chapter 8 SUMMARY

[1] Wilson et al. 1965.

APPENDICES

APPENDIX I: *Early runestones (before c. 900 A.D.) (Fig. 4)*

DR numbers 9, 15, 17, 70, 105, 144, 188, 189, 190, 192, 193, 211, 221, 239, 248, 250, 333 and 356.

APPENDIX II: *Transition runestones (c. 900 A.D. and the beginning of the tenth century) (Fig. 4)*

A. The Glavendrup group. *DR* numbers 202, 209 and 230.
B. The Læborg group. *DR* numbers 26, 29 and 34.

APPENDIX III: *Runestones related to the Jelling dynasty (Figs 4-6)*

King Gorm: Appendix II B and *DR* 41; cf. *DR* 2 and 4 (the King Knuba stones).
King Harald: *DR* numbers 36, 42 and 55.
King Sven: *DR* 1 and 3.
King Knud: *DR* 345 (?).

APPENDIX IV: *Runestones of the Jelling-type (mid-tenth century) (Fig. 5)*

DR numbers 2, 4, 30, 36, 37, 40, 41, 42, 44, 53, 55, 56, 85, 90, 106, 110, 114, 117, 118, 124, 125, 132, 133, 143, 145, 160, 161, 216, 217, 218, 219, 227, 339 and 363.

APPENDIX V: *Runestones raised over women (Figs 4-6)*

A. Early stones: *DR* 188.
B. Transition stones: *DR* 26.
C. Jelling stones: *DR* numbers 30, 40, 41, 42 (also for a man), 55, 114 and 143 (also for a man).
D. 'After Jelling' stones: *DR* 134.

APPENDIX VI: *Runestones of the 'After Jelling'-type (c. A.D. 1000) with indications of generation, some titles, etc., of the deceased) (Figs 6-8)*

Sf=Senior, father (etc.)
Sh=Senior, husband
B=Brother, etc. (same generation)
J=Junior (son, etc.)
F=Fælle (etc.)
D=Dreng
T=Thegn
dd='died'

(Double set of same or mutually excluding terms: more than one dead person on the stone.)

DR numbers: 1 F D dd, 3 dd, 6 dd, 58, 62 F, 63, 65, 66 F dd, 67 Sf, 68 F D dd, 69 B, 77 B D, 78 J D, 81, 82, 83 B B, 84, 86 B T, 91, 94 J D, 95, 96 J, 97 J, 98 Sh T, 99 Sh T, 107 B, 108 B dd, 109, 115 T, 116 Sf B, 119, 120, 121 B T, 122 Sf, 123 Sf T, 127 F D, 129 T, 130 Sf T, 131, 134, 135 B, 138 B, 149, 150, 154 Sh dd, 155 Sh, 213 Sf T, 220 B dd, 228 B, 237 B, 258, 259 B dd, 260 J, 262 F D, 265, 266 B dd, 268 B D, 269 B, 270 F, 271, 275 B, 276 B D, 277 Sh T, 278 B D, 279 F, 280 B, 281, 282 B B, 283 B, 287, 288 B D, 289 B D, 291 Sf Sh, 293 Sh T, 294 Sf T, 295 B, 296 B, 297 B, 298 Sf, 314 B B, 315, 316 F, 317 Sf Sh, 318 Sf F, 321 F, 324 B, 325 Sf, 328 Sf, 329 F, 330 F F D D, 331, 334 B dd, 335 F, 337, 338 Sf, 343 Sf T, 345 Sf.

APPENDIX VII: *Settlements with analyses of animal bone-fragments (Fig. 13)*

A. Rural settlements, etc. (Viking Age, etc.)

1. Tofting, south-west Jylland (Bantelmann 1955 (G. Nobis); the latest sample).
2. Elisenhof, south-west Jylland (Reichstein 1972, Reichstein 1973).
3. Sædding, west Jylland (unpublished; number of samples counted).
4. Viborg, north Jylland (Møhl 1968).
5. Karby, north-west Jylland (unpublished; few data).
6. Aggersborg, north Jylland (unpublished; from the settlement prior to the fortress).
7. Vejleby, Lolland (Møhl 1971[2]).
8. Löddeköpinge (Vikhögsvägen), west Skåne (Ohlsson 1975-6 (O. Persson)).
9. Karstorp, west Skåne (Ambrosiani et al. 1972 (R. Jonsson)).
10. Fosie, west Skåne (Lepiksaar 1973-4[1]).
11. Rinkaby, east Skåne (Strömberg 1961 (I. Lepiksaar)).
12. Valleberga, south Skåne (Strömberg 1961 (I. Lepiksaar)).
(13. Oxie, west Skåne (Lepiksaar 1973-4[2]; deviating site, limited in size).)

B. Fortresses (Viking Age)

1. Trelleborg, Sjælland (Nørlund 1948 (M. Degerbøl)).
2. Lembecksburg, south-west Jylland (Stampfli 1959/61 cf. Requate 1956[1] and Requate 1956[2]; the site is markedly deviating from the rest of the samples).

C. Towns (Viking Age, etc.)
1. Hedeby (Harre 1960, Reichstein 1973, Reichstein et al. 1974; several samples).
2. Ribe (unpublished, cf. Nansen et al. 1977).
3. Århus (Møhl 1971[1]).
4. Lund (Ekman 1973; etc.).

D. Slavonian town-fortresses in east Holstein (Viking Age, etc.)
1. Gikau (Stampfli 1959/61).
2. Oldenburg (Stampfli 1959/61).
3. Scharstorf (Stampfli 1959/61).

E. Early Iron Age, etc., rural settlements (sample)
1. Feddersen Wierde, at Bremerhafen (Reichstein 1972, Reichstein 1973).
2. Hodorf, Holstein (Bantelmann 1955 (G. Nobis)).
3. Tofting, south-west Jylland (Bantelmann 1955 (G. Nobis); two samples).
4. Dankirke, west Jylland (unpublished; number of samples counted).
5. Dalshøj, Bornholm (Møhl 1957).
6. Sorte Muld, Bornholm (Møhl 1957).

APPENDIX VIII: *Tenth-century cavalry graves with stirrups (all from west and mid-Denmark) (Fig. 34)*

C=Chamber grave too
S=Sword or/and spear
A=Axe the only weapon
N=No weapons, or no weapons recorded

Müller-Wille 1976[2], 56, numbers: 2 N, 3 C(?) S, 4 C S, 5 S, 6 C S (coin-dated 900-950), 8 C(?) S, 9[1] N, 9[2] S, 16 C S (coin-dated 900-950), 20 S, 28 Ship (C) N (A, but probably no weapon), 33 S (cf. Skaarup 1976, 185).

Brøndsted 1936, numbers: 7 S, 8 S, 9 N, 10 S, 12[2] S, 14 C S, 17 S, 23 N, 28 A, 33 A, 41 S, 42 N, 49 S, 67 C S, 70[1] S, 70[10] N, 82 N, 87[3] C S, 88 A, 89[2] S, 93 (probably grave) S, 95 C S, 106 S, 109 S.

New find (1978): Rosenlund, Rønninge, east Fyn, C S.

APPENDIX IX: *Tenth-century body-of-carriage graves (all from west and mid-Denmark, etc. (Fig. 34).*

C=Chamber grave too
S=Stirrup grave on the same graveyard
A=Axe grave on the same graveyard

Brøndsted 1936 numbers: 3[1] C A, 22, 24[1] C A, 32 (coin-dated 936-962), 40, 43[2] A, 55 C(?), 56 C (cf. Roesdahl 1974, Roesdahl 1975), 70[2] S, 70[3] S, 70[18] S (coin-dated 900-950), 92[1] A.

Lindholm Høje 771 A (Ramskou 1976)
Fyrkat IV C(?) A (Roesdahl 1977[1])
Fyrkat XX C(?) A (Roesdahl 1977[1])
Sdr. Onsild VII C(?) A (Roesdahl 1976)
Hørning C (Krogh et al. 1961)

Sporup (Müller-Wille 1976, 21)
Thumby-Bienebek C S (Müller-Wille 1976²)
Thumby-Bienebek C S (Müller-Wille 1976²)
Thumby-Bienebek C S (Müller-Wille 1976²)
Oldenburg, Holstein (Müller-Wille 1976², 23f.).

APPENDIX X: *Silver-hoards of the ninth century (sample discovered before 1942) (Fig. 35).*

t=terminus post quem
C=0–4 kms from open water (in the Viking Age)
i=5–9 kms from open water
I=10, or more, kms from open water

   Skovmand 1942 numbers: I A 1 C, I A 2 C, I A 3 I, I A 4 C, I A 8 C, I A 9 t 846 C, I A 10 C, I A 12 C, I B a C, I B b t 864 C, I B c t 848/49 C, I C 1 C, I C 2 t 814 C, and 133 note 2 (Koldemosen) t 890 C.

   Hoards coin-dated to the ninth century but containing tenth-century artefacts: II A 42 t 814 C, II C 8 t 809 i.

APPENDIX XI: *Coin-dated silver-hoards of the period 900-1040 (sample discovered before 1942) (Figs 36 and 54-6).*

t=terminus post quem
C=0–4 kms from open water (in the Viking Age)
i=5–9 kms from open water
I=10, or more, kms from open water

   Skovmand 1942 numbers (II: t 900–1010 A.D.; III: t 1010–1040 A.D.), cf. Hårdh 1976: II A 2 t 970 C, II A 3 t 961 C, II A 4 t 991 I, II A 5 t 952 I, II A 6 t 973 I, II A 7 t 975/80 C, II A 9 t 983 I, II A 9a t 983 I, II A 11 t 932 C, II A 13 t 910 C, II A 15 t 913 C, II A 23 t 942 I, II A 24 t 954 I, II A 26 t 975/80 i, II A 27 t 991 I, II A 28 t 975 i, II A 28a t 980 i, II A 31 t 971 I, II A 32 t 1002 C, II A 33 t 925 C, II A 36 t 936 C, II A 37 t 991 C, II A 41 t 953 C, II A 44 t 975/80 I, II A 45 t 941 I (Terslev), II A 47 t 985 I, II A 48 t 991 C, II A 53 t 1002 C, II A 54 t 1002 C, II A 55 t 954 C, II A 56 t 1004 C, II A 57 t 1002 C, II A 59 t 1000 C, II A 60 t 997 i, II A 61 t 980 i, II A 62 t 979 C, III A 3 t 1035 C, III A 6 t 1016 i, III A 10 t 1024 I, III A 16 t 1024 C, III A 17 t 1018 C, III A 39 t 1037 C, II B a t 980 i, II B b t 913 C, II B c t 900 C, II B d t 997 C, III B a t 1036 C, II C 1 t 906 C, II C 2 t 925 C, II C 3 t 916 C, II C 4 t 955 C, II C 5 t 918/936 C, II C 6 t 996 I, II C 7 t 955 i, II C 9 t 1007 I, II C 10 t 983 I, II C 11 t 983 i, II C 12 t 1002 I, II C 14 t 1002 C, II C 15 t 1002 i, II C 16 t 996 C, II C 17 t 996 I, II C 20 t 1000 i, II C 21 t 918 i, II C 22 t 927 I, II C 23 t 950 I, II C 24 a t 931 C, II C 26 t 956 I, II C 27 t 916 C, II C 28 t 942 I, II C 29 t 991 C, II C 31 t 936 C, II C 32 t 955 C, II C 33 t 1002 C, III C 10 t 1024 I, III C 11 t 1028 i, III C 12 t 1018 I, III C 13 t 1021 i.

   Hårdh 1976 numbers (more uncertain finds): 90 t 991 i, 115 t 1016 C, 116 (t 978) i (Skovmand 1942, 141 note 1, Värpinge), 125 t 954 i, 126 t 920 i.

APPENDIX XII: *Silver-hoards of the period c. 900-1010 without coins or without coins clearly dated to the period (sample discovered 1942) (Fig. 36).*

C=0–4 kms from open water (in the Viking Age)
i=5-9 kms from open water
I=10 kms, or more, from open water
    Skovmand 1942 numbers: II A 1 I, II A 8 I, II A 10 I, II A 12 I, II A 14 I, II A 16 i, II A 20 I, II A 30 i, II A 35 C, II A 39 C, II A 40 C, II A 43 I, II A 49 i, II A 50 i, II A 51 C, II A 52 C, II C 25 a C, II C 25 c C.
    The following finds contain coins of an earlier period, or undated or poorly dated coins:
    Skovmand 1942 numbers: II A 42 C (tpq 814), II A 46 C, II A 63 i, II A 64 C, II C 8 i (tpq 809), II C 24 b C (tenth century).

APPENDIX XIII: *Well-documented silver-hoards with and without coins of the ninth century (sample discovered 1942).*

C=0–4 kms from open water (in the Viking Age)
i=5-9 kms from open water
I=10, or more, kms from open water
b=below 500 g weight
a=above 500 g weight
    Skovmand 1942 I A numbers: 1 C b, 2 C b, 3 I b, 4 C a, 9 C b, 10 C b, 12 C b.
    Skovmand 1942 I B numbers: a C a, b C a, c C b.
    Skovmand 1942 I C numbers: 1 C b, 2 C b.
    Skovmand 1942, 133 note 2 (Koldemosen): C b.
Total weight 6,705 g. Average weight 516 g.

APPENDIX XIV: *Well-documented silver-hoards with and without coins employed in the regional calculations for the period 900-1010 (sample discovered 1942) (Figs 39-40).*

C=0–4 kms from open water (in the Viking Age)
i=5-9 kms from open water
I=10, or more, kms from open water
b=below 500 g weight
a=above 500 g weight

A. Northern Jylland.
    Skovmand 1942 II A numbers: 1 I b, 2 C a, 3 C b, 4 I b, 5 I b, 6 I b, 7 C b, 8 I a, 9 I b, 9a I b, 10 I b, 11 C b, 13 C a.
Total weight 4,401 g. Average weight 339 g.

B. Southern Jylland.
    Skovmand 1942 II A numbers: 14 I a, 15 C a, 16 i a, 20 I b, 22 I b, 23 I b, 24 I a.
    Skovmand 1942 II B numbers: a i b, c C b, d C a.
Total weight 11,549 g. Average weight 1,155 g.

C. Fyn, etc.

Skovmand 1942 II.A numbers: 26 i b, 27 I b, 28 i b, 28a i b, 30 i b, 31 I a, 32 C a, 33 C b.

Total weight 3,904 g. Average weight 488 g.

D. Sjælland, etc.

Skovmand 1942 II A numbers: 35 C a, 36 C a, 37 C a, 39 C a, 40 C a, 41 C a, 42 C b, 43 I a, 44 I b, 45 I a, 46 C b, 47 I b, 48 C b, 50 i a, 51 C b, 52 C a.

Total weight 32,012 g. Average weight 2,001 g.

E. Bornholm.

Skovmand 1942 II A numbers: 53 C b, 54 C b, 55 C a, 56 C b, 57 C a, 59 C b, 60 i b, 61 i a, 63 i b, 64 C b.

Total weight 3,648 g. Average weight 365 g.

F. South-west Skåne.

Skovmand 1942 II C numbers: 1 C b, 3 C a, 5 C a, 6 I b, 8 i a, 9 I a, 10 I a, 11 i b, 12 I b, 13 i b, 14 C a, 16 C a, 20 i a, 21 i b.

Skovmand 1942, 141 note 1 (Värpinge): i a.

Hårdh 1976 number 90: i b.

Total weight 11,886 g. Average weight 743 g.

G. North-east Skåne, Halland and Blekinge

Skovmand 1942 II C numbers: 22 I b, 23 I b, 24 a (find) C b, 24 b (find) C b, 26 I a, 28 I b, 29 C b, 31 C a, 32 C a.

Total weight 3,544 g. Average weight 394 g.

BIBLIOGRAPHY

A. WRITTEN SOURCES

Adam Bremensis = W. Trillmich (ed.), *Rimberti Vita Anskarii & Magistri Adam Bremensis: Gesta Hammaburgensis ecclesiae Pontificum*, in R. Buchner (ed.), *Ausgewählte Quellen zur deutschen Geschichte des Mittelalters* XI, Berlin 1961.

Anglo-Saxon Chronicle = D. Whitelock (ed.), *The Anglo-Saxon Chronicle*, London 1961.

Annales Francorum = R. Rau (ed.), *Annales Regni Francorum, Annales Bertiniani & Annales Fuldenses* (= *Quellen zur karolingischen Reichsgeschichte* I–III), in R. Buchner (ed.), *Ausgewählte Quellen zur deutschen Geschichte des Mittelalters* V–VII, Berlin 1955–60.

Annales Fuldenses = *Annales Francorum*.

Diplomatarium Danicum = Christensen & Nielsen 1975 = C. A. Christensen & H. Nielsen (eds), *Diplomatarium Danicum*, 1 række, 1 bind, Copenhagen 1975.

Ethelwerdi Chronicorum = R. Pauli (ed.), *Ethelwerdi Chronicorum Libri Quatuor*, in G. H. Pertz et al. (eds), *Monumenta Germaniae Historica, Scriptorum* XIII, Hanover 1881.

Gregorius Turonensis = R. Buchner (ed.), *Gregorii episcopi Turonensis Historiarum Libri Decem*, in R. Buchner (ed.), *Ausgewählte Quellen zur deutschen Geschichte des Mittelalters* II–III, Berlin 1955–6.

King Alfred = J. Bosworth (ed.), *A Description of Europe and the Voyages of Othare and Wulfstan, written in Anglo-Saxon by King Alfred the Great*, London 1853.

Thietmar = W. Trillmich (ed.), *Theitmari Merseburgensis Episcopi Chronicon*, in R. Buchner (ed.), *Ausgewählte Quellen zur deutschen Geschichte des Mittelalters* IX, Berlin 1957.

Widukind = A. Bauer & R. Rau (eds), *Widukindi res gestae Saxonicae*, in R. Buchner (ed.), *Ausgewählte Quellen zur deutschen Geschichte des Mittelalters* VIII, Darmstadt 1971.

Vita Ansgarii = see Adam Bremensis or *Vita Rimberti*.

Vita Bernwardi = Thangmarus decanus Hildesheimensis, *Vita Bernwardi episcopi Hildesheimensis* = G. H. Pertz et al. (eds), *Monumenta Germaniae Historica, Scriptores* IV = *Annales aevi Carolini et Saxonici Historiae aevi Carolini et Saxonici*, Hanover 1841.

Vita Rimberti = G. Waitz (ed.), *Vita Anskarii auctore Rimberto, Scriptores rerum Germanicarum*, Hanover 1884. (Includes *Vita Rimberti*)

The reader with a knowledge of Nordic languages may benefit from the translations of selected texts in J. Bjernum, *Kilder til vikingetidens historie*, 2nd ed., Copenhagen 1965.

B. SECONDARY SOURCES

B. Aaby, 'Cyclic climatic variations in climate over the past 5,500 yr reflected in raised bogs', *Nature* 263 (no 5575) 23 Sep. 1976, 281ff.

S. Aakjær, 'Old Danish Thegns and Drengs', *Acta Philologica Scandinavica* II, 1927, 1ff.

V. Aalkjær, 'Egnen under Århus', *Skalk* 1976, 1, 11ff.

Aarbøger = *Aarbøger for nordisk Oldkyndighed og Historie*.

Acta Arch. = *Acta Archaeologica* (Copenhagen).

E. Albrectsen, *Fynske jernaldergrave IV, Gravpladsen på Møllegårdsmarken ved Broholm*, Odense 1971.

B. Ambrosiani, G. Magnussen (& R. Jonsson), *Arkeologisk undersökning, 1968-9*, Karstorp, Lomma köping, Skåne. *Riksantikvarämbetet rapport* 1972 B9 (Stockholm).

H. Andersen, 'Grydehøj', *Skalk* 1958, 4, 15ff.

H. H. Andersen, P. J. Crabb & H. J. Madsen, 'Århus Søndervold, en byarkæologisk undersøgelse', *Jysk Arkæologisk Selskabs skrifter* IX, 1971.

H. H. Andersen, H. J. Madsen & O. Voss, 'Danevirke' = *Jysk Arkæologisk Selskabs skrifter* XIII, 1976.

S. W. Andersen, 'Vikingerne i Lejre', *Historisk årbog fra Roskilde amt* 1977, 11ff.

A. Andrén, 'Stadsbilden', in Mårtensson 1976, 21ff.

E. Aner, 'Das Kammergräberfeld von Haithabu', *Offa* 10, 1952[1] (Neumünster), 61ff.

E. Aner, 'Die wikingerzeitlichen Kammergräber am Thorsberger Moor', *Offa* 11, 1952[2] (Neumünster), 60ff.

H. Arbman, *Birka, Sveriges äldste handelsstad*, Stockholm 1939.

H. Arbman, *Birka I, Die Gräber*, Stockholm 1943.

T. J. Arne, 'La Suède et l'Orient', *Archives d'Etudes orientales* 8, Uppsala 1914.

G. Balandier, *Anthropologie Politique,* Paris 1967.

A. Bantelmann, 'Tofting', *Offa Bücher* N.F.12, 1955 (Neumünster).

A. Bantelmann, 'Die frühgeschichtliche Marschensiedlung beim Elisenhof in Eiderstedt', *Studien zur Küstenarchäologie Schleswig-Holsteins,* Serie A, Band 1, Frankfurt am Main 1975.

M. W. Barley (ed.), *European Towns: Their Archaeology and Early History,* London 1977.

C. J. Becker, 'Lousgaard 28. Ein Kammergrab des 10 Jahrhunderts am Bornholm', *Acta Arch.* XXIV, 1953, 155ff.

C. J. Becker, 'Ein früheisenzeitliches Dorf bei Grøntoft, Westjütland', *Acta Arch.* XXXVI, 1965, 209ff.

M. Bencard, 'Ribes vikingetid', *Mark og Montre* 1973, 28ff.

B. E. Berglund, 'Vegetation and human influence in south Scandinavia during prehistoric times', *Oikos* (Suppl.) 12, 1969, 9ff.

M. Biddle, 'The towns', in Wilson 1976, 99ff.

H. Birkeland, 'Nordens historie i middelalderen etter arabiske kilder', *Skrifter utgitt av Det Norske Videnskaps-Akademi i Oslo,* II. Hist.- Filos. Klasse, 1954, no 2, Oslo 1954.

C. Blindheim, 'Kaupang in Skiringssal', in Jankuhn et al. 1974, 40ff.

G. A, Blom (ed.), *Urbaniseringsprosessen i Norden; Del 1, Middelaldersteder,* Oslo 1977.

R. Blomqvist, 'Die älteste Geschichte der Stadt Lund', in Jankuhn et al. 1974, 128ff.

S. Bolin, 'Mohammed, Charlemagne and Ruric', *Scandinavian Economic History Review* 1953, 5ff.

A. W. Brøgger, H. Falk, S. Grieg & H. Shetelig, 'Osebergfunnet', Utgitt av Den norske stat I-IV, Christiania (Oslo) 1917-28.

H. C. Broholm, *Danmarks Bronzealder* I-IV, 1943-9 (Copenhagen).

J. Brøndsted, 'Danish inhumation graves of the Viking Age', *Acta Arch.* VI, 1936, 81ff.

J. Brøndsted, *Danmarks Oldtid III, Jernalderen,* 2nd ed., Copenhagen 1960[1].

J. Brøndsted, *Vikingerne,* Copenhagen 1960[2].

A. Brown & P. Foote (eds), *Early English and Norse Studies, presented to Hugh Smith in honour of his sixtieth birthday,* London 1963.

K. Carlqvist, 'Vad säger runstenarna?' *Meddelanden från arkivet för Folkets historia* 5, 4, 1977 (Stockholm).

A. E. Christensen, *Vikingetidens Danmark,* Copenhagen 1969.

A. E. Christensen, 'The Jelling monuments', *Mediaeval Scandinavia* 8, 1975, 7ff.

A. E. Christensen, H. P. Clausen, S. Ellehøj & S. Mørch (eds), *Danmarkshistorie* 1ff., Copenhagen 1977.

T. E. Christiansen, 'Træningslejr eller tvangsborg', *Kuml* 1970, 43ff.

M. Claus, W. Haarnagel & K. Raddatz (eds), *Studien zur europäischen Vor- und Frühgeschichte*, Neumünster 1968.

H. J. M. Claessen & P. Skalník (eds), *The Early State*, The Hague 1978.

R. Cohen & E. R. Service (eds), *Origins of the State*, Philadelphia 1978.

W. Dansgaard, S. J. Johnsen, N. Reeh, N. Gundestrup, H. B. Clausen & C. V. Hammer, 'Climatic changes, Norsemen and modern man', *Nature* 255, 1 May 1975, 24ff.

W. Dansgaard, 'Klima, is og samfund', *Naturens Verden* 1977, 17ff.

R. H. M. Dolley, *The Hiberno-Norse Coins in the British Museum* = *Sylloge of Coins of the British Isles*, London 1966.

P. Donat & H. Ullrich, 'Einwohnerzahlen und Siedlungsgrösse der Merowingerzeit', *Zeitschrift für Archäologie* 5, 1971, 234ff.

DR = Jacobsen et al. 1941-2 (usually referred to by number of runestone).

J. Duplessy, 'La circulation des monnaies arabes en Europe occidentale du VIIIᵉ an XIIIᵉ siècle', *Revue Numismatique*, 5 ser., vol. 18, 1956, 101ff.

K. Düwel, 'Runische Zeugnisse zu 'Bauer'', in Wenskus et al. 1975, 180ff.

E. Dyggve, 'La fouille par le Musée National Danois du tertre royal Sud a Jelling en 1941', *Acta Arch.* XIII, 1942, 65ff.

E. Dyggve, 'Gorm's temple and Harald's stave-church at Jelling', *Acta Arch.* XXV, 1954, 221ff.

K. Eder, *Die Entstehung staatlich organisierter Gesellschaften, ein Beitrag zu einer Theorie sozialer Evolution*, Frankfurt am Main 1976.

J. Ekman, 'Early mediaeval Lund – the fauna and the landscape', *Archaeologica Lundensia* V, 1973.

F. Engels, *Der Ursprung der Familie, des Privateigentums und des Staats,* 1st ed., Hoffingen-Zürich 1884. Later editions (especially 1892) and numerous later printings.

K. V. Flannery, 'The cultural evolution of civilisation', *Annual Review of Ecology and Systematics* 3, 1972.

P. G. Foote & D. M. Wilson, *The Viking Achievement*, London 1970.

M. Fried, *The Evolution of Political Society*, New York 1967.

G. Galster, 'Møntfundet fra Over Randlev', *Numismatisk Forenings Medlemsblad* XIV, 1934, 18ff. & 33ff.

F. L. Ganshof, *Qu'est-ce que la féodalité?* Paris 1944 = *Feudalism*, 3rd ed., London 1964.

P. Grierson, 'Commerce in the Dark Ages: a critique of the evidence', *Transactions of the Royal Historical Society*, 5 ser., 9, London 1959, 123ff.

P. Grierson, 'The monetary reforms of 'Abd Al-Malik', *Journal of the Economic and Social History of the Orient* III, 1, April 1960, 241ff.

W. Haarnagel, *Die Wurtensiedlung Feddersen Wierde im Nordsee-Küstengebiet, Ausgrabungen in Deutschland* 2 = *Römisch-germanisches Zentralmuseum zu Mainz, Monographien* 1, 2, Mainz 1975, 10ff.

K. Hald, 'The cult of Odin in Danish place-names', in Brown et al, 1963.

K. Hald, *Vore stednavne*, 2nd ed., Copenhagen 1965.

B. Hårdh, *Wikingerzeitliche Depotfunde aus Südschweden*, Lund 1976 = *Acta Archaeologica Lundensia*, serie in 8to, no 6, & serie in 4to, no 9.

H.-J. Hässler (ed.), *Studien zur Sachsenforschung*, Hildesheim 1977.

G. Hatz, *Handel und Verkehr zwischen dem Deutschen Reich und Schweden in der späten Wikingerzeit*, Stockholm 1974.

P. Hauberg, *Myntforhold og Udmyntninger i Danmark indtil 1146*, Copenhagen 1900.

P. Hauberg & J. Østrup, 'Terslev-Fundets Mønter', *Aarbøger* 1914, 63ff.

H. Helbæk, 'The Fyrkat grain', in Olsen et al. 1977, (1)f.

W. Harre, 'Die Haustiere von Haithabu', *Die Ausgrabungen in Haithabu* 3, 1960 (Neumünster).

J. Herrmann, 'Slawische Stämme zwischen Elbe und Oder, Siedlung, Wirtschaft und Gesellschaftliche Verhältnisse der slawischen Stämme zwischen Oder/Neisse und Elbe', *DAW Schriften der Sektion für Vor- und Frühgeschichte* 23, Berlin 1968. (*DAW = Deutsche Akademie der Wissenschaften zu Berlin.*)

I. Hodder & C. Orton, *Spatial Analysis in Archaeology*, Cambridge 1976.

W. Holmqvist, 'Die Ergebnisse der Grabungen auf Helgö (1954-74)', *Prähistorische Zeitschrift* 51, 1976, 127ff.

W. Hübener, 'Die Keramik von Haithabu', *Die Ausgrabungen in Haithabu* 2, 1959 (Neumünster).

S. Hvass, 'Das eisenzeitliche Dorf bei Hodde, Westjütland', *Acta Arch.* XLVI, 1975, 142ff.

S. Hvass, 'Udgravningerne i Vorbasse', *Mark og Montre* 1976, 38ff.

S. Hvass, 'Vikingebebyggelsen i Vorbasse', *Mark og Montre* 1977[1], 18ff.

S. Hvass, 'Udgravningerne i Vorbasse', *Fra Ribe Amt* 1977[2] (no page).

Å. Hyenstrand, 'Production of iron in the outlying districts and the problem of Järnbäraland', *Early Medieval Studies* 4, = *Antikvarisk Arkiv* 46, 1972.

J. Iversen, 'The development of Denmark's nature since the last glacial', *Geology of Denmark* III, *Danmarks Geologiske Undersøgelse*, 5 række, no 7 - C, Copenhagen 1973.

G. Jacob, *Welche Handelsartikel bezogen die Araber des Mittelalters aus den nordisch-baltischen Ländern*, 2nd ed., Berlin 1891; with G. Jacob, *Die Waaren beim arabisch-nordischen Verkehr im Mittelalter*, Berlin 1891.

L. Jacobsen & E. Moltke: *Danmarks Runeindskrifter*, Copenhagen 1941-2.

H. Jankuhn, *Die Ausgrabungen in Haithabu 1937-9*, Berlin 1943.

H. Jankuhn & R. Schütrumpf, 'Siedlungsgeschichte und Pollenanalyse in Angeln', *Offa* 10, 1952[1], 28ff.

H. Jankuhn, 'Ein Münzfund der Wikingerzeit aus Steinfeld, Kr. Schleswig', *Offa* 11, 1952[2], 82ff.

H. Jankuhn, W. Schlesinger & H. Steuer (eds), 'Vor- und Frühformen der europäischen Stadt im Mittelalter II', *Abhandlungen der Akademie der Wissenschaften in Göttingen* 84, Göttingen 1974.

H. Jankuhn, *Haithabu, Ein Handelsplatz der Wikingerzeit*, 6th ed., Neumünster 1976.

H. Jankuhn, R. Schützeichel & F. Schwind, 'Das Dorf der Eisenzeit und des frühen Mittelalters', *Abhandlungen der Akademie der Wissenschaften in Göttingen, Philologisch-historische Klasse*, Dritte Folge, 101, Göttingen 1977.

S. B. F. Jansson, *Runeinskrifter i Sverige*, Uppsala 1976.

S. Jelgersma & J. F. van Regteren Altena, 'An outline of the geological history of the coastal dunes in the western Netherlands', *Geologie en Mijnbouw* 48 (3), 1969, 335ff.

S. Jelgersma, J. de Jong, W. H. Zagwijn & J. F. van Regteren Altena, 'The coastal dunes of the western Netherlands: geology, vegetational history and archaeology', *Mededelingen Rijks Geologische Dienst*, n.s. 21, 1970, 93ff.

G. Jones, *A History of the Vikings*, Oxford 1968.

E. Jørgensen, 'Tuernes mysterier', *Skalk* 1975, 1, 3ff.

T. D. Kendrick, *A History of the Vikings*, London 1930.

K. Kersten & P. La Baume, *Vorgeschichte der nordfriesischen Inseln, Die vor- und frühgeschichtlichen Denkmäler und Funde in Schleswig-Holstein* IV, Neumünster 1958.

O. Klindt-Jensen, 'Bornholm i Folkevandringstiden, og forudsætningerne i tidlig jernalder', *Nationalmuseets skrifter, Større beretninger II*, 1957.

G. Kossack, O. Harck, J. Reichstein et al., 'Zehn Jahre Siedlungsforschung in Archsum auf Sylt', *Berichte der römisch-germanische Kommission* 55, 1974, 355ff.

D. K. Kouymjian (ed.), *Near Eastern Numismatics, Iconography, Epigraphy and History: studies in honor of George C. Miles*, Beirut 1974.

K. J. Krogh & O. Voss, 'Fra hedenskab til kristendom i Hørning', *Nationalmuseets Arbejdsmark* 1961, 5ff.

K. J. Krogh, 'Kirken mellem højene', *Skalk* 1966, 2, 5ff.

KLNM: Kulturhistorisk Leksikon for Nordisk Middelalder I-XXI, Malmö 1956-78.

E. Lange, 'Botanische Beiträge zur mitteleuropäischen Siedlungsgeschichte', *Schriften zur Ur- und Frühgeschichte* 27, Berlin 1971.

J. Lepiksaar, 'Tierreste der siedlungen von Valleberga und Rinkaby', in Strömberg 1961, 220ff.

J. Lepiksaar, 'Trehögsparken, Fosie sn, Skåne: Osteologisk undersökning, *Kring Malmöhus* 4, 1973-4[1], 104ff.

J. Lepiksaar, 'Grophus i Oxie by: Osteologisk undersökning', *Kring Malmöhus* 4, 1973-4[2], 132ff.

E. L. Nielsen, *Pedersstræde i Viborg*, Kuml 1968, 23ff.

T. Lewicki, 'La commerce des Samanides avec l'Europe orientale et centrale à la lumière des trésors de monnaies coufiques', in Kouymjian 1974, 219ff.

U. S. Linder, 'En uppländsk silverskatt från 800-talet', *Nordisk Numismatisk Årsskrift* 1938, Copenhagen, 109ff.

K. G. Ljunggren, '*Landmand* och *bomand* i vikingatida källor', *Arkiv för Nordisk Filologi* 74, 1959 (Lund), 115ff.

H. R. Loyn, *Anglo-Saxon England and the Norman Conquest*, London 1962.

M. Lombard, *L'Islam dans sa première grandeur*, Paris 1971 Eng. tr. *The Golden Age of Islam*, Amsterdam 1975.

L. Lundström, 'Bitsilver och betalingsringar', *Theses and Papers in North-European Archeology* 2, Stockholm 1973.

H. J. Madsen, *Vikingernes Århus*, Århus 1975.

B. Malmer, *Nordiska mynt före år 1000*, Lund 1966 = *Acta Archaeologica Lundensia*, serie in 8to, no 4.

A. W. Mårtensson (ed.), 'Uppgrävt förflutet för PKbanken i Lund', *Archaeologica Lundensia* VII, Lund 1976.

G. C. Miles, 'A ninth-century hoard of dirhems found at Susa', *Mémoires de la Mission Archéologique en Iran* XXXVII, 1960, 69ff.

B. Magus & B. Myhre, *Forhistorien*, Oslo 1976 = *Norges Historie* 1 (ed. K. Mykland).

U. Møhl, 'Zoologisk gennemgang af jernalderbopladserne Dalshøj og Sorte Muld, Bornholm', in Klindt-Jensen 1957, 279ff.

U. Møhl, 'Knoglematerialet fra Pederstræde i Viborg', *Kuml* 1968, 83ff.

U. Møhl, 'Et knoglemateriale fra Vikingetid og Middelalder i Århus', in H. H. Andersen et al. 1971[1], 321ff.

U. Møhl, 'Vejleby-fundets dyreknogler', *Lolland-Falsters Stiftsmuseum* 1971[2], 17ff.

E. Moltke, *Runerne i Danmark og deres oprindelse*, Copenhagen 1976.

M. Müller-Wille, 'Das Bootkammergrab von Haithabu', *Bericht über die Ausgrabungen in Haithabu* 8, 1976[1].

M. Müller-Wille, 'Das wikingerzeitliche Gräberfeld von Thumby-Bienebek (Kr. Rendsburg-Eckernförde) Teil I', *Offa Bücher* 36, 1976² (Neumünster).

M. Müller-Wille, 'Der frühmittelalterliche Schmied im Spiegel skandinavischer Grabfunde', *Frühmittelalterliche Studien* 11, 1977, 127ff.

E. Munksgaard, *Oldtidsdragter*, Copenhagen 1974.

P. Nansen & R. J. Jørgensen, 'Fund af parasitæg i arkæologisk materiale fra det vikingetidige Ribe', *Nordisk Veterinærmedicin* 29, 1977, 263ff.

H. Neumann, 'Die Befestigungsanlage Olgerdige und der jütische Heerweg,' in *Hässler* 1977, 295ff.

K. M. Nielsen, 'Var Thegnerne og Drengene Kongelige Hirdmænd', *Aarbøger* 1945, 111ff.

K. M. Nielsen, 'Om dateringen af de senurnordiske runeindskrifter, synkopen og 16 tegns futharken', *Aarbøger* 1969, 5ff.

K. M. Nielsen, 'Jelling problems: a discussion', *Mediaeval Scandinavia* 7, 1974, 156ff.

L. C. Nielsen, 'Omgård – en vestjysk landsby fra vikingetid', *Hardsyssels Årbog* 1976, 37ff.

L. C. Nielsen, 'Omgård – en vestjysk landsby fra vikingetid', *Hardsyssels Årbog* 1977, 59ff.

E. Nöbbe, 'Münzfunde vom Stadtplatz Haithabu 1905-31', in Schwantes 1936, 131ff.

P. Nørlund, *Trelleborg*, Copenhagen 1948 = *Nordiske Fortidsminder* IV, 1.

T. Ohlsson, 'Rapport från Västra Karaby', *Ale* 1971, 2, 29ff.

T. Ohlsson, 'Vikingatid och medeltid i Löddeköpinge', *Ale* 1973, 1, 27ff.

T. Ohlsson, 'The Löddeköpinge Investigation I: the settlement at Vikhögsvägen', *Meddelanden från Lunds Universitets Historiska Museum*, 1975-6, 59ff.

J. Olrik, *Drikkehorn og Sølvtøj fra Middelalder og Renaissance udgivet af Nationalmuseets Anden Afdeling*, Copenhagen 1909.

O. Olsen, 'St. Jørgensbjerg Kirke, Arkæologiske undersøgelser i murværk og gulv', *Aarbøger* 1960, 1ff.

O. Olsen & O. Crumlin-Pedersen, *Fem vikingeskibe fra Roskilde Fjord*, Roskilde 1969.

O. Olsen & H. Schmidt, 'Fyrkat, en jysk vikingeborg I. Borgen og bebyggelsen', *Nordiske Fortidsminder* serie B, in 4to, no 3, Copenhagen 1977.

T. Ramskou, 'Viking Age cremation graves in Denmark', *Acta Arch.* XXI, 1950, 137ff.

T. Ramskou, 'Vikingerne ofrede mennesker', *Nationalmuseets Arbejdsmark* 1963-5, 79ff.

T. Ramskou, 'Lindholm Høje Gravpladsen', *Nordiske Fortidsminder* serie B, in 4to, no 2, Copenhagen 1976.

T. Ramskou, 'Vikingebroen', *Skalk* 1977; 1, 3ff.

K. Randsborg, 'Social stratification in early Bronze Age Denmark: a study in the regulation of cultural systems', *Prähistorische Zeitschrift* 49, 1974, 38ff.

Reallexikon der germanischen Altertumskunde 1ff., Berlin 1968ff.

H. Reichstein, 'Einige Bemerkungen zu den Haustierfunden auf der Feddersen Wierde und vergleichbarer siedlungen in Nordwestdeutschland', *Die Kunde* 23, 1972, 142ff.

H. Reichstein, 'Die Haustier-Knochenfunde der Feddersen Wierde (Allgemeiner Teil)', *Probleme der Küstenforschung im südlichen Nordseegebiet* 10, 1973, 95ff.

H. Reichstein & M. Tiessen, 'Ergebnisse neuerer Untersuchungen an Haustierknochen aus Haithabu (Ausgrabung 1963-4)', *Berichte über die Ausgrabungen in Haithabu* 7, 1974, 9ff.

H. Requate, 'Zur Geschichte der Haustiere Schleswig-Holsteins', *Zeitschrift für Agrargeschichte und Agrarsoziologie* 4, Heft 1, 1956[1] (April), 2ff.

H. Requate, 'Die Jagdtiere in den Nahrungsresten einiger frühgeschichtlicher Siedlungen in Schleswig-Holstein', *Schriften Naturwissenschaft. Vereins Schleswig-Holstein* 29, 1956,[2] 21ff.

E. Roesdahl, 'The northern mound: burial chamber and grave goods', in K. M. Nielsen 1974, 208ff.

E. Roesdahl, 'A forgotten casket hinge from the burial chamber at Jelling, *Mediaeval Scandinavia* 8, 1975, 21ff.

E. Roesdahl, 'Otte vikingetidsgrave i Sdr. Onsild', *Aarbøger* 1976, 22ff.

E. Roesdahl, 'Fyrkat, en jysk vikingeborg II. Oldsagerne og gravpladsen', *Nordiske Fortidsminder*, serie B, in 4to, no 4, Copenhagen 1977[1].

E. Roesdahl, 'Borgenes borg', *Skalk* 1977[2], 2, 3ff.

A. Ruprecht, 'Die ausgehende Wikingerzeit im Lichte der Runeninschriften', *Palaestra* 224, Göttingen 1958.

J. A. Sabloff & C. C. Lamberg-Karlovsky (eds), *Ancient Civilisation and Trade*, Albuquerque 1975.

M. D. Sahlins, *Tribesmen*, Englewood Cliffs 1968.

P. H. Sawyer, *The Age of the Vikings*, 2nd ed., London 1971.

U. Schaefer, 'Anthropologische Untersuchung der Skelette von Haithabu', *Die Ausgrabungen in Haithabu* 4, 1963 (Neumünster).

K. Schietzel, 'Zur Frage einer wirtschaftlichen und sozialen Gliederung Haithabus', in M. Claus et al. 1968, 253ff.

K. Schietzel, 'Die archäologischen Befunde der Ausgrabung Haithabu 1963–4', *Berichte über die Ausgrabungen in Haithabu* 1, 1969, 9ff.

K. Schietzel, 'Haithabu', *Ausgrabungen in Deutschland 3, Römischgermanisches Zentralmuseum zu Mainz, Monographien* 1, 3, Mainz 1975, 57ff.

G. Schwantes (ed.), *Beiträge zur Vor- und Frühgeschichte anlässich der Hundertjahrfeier des Museums vorgeschichtlicher Altertümer in Kiel*, Neumünster 1936.

E. R. Service, *Primitive Social Organisation: an evolutionary perspective*, 2nd ed., New York 1971.

E. R. Service, *The Origins of the State and Civilisation*, New York 1975.

K. Skaare, *Coins and Coinage in Viking-Age Norway*, Oslo 1976.

J. Skaarup, *Stengade II*, Rudkøbing 1976.

P. Skautrup, *Det danske Sprogs Historie I*, Copenhagen 1944.

I. Skovgaard-Petersen, 'Vikingerne i den nyere forskning', *Historisk Tidsskrift* 12 række, 5, 1971 (Copenhagen), 651ff.

I. Skovgaard-Petersen, 'Oldtid og Vikingetid', in A. E. Christensen et al. 1977, 15ff.

R. Skovmand, 'De danske Skattefund fra Vikingetiden og den ældste Middelalder indtil omkring 1150', *Aarbøger* 1942, 1ff.

H. R. Stampfli, 'Die Tierreste der slawischen Siedlungen Oldenburg in Holstein und Scharstorf', *Offa* 17/18, 1959/61, 109ff.

M. Stenberger, *Det forntida Sverige*, Stockholm 1964.

H. Steuer, 'Die Südsiedlung von Haithabu', *Die Ausgrabungen in Haithabu* 6, Neumünster 1974.

H. Stiesdal, 'Kanalen der skærer Samsø over', *Skalk* 1960, 4, 6ff.

I. Stoumann, 'Vikingetidslandsbyen i Sædding', *Mark og Montre* 1977, 30ff.

M. Strömberg, 'Untersuchungen zur jüngeren Eisenzeit in Schonen I-II', *Acta Archaeologica Lundensia*, series in 4to, no 4, Lund 1961.

M. Strömberg, 'Grubenhäuser in Valleberga', *Meddelanden från Lunds Universitets Historiska Museum*, 1969-70, 192ff.

M. Strömberg, *En kustby i Ystad*, Ystad 1978.

C. J. Thomsen & J. C. Lindberg, 'Fund ved Vaalse paa Falster', *Annaler for Nordisk Oldkyndighed* 1842-3, 21ff.

E. Thorvildsen, 'Dankirke', *Nationalmuseets Arbejdsmark* 1972, 47ff.

K. Thorvildsen, 'Ladby-skibet', *Nordiske Fortidsminder* VI, 1, Copenhagen 1957.

J. A. Trimpe Burger, 'Oost-Souburg, Province of Zeeland: a preliminary report on the excavation of the site of an ancient fortress (1969-1971)', *Berichten van de Rijksdienst voor het Oudheidkundig Bodemonderzoek* 23, 1973, 355ff.

P. J. Ucko, R. Tringham & G. W. Dimbleby (eds), *Man, Settlement and Urbanism*, London 1972.

M. Abu-L-Faraj AL-'USH, *Trésor de monnais d'argent trouvé a Umm-Hajarah*, Damas 1972.

E. Vedel, *Efterskrift til Bornholms Oldtidsminder og Oldsager*, Copenhagen 1897.

H. C. Vorting, 'Inden Esbjerg', *Skalk* 1972, 4, 3ff.

V. Vogel, 'Die archäologischen Ausgrabungen im Stadtkern von Schleswig, Ausgrabungen in Deutschland 3', *Römisch-germanisches Zentralmuseum in Mainz, Monographien* 1, 3, Mainz 1975, 72ff.

M. C. Webb, 'The flag follows trade: an essay on the necessary interaction of military and commercial factors in state formation', in Sabloff et al. 1975, 155ff.

M. Weber, *The City*, New York 1958 (Eng. tr. of *Die Stadt*).

D. Webster, 'Warfare and the evolution of the state: a reconsideration', *American Antiquity* 40, 4, 1975, 464ff.

H. Weitemayer, G. Knudsen et al., *Trap: Danmark, I-X*, 4th ed., Copenhagen 1920-30.

R. Wenskus, H. Jankuhn & K. Grinda (eds), 'Wort und Begriff 'Bauer'', *Abhandlungen der Akademie der Wissenschaften in Göttingen, Philologisch-Historische Klasse*, Dritte Folge 89, 1975, 180ff.

D. M. Wilson & O. Klindt-Jensen, *Vikingetidens kunst*, Copenhagen 1965.

D. M. Wilson, 'Archaeological evidence for the Viking settlements and raids in England', *Frühmittelalterliche Studien* 2, 1968, 291ff.

D. M. Wilson (ed.), *The Archaeology of Anglo-Saxon England*, London 1976.

L. F. A. Wimmer, *De danske Runemindesmærker I*, Copenhagen 1893 (1895).

H. T. Wright, 'Recent research on the origin of the state', *Annual Review of Anthropology* 6, 1977 (Palo Alto).

J. Żak, 'Kontakte zwischen Skandinavien und Westslawen des 9.-11. Jahrhunderts n. Chr. im Lichte der archäologischen Quellen', *Offa* 32, 1975 (Neumünster), 48ff.

INDEX OF PLACE NAMES

INDEX OF SUBJECTS